ASTR

MW01491884

# THE SPIRITUAL STUDY OF THE TAROT

## *INCLUDING THE KABALAH*
## *TREE OF LIFE*
## *NUMEROLOGY*
## *ASTROLOGY*

LOUISE FIMLAID, p.m.a.f.a.

"The Rider (Waite) Tarot Deck" of cards is used for interpretation.

Galaxy Publishing House
St. Petersburg, Florida

ISBN 0-9630409-3-6
TX 5-893-418

Copyright ©️ 1997 by Louise Fimlaid
First Edition - June, 1997
Second Edition – March, 1998
Third Edition – September 2001
Fourth Edition – September 2005

727-723-0120
**Galaxy Publishing House**
-D

**Louise Fimlaid**
Apt. A14
2632 Enterprise Rd. E
Clearwater, FL 33759

# ACKNOWLEDGEMENTS

My first thanks goes to The Temple of the Living God, where I was asked to teach the Tarot to a group of students studying the Kabalah. Twenty pages of handouts later turned out to be the book that you are holding in your hands. The Temple, a metaphysical church, has allowed me to fulfill my lifelong dream of combining my spiritual knowledge with the teachings of Astrology, Numerology, Dream analysis, the Tarot and the Kabalah.

To John, a very special person in my life, I say thank you......for putting up with the time spent in writing this book and the eternal array of papers scattered about.

To Susan, who without her artistic ability this book would only be a book of pages with letters and numbers on them. The cover was also designed by her.

Thanks to Judy for her quick response when help was needed.

Thanks to all those who came before me for their wisdom and insight which allowed me to re-light my beacon in my journey through this life.

Last but not least, a thank you to that special someone whom I walked with in another life and continue to do so in this life. Without that connection I would not be what I am today.

# THE

# SPIRITUAL

# STUDY OF

# THE TAROT

# TABLE OF CONTENTS

# CARDS PART TWO: THE MINOR ARCANA

## TABLES

## FIGURES

# PREFACE

While considering this preface, it brought to mind a sermon given by the Reverend LeRoy Zemke at the Temple of the Living God (St. Petersburg, Florida), *LIVING IN THE ETERNAL*, from which I quote the following excerpts with his kind permission. Reverend Zemke is renowned for his great insights and spiritual knowledge. He starts his sermon by quoting scripture, Matthew chapter 5 verses 14 -17.

*"Ye are the light of the world. A city that is set on a hill cannot be hid. Neither do men light a candle, and put it under a bushel, but on a candlestick; and it giveth light unto all that are in the house. Let your light so shine before men, that they may see your good works, and glorify your Father which is in heaven. Think not that I am come to destroy the law, or the prophets: I am not come to destroy, but to fulfil."* **(Matthew 5:14-17)**

Rev. Zemke continues, "These famous statements are part of the great body of the teachings that were given by Jesus in his famous Sermon On the Mount and they comprise the 5th 6th and 7th chapters of the Book of Matthew.

"This body of writing, attributed to Jesus, is essentially the basic structure of his teaching. Any sense of his purpose in his life, as far as what he was about as a teacher, is summed up in these writings.

"Jesus talks about the idea of being the expression of a divine Source in one's self when he says 'Let your light so shine before men.....' Being a beacon, a city which is on a hill cannot be hidden, and therefore, the light which is within each of us cannot be hidden."

Note to the reader: in the author's opinion this is like unto The Hermit in the Tarot cards. He holds the lantern with the light from the Star of David shining out. It is also Sephirah #6 Tiphareth and the Sun (Son, Christ) which is the center of The Tree of Life, the Kabalah. Both the Hermit and Christ attained knowledge and became beacons (Great Lights) for others.

Rev. Zemke goes on to say, "The idea of living in the Eternal is a very difficult concept when we think about, what *is* eternity? From a philosophical point of view we can't answer that. Philosophers over the centuries have attempted to define eternity. They came up with words such as timelessness, changelessness, unlimited ending.

"Now, what does unlimited ending mean? Where do we go with that term? How do we put that which is unlimited into the finite? How do we speak to that which is eternal in the broadest, fullest, largest sense that our minds can grasp into the present time? Into a word? Into a phrase? From a practical point of view, we can't do it. Even so, it is useful to examine this idea because it gets us to look at our lives in a larger context which enables us to enjoy our journey.

"Very frequently in our life's journey we become tied to viewpoints, structures, concepts, families, groups and organizations. We get overly involved in what is often called 'the livingness of our lives.' I propose that in order for us to come into a sense of esoteric learning, we must first learn to live in the here now and then in the Eternal now. I offer the following ideas.

"1st: God is all that is identified as Energy. God is all there is, or is that which we think of as Unlimited Source. We may give this Source a scientific label, but in reality when we think about it, all that we can sense, all that we can see, all that we can know, and all that is unknown to us is the great body of God.

"We start with the premise: there is this Presence, this Power which we identify so clearly when we say God is all that is visible and invisible. One Presence, One Power, One Mind. The One that is All.

"That is a philosophical statement of belief and a statement of how we begin to approach what we think of as the Divine. It is an essential statement of fundamental comprehension if we are going to begin to have any sense of direction in our lives and understanding that God is the Power that motivates the whole *modus operandi* of life.

"2nd: We must accept that man/woman is a living child of God and learn to feel the living energy of God within us. We are a spark of divinity, a spark of this Power, of this Energy, this Presence. All metaphysical teachings talk about this in a variety of ways: Yoga, Numbers, Kabalah, Unity, Science of Mind, Astrology, etc., which says we are each a child of God. Being a child of God means that we are heirs of this Being flowing in and through us. It means that we have access, that we have the creative capacity, the mind, the ability, sensitivity and the capability of expressing this Energy in us, in our lives. When we do that, we live in the Now. When we do it, when we are honestly expressing it, that's when we begin to own it."

Note to the reader: in the author's opinion, this is like The Magician who realized that his connection with that above gave him the power here on earth to work through his journey.

Rev. Zemke concludes, "3rd: We are invited into working with our capabilities, our talents, our skills, our deepest innate capacities in order to develop them. We are invited, we are given this as an opportunity over and over again within the context of our lives. We are all invited into that in a variety of ways.

"Whatever the diversity of our abilities, if a talent is meaningful to us, we have to do something about it. We have to develop it. We have to express it. It cannot happen for us if we do not do something about it. Now, the amount of the effort, time, circumstances in which we create the effort, and put it to work, is all part of the dynamics which has to do with being invited into the working with our own capabilities. We must stay focused if we want to make a difference in our life. If we don't sample the energy of our life, we never really engage in it.

"4th: Practice our connection to God daily through prayer, meditation or other spiritual practices. Why is that important? God knows our thoughts before we think them. What is important is that *we* become conscious of that connection, we become conscious of our *power* with that connection and its *presence* within us."

Final note to the reader: The author emphasizes that through studying any of the metaphysical subjects one is lead along the path to 'Living in the Eternal.' This book, "The Spiritual Study of the Tarot," is written with just that concept in mind. It incorporates knowledge of Astrology, Numerology and the Kabalah and shows how all studies are intertwined in the Tarot cards. Many roads lead to the same place. I am pleased to be able to open the gate to the path of "YOUR" SPIRITUAL JOURNEY by sharing my insights with you. ENJOY!

# BIOGRAPHY

For over 25 years (plus many lifetimes) I have acquired knowledge that has allowed me to be a Metaphysical teacher and counselor. Besides The Tarot, I teach Astrology, Numerology, Dream analysis and the Kabalah.

Being a certified Astrologer with the American Federation of Astrologers and a member of the National.Council for Geocosmic Research has allowed me many exciting adventures. While living in Massachusetts I wrote for newspapers and television guides. At one time I had an astrological call-in radio program as well as a metaphysical store called 'The House of Zodiac.' Teaching the subject of Astrology was accomplished in the high schools and at the present time an accredited course is being taught in the Temple of the Living God in St. Petersburg Florida, where I now reside. My lecturing and teaching has taken me to Astrological conferences and groups throughout the country. From time to time I have had the honor of being the guest speaker for organizations as well as on cruise ships.

During this time I have compiled two sets of courses on cassette tapes. Study Astrology with Louise #1 (beginners astrology) and Study Astrology with Louise #2 (lectures and workshop tapes with a book of handouts). In 1991 "Timetable of Life," an intermediate astrology text, was written. In 1997 came "The Spiritual Study of the Tarot" which you are now reading. In 1998 there will be a beginners astrology text book called 'Filling in the Gaps', which is everything that you were not told about in Astrology. Your spiritual journey in life shown through the study of Astrology. (See the back of this book for ordering instructions.)

I always say that will be it! However, being a Gemini I have the unique ability to see a concept and have total understanding of it. My head is always full of knowledge that I want to share with others. There was a time in 1978 when I traveled to Greece and Egypt and felt right at home in the temples and pyramids. While in Egypt I had the honor to sit and meditate in the King's Chamber, in the same spot that Napoleon and Alexander the Great once sat. At that time, I was in contact with the Universe and felt surrounded by all of its knowledge. This experience profoundly affected my whole life. I found that I would talk about things of which I really had no conscious knowledge, and at a later time, would open one of the books in my library and find verification of what I intuitively had known. I have been lead to write this book for you.

So until we meet again in one of my books, or in this journey of life, Enjoy!!!!!!

# INTRODUCTION

I want to welcome all of you to the spiritual study of the Tarot. This study includes knowledge of Astrology, Numerology, and The Kabalah. This is a very important time in your life! Since you were led here to seek this knowledge, this means that you are ready for the next step in your spiritual evolution. A new awareness is opening up to you. I feel honored that I will be your teacher and share my knowledge and wisdom with you. You, as the student of this new subject, may choose to immerse yourself in the system until it is fully understood. Put yourself into a meditative state of mind and tune in. Ask for Divine enlightenment to come through. It will come in many forms depending upon the level of spiritual understanding that you have reached. For some, you may find that you study all these subjects and then put them aside only to come back again at a later time in your life. At that time your understanding will be on a different level and you may comprehend it completely. As one studies all of these subjects, the Kabalah, Numerology, Astrology and the Tarot, the higher consciousness will begin to unfold.

The Kabalah is as old as man's history, it is from the beginning of time. It is said that Adam received a Kabalistic book from the angel Raziel. The book was handed down to Enoch, (seventh master of the World after Adam). It was then passed down to Solomon who used it. The Book of Yetzirah states, "The uniting bond in creation are the 22 letters of the Hebrew alphabet and the first 10 numbers. These two types of signs are called 'the 32 marvelous ways of wisdom." Through word and writ man can penetrate the most divine secrets and with words and signs work wisdom."

Eliphas Levi, Christian, Fabre d'Olivet, Paracelsus, Wirth, and Papus feel the Tarot's true symbolism comes from Ancient Egypt. Moses, who was born and raised in Egypt, was knowledgeable in all occult subjects. He was an astrologer and much of his knowledge also relates to the Kabalah. When he went to the top of Mt. Sinai to receive the Ten Commandments he also received The Spiritual laws of the Kabalah. The Ten Commandments can be likened to the Ten Sephiroth on the Tree of Life. Moses caused 70 scribes to record 70 books (5 of which remain); two books were transmitted orally to the High Priests, to be held in secrecy and transmitted to a chosen few, orally. This was the 'oral tradition' of the Hebrews, i.e., The Kabalah.

Another story was that Thoth was responsible. He is symbolized by the head of the Ibis and was counselor to Osiris and the scribe of the Egyptian gods. He was the measurer of time and invented numbers and performed magic. The Greek god Hermes Trismegistus also gets credit. His ideas appear in the studies of Astrology, Kabalah, Alchemy and Magic. These two men are believed to be the same person. It is said that Hermes invented the first Tarot in order to preserve and secure the secrets of the Kabalah. Kabalah means to receive the inner knowledge. The Tarot is the key to the Kabalah and the Kabalah is the key to the Tarot.

In traditional Western Occultism, the Tarot cards are recognized as the keystone of an entire philosophical system called Hermetism. Before the cards came into being, the knowledge was handed down by word of mouth from initiate to initiate. The Tarot cards are the first set of cards in existence. They came about when all higher knowledge was forbidden to be discussed. Many languages were spoken, so when the cards were drawn, the wisdom was seen in pictures so all could understand.

They seemed to be first heard of in Austria in the 12th century. Some say the Chaldeans and Egyptians were the first to use the cards, and that they were later transported by the Gypsies into Israel and Greece. The 'Masters', then known as the Hierophants (priests of the Eleusinian Mysteries), gave their knowledge to the Gypsies in order to preserve it. They designed the cards to hold the spiritual esoteric lessons. These cards linked together God, the Universe and Man. The Gypsies pretended that they were designed for entertainment in order to hide their true meaning.

In a sense, all sacred books of the world (including the Avesta, the Vedas and the Bible) are largely kabalistic. They all set forth traditions that are capable of an inner, or esoteric, interpretation. Many interpretations are possible, each revealing a deeper truth to those who have advanced along the path.

The ancient races preserved the remembrances of a primitive book which was written in hieroglyphics by Sages of the earliest epochs of our world. Changed and altered by the centuries, the symbols became the letters of our alphabet.

It is said that in the Tarot, the 22 Major Arcana lessons were part of the initiation ceremonies for the Egyptian priesthood. These cards, placed on the paths of the Tree of Life in the Kabalah, have also been used by the Hebrew masters with their higher spiritual learning. The Masons and the Eastern Star also use these paths as degrees. You may have heard of the 32nd degree Mason: one who went through all the lessons, or paths, became a 32nd degree Mason. There is a 33rd degree which is the highest one can become. I have been fortunate to know a man that did achieve this rating. He was my father-in-law. The right pillar on the tree is sometimes called Jachin and the left one Boaz, named by the Masons. You will see the letters J and B representing these words on the pillars that the High Priestess sits between.

Whomever is responsible certainly knew ancient religions and philosophies. The Tarot cards not only display the symbolism depicted in the scenes, but also the subjects of the Kabalah, Numerology, Astrology, color, musical tones and Hebrew letters to bring the message of spiritual wisdom. The Kabalah was also handed down by word of mouth, and finally came into existence in written form about 600 A.D. It became more important during the 15th century when philosophers wanted to incorporate Jewish mysticism into Christian thought. The final outcome for the Kabalah was that it incorporated all religions into it. All major religions (Christianity, Buddhism, Krishna, Hinduism, Judaism etc.) teach us that there is only one Primal Point, one Source. All roads lead to the same one universal energy. It may help if we change the word religion to spirituality. The Kabalah is a spiritual study which uses the subjects of Numerology, Astrology and the Tarot to tell its story.

Man and the universe is in perfect order, which one can see and understand. There are no such things as accidents. Everything has a planned order. Through Astrology, I have found that the soul chooses the moment to be born. Before that takes place the soul sees a flash picture of its whole life. It has to agree to what it sees in order to be born. What is chosen for life is what is needed for the Soul's evolution. The pattern is set and put into motion when the soul is born and the parents, as well as everyone in the life, help that pattern to unfold. The clock's alarm is set when you come in and goes off when it is time to leave. I know this may seem difficult for you to believe or understand, but we must take full credit or blame for our lives.

People will be heard saying, "Why has God done this to me?" Why doesn't He help me? We must understand that everyone was given intelligence, energy and feelings to use. How we use them is up to us.

The Soul knows the whole story. The human mind does not know what the Soul does and therefore, not being aware of the pattern, allows life to just happen. The Soul is always in charge and will get the person where they are supposed to be at the right time. The time then comes in the life when there is an awakening and the two are united and the human awareness works with the Soul. Every moment in life is interrelated. The past is a great part of the present and has a direct influence on the future. Past, present and future are all part of the great unity.

The deck of cards that you will be learning from is called the Rider Waite deck. This deck is the best to learn from because the pictures on the cards are designed to show all the meanings that the card represents. After you learn this deck you may then apply your knowledge to other decks. The same knowledge will apply to those cards. These cards were drawn in 1910 by Pamela Colman Smith under the direction of Arthur Edward Waite. Mr. Waite was a member of the Golden Dawn society and a student of ancient myths and religions. He designed these cards to contain as many of the esoteric studies as he could. He was able to restore a lot of the original symbolic meanings that had been lost or changed over time. The Tarot represents the universal truths in man's evolution for all to understand.

The care of the cards is important. These are spiritual cards and should be treated with respect. They should always be stored in a natural material such as a silk cloth or bag, or a wooden box. (Silk is natural and comes from a silk worm.) They can also be placed in a wooden box. The box should be made from an evergreen tree as evergreen trees are always alive and considered everlasting. Before there were coffins, a piece of pine was placed over the body when it was put into the ground. This was to keep the evil spirits and animals from getting to it. The same will be true for the cards.

It is all right for you to pick your own deck of cards. Some people believe that they should be given to you or they will bring bad luck. This is a superstition. Living in the spiritual world does not leave room for superstitions. Bless your cards! Before you shuffle your cards, make sure that they are all facing in the same direction. Shuffle them and while doing so, say a prayer or affirmation. Give them to your client and let him/her shuffle them. After each reading, you can shuffle them again to release the energy of the person who handled them before.

When a person shuffles the deck, their Soul (through their fingers) is stacking the deck in order to have the right cards come out for their message. When the unconscious mind has its attention focused on obtaining certain information, the psychic senses are active to obtain that information. The Tarot cards afford both a means by which the attention of the Soul is directed to acquire such information, and a means by which this information can be raised into the objective consciousness. While shuffling the cards, one may end up reversing them. When they are placed down some may be upside down. If this is the case you will interpret them differently. Some people's lives are upside down and a little confusing and some are not. Since we deal with the polarity in life of positive and negative, when the card is upright it will be read in a positive manner. When upside down there is a delay or there is more work to be done before completion. The cards will come out the way they are meant to. Sometimes they even jump out to be chosen.

In studying the Tarot cards I am going to integrate three major studies into the lessons: Astrology, Numerology, and The Kabalah. For the layman I hope to make this as clear as possible, with the hope that it will spark the curiosity to allow one to study each subject further.

The Tarot is a hieroglyphic and numerical alphabet expressed by characters and numbers and a series of universal and absolute ideas. It is a philosophical machine, which keeps the mind from wandering while leaving it initiative and liberty to create its own understanding. It was put together by human genius and is universal principal which manifests itself in every sphere of life. The symbols used are letters of the old Hebrew alphabet, plus figures, numbers, planets and signs of the Zodiac. Knowing the fixed idea behind it, we can operate as mathematicians using formulas and terms.

The Tarot is an interpretative system involving a set of 78 cards. 22 are called the Major Arcana. Arcana means secret and spiritual. The 22 Major Arcana are more related to our spiritual mission rather than to the mundane. Therefore, the paths of the Tree in the Kabalah are important since the Major Arcana is placed on the paths. It is the main potency in ourselves and the universe which we strive to bring into consciousness. 56 of the cards are called the Minor Arcana and deal with the mundane part of life. These cards unlock the wisdom of the ancient philosophers. The symbolism depicted by the pictures- the numerological, astrological, color, musical tone, Hebrew letters and their placement on the Tree...of the Kabalah-are fascinating. They all combine to give us the spiritual basis for life in this world, and the world of spirit above. The Kabalah, Numerology, Astrology and the Tarot are more than devices for telling fortunes. After reading this book and seeing how they work, one will want to explore each of them in more depth.

# ESSENTIALS

On the following pages are some essentials that *must* be understood in order to get the most out of interpreting the cards.

## THE FIRST IS:
## THE UNDERSTANDING OF *THE FOUR ELEMENTS.*

*Everything* in life is made up of the **four elements: Air, Fire, Water, and Earth.**

The four elements are the substance of life as well as spiritual substance. Plants, minerals, animals, and man are composed of these four elements in combination of various proportions to construct their living organisms.

All organic structures are built of cells which in their simplest form are hexagonic (6 sided) spheroids, similar to those of the honeycomb. In Astrology this hexagon is called a sextile aspect which represents an opportunity and is of positive influence. Therefore, the hexagon is the primary structural pattern of benefit. When light (substitute the word **Fire**) enters at the external angle of 60 degrees, and the internal angle of 120 degrees, it necessarily **illuminates all parts of the structure** in equal lines of influence. **The light that pours in at either of these angles imparts exhilarating and harmonious vibrations which stimulate its continuous growth.** 120 degrees forms the Astrological aspect called the trine which is also beneficial.

Opposed to this is the process of crystallization, recognized in magnetism and electricity, wherein the two forces operate at right angles to each other - a geometrical relationship that is destructive to organic form. This is called a square aspect in Astrology. It causes friction which creates results. **As a result, side by side through nature two mutually antagonistic forces exist, which, despite their antipathy to each other, work together toward the ordered disposition of the whole: one based upon the quadrature, the other upon the hexagon, i.e., the square and the sextile.** This happens when one mixes **Fire and Water** together. These elements and astrological signs of these elements do not blend and cause friction. This friction, as said above, despite its antagonistic forces, works together toward the ordered disposition of the whole. It is important to totally understand the blending of the elements Fire and Water. The entire Tree of Life is constructed by blending the masculine and feminine, positive and negative, Fire and Water elements together. Water is the feminine, receptive/negative energy representing the subconscious mind which perceives ancient wisdom. Fire is the masculine, positive, conscious mind. Fire is intense and will automatically consume and sterilize but does not progress without the help of Water. Will, represented by the Fire, is the strongest attribute of Fire. Use *your* will to push yourself onward and upward. Fire awakens and energizes.

Until the conscious (Fire) mind unites with the understanding of the subconscious (Water) mind, there is no balance. When this blending does occur one has awareness which is then represented by the super-conscious mind. Throughout the Tarot cards you will see different combinations of a woman, man or child. The man is the conscious mind. The woman is the subconscious mind. The child is the product which comes from the blending of the two to create the super-conscious mind. These three combined represent the Trinity.

Astrology postulates that the quadrate (square) relationship between energy sources is destructive to form. However, it creates friction in order to change. Think of it as a catalyst. Through releasing this energy that is locked up in the various structures nature has built, it allows the sextile and the trine aspects to constitute the constructive side of nature, whereby organic forms are created, nourished and perpetuated, and can be released when subsequent destructive configurations are encountered. The combination of Fire and Water, or Fire and Earth are considered catalysts and form agitation. Fire and Air are compatible energies. Earth and Water are compatible. Earth and Air and Earth and Fire are not. The Earth can smother the Fire, and the Air can blow away the Earth.

Henry Drummond, in "Natural Law in Spiritual World," describes this process as follows: "If we analyze this material point at which all life starts, we shall find it to consist of a clear structureless, jelly-like substance resembling albumen or white of egg. **It is made of Carbon, Hydrogen, Oxygen and Nitrogen.** Its name is **protoplasm.** And it is not only the structural unit with which all living bodies start in life, but with which they are subsequently built up. Protoplasm is the formal basis of all life. It is the clay of the Potter." **The Water element** according to ancient philosophers has been metamorphosed into the hydrogen of modern science; **the Fire,** nitrogen; **the Earth,** carbon; **the Air** has become oxygen.

**You will see that this is the first project of The Fool. He needed a physical body,** the same way that you did when you decided to make your journey. He came in and first went to the Fire Pillar on the Tree of life, path #11 (1). Here he obtained nitrogen. Then he traveled to path #12 (2) where he found The Magician and connected to the Water Pillar and obtained hydrogen. Then he went to path #13 (3) and met The High Priestess on the Air Pillar and obtained oxygen. The lungs are like the bellows to Fire. When these three substances are combined they create the element Earth (carbon). Earth is the element which digests and forms matter. He now had his body.

Paracelsus believed that there was one vital force in life. It is called the vital life force. This is like the astral or spiritual light. Eliphas Levi seconded this belief, saying that "Light, that creative agent, the vibrations of which are the movement of life of all things: light, latent in the universal ether, radiating about absorbing centers which, being saturated thereby, project movement and life in their turn, so forming creative currents; light, astralized in the stars, animalized in animals, humanized in human beings; light, which vegetates all planets glistens in metals, produces all forms of nature and equilibrates all by the laws of universal sympathy. This is the light which exhibits the phenomena of magnetism, divined by Paracelsus, which tinctures the blood, being released from the Air as it is inhaled and discharged by the hermetic bellows of the lungs." (*The History of Magic.*)

Dr. Sigismund Bacstrom believed that if a physician could establish harmony among the four elements of Air, Fire, Water, and Earth and unite them into a stone (the Philosopher's Stone), symbolized by the six pointed star or two interlaced triangles, he would possess the means of healing all disease.

Dr. Bacstrom further stated that there was no doubt in his mind that the universal, omnipresent Fire (Spirit) of nature "does all and is all in all." By attraction, repulsion, motion, heat, sublimation, evaporation, coagulation, and fixation, the Universal Fire (Spirit) manipulates matter, and manifests throughout creation. Any individual who can understand these principles and adapt them to the three departments of nature becomes a true philosopher.

James Gaffarel in 1650 told how he chopped up, mortared and burnt flowers. Even in doing this both the juices and ashes remained in the same form. This was followed by M. du Chesne and S. de la Violette, chemists who saw a Polish physician who kept herbs as ashes in glass containers. He lit a FIRE under the ashes of a rose. As it felt the heat, the ashes began to move in the glass container. After rising up it formed a rose. This theory is what alchemy and homeopathy are all about, namely that the most minute drop of substance contains the whole essence. Heat (Fire) is a requisite for manifestation. Heat increases vibrations and as it gets hotter light appears.

Think about this! We now have a means of healing which is acupuncture. Through the insertion of needles the acupuncturist tries to get the body back in balance. He also heats the needles. The acupuncturist uses the knowledge of Air, Fire, Water and Earth to stimulate the body's meridians in order to heal.

If we could keep a balance of these elements we would not die. Sickness, disease and old age appear when the body cannot maintain its balance. Today there is much talk about stimulating the hormones of our body which have shut down at early ages. It is believed that if we can once more put these on line then we would not age or become unhealthy. If a balance can be kept, then it is believed that we can live to be at least 125 years old and in perfect health.

Every created thing has two bodies, one visible and one invisible which is transcendent. The latter consists of an ethereal counterpart of the physical form, and dissipates at death. The outer sheath is not dissipated at death. It remains until it knows the physical form is completely disintegrated. This outer sheath is the one that is the most susceptible to the energies of the world.

The Fool had the outer sheath when he arrived. He had to obtain the physical form. When he left the world he shed the physical form and kept the outer sheath. All of us have done this and will do it again when we transcend from this life to that above.

You will become a true philosopher when you understand the true meanings of Air, Fire, Water and Earth. Air, Fire, Water and Earth are the ingredients that everything is made of. You yourself eat, drink, and breathe, and in you the inert earth and air are transfigured into life and take the living form which is you.

## ELEMENTAL SPIRITS

Our bodies are made up of all the elements and therefore can be visible. Because an element consists of only one element it is impossible to see it, it is invisible. The only time that they can be seen is when they interact with another element and cause an action such as banging into one another. There are humans who are able to see in this dimension and visualize them. Each element can have its own mental/physical body but belongs to a more subtle subdivision that is invisible to humans. There is a spirit for each of the elements. They direct special involuntary activities such as chemical and physical phenomena.

The spirits of the Fire element are represented by the Salamanders. They are sometimes seen as a small ball of light. Without them it is said that material fire cannot exist or a match to be struck. A salamander can be evoked by friction.

The spirits of the Earth element are called Gnomes. They look like a brownie or elf.

The spirits of the Air element are called Sylphs. They are tiny winged cherubs and delicate fairies. They work through the gases and ethers of the earth.

The spirits that relate to the Water element are called Undines. They appear in the form of mermaids, sea maidens and water nymphs.

When these spirits show up in the Tarot cards I will call them to your attention.

## ELEMENTAL SPIRITS

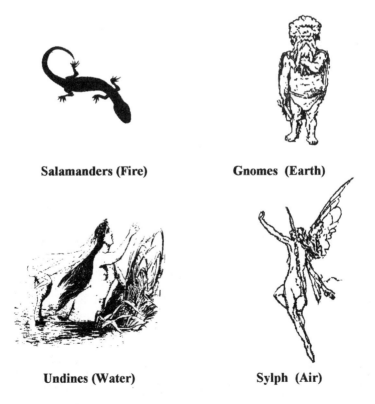

**Salamanders (Fire)**          **Gnomes (Earth)**

**Undines (Water)**          **Sylph (Air)**

## THE SPHINX

The Sphinx is made up of a man, an eagle, a lion, and a bull which represent the four elements of Air, Water, Fire and Earth as well as the four gospels. These four symbols, with all their analogies, explain the one word hidden in all sanctuaries which is God. Moreover, the sacred word, Jehovah, was not pronounced but spelt in Hebrew and expressed in four words which are the four sacred letters: Yod He' Vau He'.

I refer to the Kabalah often. As we proceed I will explain it as simply as possible so that you, the student, can understand. There are examples of the Tree for you to refer to on pages 37, 38, and 42.

All matter is composed of energy. Energy requires two forces, positive and negative, in order to exist. The balance of these two forces is essential for all life. It is the same as the energy involved in the Yin and Yang. Negative is drawing in and receptive. Positive is outgoing and aggressive.

It should be understood here that positive can be good or bad and negative can be bad or good. There are times when too much of a good thing can create a problem. Bad becomes good when the difficult energy creates a change that works out to be beneficial. There are always the two forces at work. The Tree of Life is a typical example of this. The whole tree continually balances the positive + and the negative - energies.

## THE FOUR SACRED HEBREW LETTERS ARE:

**יׂ YOD (Y)** - is the positive **Fire** element and the primary energy. It must be in all that exists. Nothing exists without it. It represents the sense of hearing. It is #10 in the Hebrew letters. When #10 is reduced (10=1+0=1) it becomes #1. So the Yod is like the #1. Read about #1 in the section on numbers. All the Hebrew letters are created with the Yod. The odd numbers, when divided by 2, have a remainder of 1. Therefore, the odd numbers are said to be from spirit. The Yod is like the right hand Fire pillar of the Tree of Life in the Kabalah. It represents the Kings and Wands in the Tarot. The King is a man over 30, and the Wands represent drive, energy, ambition and all disciplined activity such as business, profession, and sports.

**ה HE' (H)** - is the negative **Water** element and is the emergence of the Fire energy into form. It is the opposite of Fire. It represents the receptive, maternal, all-productive element. It is the sense of taste in the organs, nerves, and brain centers in which the element of Water predominates. The sense of taste is dependent upon the presence of Water for its operation. He' is like the #2. It is #5 in the Hebrew letters. It takes two 5's to make a 10. The #2 represents polarity and duplication or opposites. The He' is like the left hand Water pillar of the Tree of Life in the Kabalah. It represents the Queens and Cups in the Tarot. The Queen is a woman over 30, the Cup represents the nurturing, sensitive, passive, emotional nature. "Truly truly, I say unto you, unless one is born of Water and the Spirit he cannot enter the kingdom of God." John III, 5.

**ו VAU (V)** - is the positive **Air** element and is the stabilization of the process of formation. It is like the #3 bringing completion. It is the middle Air pillar on the Tree of Life in the Kabalah. This middle pillar represents the spine in the body and the chakras. Air has to do with oxygen and breathing. Before one learns to breathe and evoke the different chakras, it is important to understand Sephirah #6 which relates to the Sun and the Christ center or consciousness. When air is still, it corresponds to the faculty of intuition. Rushing air sometimes refers to disturbed mental and emotional states. It wants to stir things up and create a change. Vau and Air represents the Knights and Swords in the Tarot. The Knight is older than the Page but younger than the King or Queen. The age is around 20-30. It is a youth and can be either male or female. The Swords represent intelligence.

ה HE' (H) - is the negative **Earth** and is the final element which reveals the completion of the movement of energy into form. Since it is a duplicate of the He' it now starts a new beginning. What is completed by the #3 Vau, can be continued as a new cycle in the second He'. Earth is placed on Sephirah #10 in the Tree of Life. This Sephirah is called Malkuth. Earth, meaning all solid ground and substances, corresponds to form and to the body. It represents the sense of smell. All solid objects refer to states of waking bodily consciousness. Mountains, which you will see often in the cards, represent exalted states. Gardens mean fruitfulness and abundance. He' represents the Pages and Pentacles in the Tarot. Read about the meaning of the Pentacle in the card of the Ace of Pentacles. The Page is young, representing adolescence and can be either male or female. The Pentacles represent values, often money.

**Yod He' Vau He' -** י ה ו ה The name for God or Jehovah. This is the pronunciation of the Hebrew. However, it is written and read in Hebrew from right to left (He' Vau He' Yod).

There is one more sense which is the fifth and it is touch. Touch involves the total life principle of the whole human organism from highest Spirit to the dense physical body. This could be the Auric envelope. One's sense of things close to them is felt as the aura senses the change of energy.

## WHITE CLOUD

When the consciousness is exalted to the level of pure wisdom and spiritual intuitiveness, it is sometimes symbolized by a white cloud. At that point the omnipotent power of the Will of man is used. Man has raised his consciousness up to the spiritual level. This white cloud (although it appears as gray in the cards) is seen around the hand of God in the Aces. It is also seen in the cards of the King, Queen, and Page of Swords since the Swords are of the Air element. It can be seen around Gabriel in the card of Judgement. The cloud is around the four creatures in the corners of the cards of the Wheel of Fortune and The World. Air seems to be the strongest of all elements because of its influence in helping us to raise our consciousness. That is why studies, breathing and meditation are so important. Fire rises, Water descends, and Air is the regulatory medium between the two.

## ALCHEMY

There will be times when symbols for Alchemy appear in the cards. They relate to the elements of Air, Water, Earth, and Fire. More information about azoth, mercury, salt and sulfur can be found on the page of the Wheel of Fortune.

When talking about alchemy the elements represent the following:

Air    is universal solvent Azoth
Water  is the Liquid mercury ☿
Earth  is salt ⊖
Fire   is sulfur ♄

## ANOTHER SUBJECT THAT WILL BE SEEN IN THE CARDS IS *ASTROLOGY.*

The Tarot and the astrological planet, the Moon, is the Silver Key. Astrology and the planet, the Sun, is the Gold Key. These keys open the trunks of spiritual knowledge as well as the lessons of the Bible. You will see these keys in card #5, The Hierophant. Astrology is intermingled in the Tarot. If you have some knowledge of Astrology it will be helpful. If you do not, you may be interested in taking a course in Astrology to learn more. A short synopsis of each of the signs and planets follows. This will help you when interpreting the cards and also when you describe people represented by the court cards. The court cards are the cards in the Minor Arcana that represent people.

## ASTROLOGICAL SIGNS

**ARIES** 3/21-4/19. The glyph for Aries is ♈. Aries is a Cardinal/active Fire sign. Aries people are like the spring. They are like a young plant springing from the seed. They jump into life with eagerness and impulsiveness. They love to be the starters and initiators of anything that is new. They are adventurous, impatient, self-expressive, open, direct and not always sensitive to anothers feelings. Mars ♂, the aggressive planet, is the ruling planet for Aries. The Ram is the animal symbol.

**TAURUS** 4/20-5/20. The glyph for Taurus is ♉. Taurus is a Fixed Earth sign. They are practical, materialistic and steady, persistent, cautious and stick-to-it until it is done. They have patience. Through their hard work and determination they accomplish, accruing an abundance in worldly possessions. The social, love planet Venus ♀ is the ruling planet for Taurus. The Bull is the animal symbol.

**GEMINI** 5/21-6/20. The glyph for Gemini is ♊. Gemini is a Mutable Air sign and is, therefore, an intellectual sign. They are curious and always questioning. Gemini likes movement and change. The Twins are its astrological symbol representing duality. The intellectual planet Mercury ☿ is its ruling planet. Mercury was the messenger who delivered the messages of the gods. Gemini is the communicator and the teacher.

**CANCER** 6/21-7/22. The glyph for Cancer is ♋. Cancer is a Cardinal/active Water sign. Water represents emotions and gives Cancer a sensitive nature. The family unit is important as well as security. They love to nurture and be nurtured. They have an intuitive nature. Their ruling planet is the reflective Moon ☽. The Crab is their animal symbol.

**LEO** 7/23-8/22. The glyph for Leo is ♌. Leo is a Fixed Fire sign. They love to be on stage and get their applause. They are star performers. They have a warm majestic nature. They are admired and respected, dress well and are well poised. The Sun ☉ is their ruling planet. The Sun represents the will and ego of the individual. The Lion is their animal symbol.

**VIRGO** 8/23-9/22. The glyph for Virgo is ♍. Virgo is a Mutable Earth sign. Virgo likes to work. They are practical and love details and are very methodical. They tend to their duties and take pride in their accomplishment. They are critical and intellectual people. If you want something done right, ask a Virgo or someone with the intellectual Mercury or energetic Mars in the sign of Virgo. Mercury ☿ the intellectual planet is their ruling planet. The Angel or Virgin is their symbol.

**LIBRA** 9/23-10/22. The glyph for Libra is ♎. Libra is a Cardinal Air sign. They are artistic and musically inclined. They like peace and harmony and are good at seeing both sides of a situation. Partnerships are important to them. Libra rules the lower courts. Venus ♀ the social and love planet is their ruling planet. The Scales are their symbol.

**SCORPIO** 10/23-11/21. The glyph for Scorpio is ♏. Scorpio is a Fixed Water sign. They become very attached to what intrigues them emotionally. They love to transform anything. They are great at taking something that is discarded and giving it new life. They make good detectives, policemen, doctors and psychologists. Investigation is easy for them. The planet Pluto ♇ is their ruling planet. The Scorpion, Eagle, Serpent, and Phoenix are the symbols for Scorpio.

**SAGITTARIUS** 11/22-12/21. The glyph for Sagittarius is ♐. Sagittarius is a Mutable Fire sign. Freedom and the wide open spaces are what they like. They are happy, jovial and optimistic people. Sports interest them. They love to travel. Jupiter ♃ is their ruling planet. The symbol is a Centaur which is half horse and half man shooting an arrow upward.

**CAPRICORN** 12/22-1/19. The glyph for Capricorn is ♑. Capricorn is a Cardinal Earth sign. They are quiet, reserved and accurate in what they do. They are late bloomers and usually marry later in life. They make good business people and are very dependable. Their ruling planet is Saturn ♄. The Mountain Goat is their animal. Capricorns set their goal, pace themselves, and get there.

**AQUARIUS** 1/20-2/18. The glyph for Aquarius is ♒. Aquarius is a Fixed Air sign. They are inventors, pioneers and people of the future. They are unique and independent. Some are scientific, astrologers, electricians and teachers. Their ruling planet is Uranus ♅. Their symbol is a man pouring from a jug. This sometimes causes it to be mistaken for a Water sign, but it is Air. Being an intellectual sign it is cosmic knowledge that is being poured on the parched earth below.

**PISCES** 2/19-3/20. The glyph for Pisces is ♓. Pisces is a Mutable Water sign. Pisces is the sign of the Good Samaritan. They always want to be of service to those in need. Neptune ♆, their ruling planet, makes them imaginative. They can be poets, writers, artists, religious leaders, composers and dancers. The symbol for Pisces is the two Fish tied together.

## THE MEANING OF THE PLANETARY GLYPHS *(hieroglyphics)*

Man consists of Spirit (solar), Soul (lunar) and Body (terrestrial).  He is capable of responding to impulses from the Solar, Lunar and Terrestrial planes of existence.

The Ancient symbolism of the **Circle**, **Crescent** and the **Cross** relates to the above mentioned.

The Circle stands as a symbol for the Spirit or the Sun, which is the source of life.  The circle has no beginning or ending.  It is continual, and is all encompassing.  It is the seed of the God force.  It is the supreme source which finds expression in the life of mankind.  In Eastern Indian religion, the circle was made by the snake holding its tail in its mouth.  This represented eternal life, infinity, no beginning or ending, just one supreme atom-the totality of all matter.  The circle is the life giver.

The Crescent stands for the symbol of the Soul of Man and the Moon.  Just as the Moon changes signs every 2 1/2 days, man goes through various phases.  The Moon receives its light from the Sun.  The Moon is like the Cups in the Tarot or a chalice.  They are containers.

The Cross is the symbol of the body of man and of the Earth.  It is the physical cross that the Soul suffers or works through while on the earth.  The cross of matter reminds us of the four seasons of the equinox: Spring, Summer, Fall and Winter, as well as sunrise, noon, sunset, midnight and cardinal activity.  It is also the polarity of the positive + and the negative - The square aspects in a chart are our crosses to bear.

All the planets are made from combinations of the Circle, Moon/Crescent and the Cross.

⊙ The Sun/circle is the infinite that encloses all.  It is spirit: a perfect circle with no beginning or ending.  The dot is the sperm or seed of man which is encompassed by the circle of the infinite, the God force. The central point denotes the highest spiritual aspect **WILL,** or Divine **SPIRIT,** or spark.  It represents the highest expression of the individual self; the self-conscious realization of ourselves and the universe.  Christians base their belief on a 3-fold aspect of the trinity.  There are 3 major phases of the Sun: dawn, noon, and sunset.  The rising Sun, dawn is the beginning and the promise of the day.  It is the giver of life and represents the father in the trinity.  Noon is when the Sun reaches maturity and shines upon everyone and helps things to grow and is the Son. The sunset is the end of the work day and a time of rest and represents the Holy Ghost. The Sun and the circle represents the totality of the Supreme Intelligence, the motivating force of creation.

☽ The Moon/crescent symbolizes the reflection of the Sun. It has no light of its own. It reflects the light of the Sun. It is the emotional, receptive plane. It is the Soul and the personality. It is our subconscious emotions, behavioral instincts and collective memory. It is the link between spirit and matter. The Moon rules the brain cells. It is the memory of the most important part of man: where he came from. This, joined with Pluto, gives the total information to the Soul. The Moon represents woman (Water) and the subconscious.

☿ Mercury uses all three parts. The Moon/crescent, the circle and cross. Mercury, the intellectual planet, shows the emotional or receptive nature is on top of the circle of the divine. By being the most elevated, it shows the Soul emerges and collects by the intuitive process. The Moon will be a receptacle like a satellite disk bringing information from the divine, which will have an impact on the cross of matter. The cross of matter on the bottom shows that our thinking is a struggle, and hard work brings out our higher self, the circle(spirit). The Moon and circle are trying to spiritualize matter.

♀ Venus, the love planet, only has the circle of the divine over the cross of matter/activity. The self (spirit) surmounts the cross of matter. The foundation brought by the hard stress allows the spirit to be elevated. Love conquers all. Until love enters our hearts, we are not in touch with anything in nature. Love produces harmony. The divine is superior to the cross of matter/activity. The divine is influencing matter. Venus has spirituality as its highest principle.

♂ Mars, the energy or will planet, reverses what is said of Venus. We have the cross of matter/activity superior to the divine. The activity or will is stronger than the spiritual. Desire and material is elevated above the self and creates outgoing energy. Passion and emotional aspects cause man to work outwards in the world. The spirit propels the cross of matter to accomplish. The spirit is held down until this happens. Mars used to be made with a cross and has now been changed to an arrow.

♃ Jupiter, the planet of growth, has the Moon/crescent to the side of the cross. When drawing this symbol make the Moon higher than the cross. The reflective Moon is superior to the cross. The soul has risen over matter. The result is that soul has passed through experience and profited by the trials and temptations. Soul conquers matter and is free. It knows the value of mercy and has tasted the divine. The true religious spirit comes from Jupiter. Through reflection and activity we grow. The Moon is trying to elevate the cross of matter.

♄ Saturn, the structure planet, has the cross of matter at the highest point and two crescents, or Soul, below it. This is just the opposite of Jupiter. Just turn Saturn's glyph upside down and you have Jupiter. The discipline of the cross of matter is placed as a heavy weight on the reflective nature. Saturn is the reaper and is cold and calculating. Saturn is the planet of limitation. Saturn helps to distinguish between truth and illusion. The Moon is your intuition and the cross of matter being elevated makes you prove everything. Interestingly, the Moon is Sat-upon.

♅ Uranus, the intuitive planet, has two Moons/crescents which absorb and reflect on each side. They are joined by the cross of matter/activity with the circle at the bottom of the cross. This shows that the cross of matter/activity needs the two satellites to bring in the reflective energy to then filter down to the circle of spirituality. The cross of matter holds down the spirit. The conscious and subconscious minds are united by the cross of matter. It is perfectly balanced. When intuition is used in a practical way, it will allow the spirit to rise. The head of the baby emerges: a breakthrough and a new birth.

♆ Neptune, the planet that rules our imagination and picture-making ability, has the crescent on the top and is pierced by the cross of matter. This shows the joining of the emotions and imagination and the need for the cross to anchor it. When we understand our Karma (cross) and we are in tune with the past (Moon), we have made a break through. (Practical intuition.) If the cross of matter does not anchor the Moon, our fears, emotions and imagination run away with themselves.

♇ Pluto, the planet of transformation and the planet that represents the memory of the Soul (as well as the Moon), has the circle of spirituality the highest and is not even connected to the crescent or cross. This shows that the spiritual is the ultimate and is cradled by the crescent/receptive Moon. Both are superior to the cross of matter. However, the cross is connected and becomes the foundation that holds the perception. The process that we go through in our physical life allows our Soul to be elevated which then becomes the chalice to hold the spirit. The spirit emerges and all has been completed. We work through our cross of matter/activity and accomplish the ultimate. Remember to keep your head in the spiritual while your feet are on the ground.

⊕ Earth is a combination of the circle and the cross. The cross of matter (karma) which represents the earth is encircled by the spiritual. The only way out is the spiritual. The two are joined together. Lift the cross out of the circle and you get the planet Venus ♀. This is seen on the box at the feet of the Hierophant.

## DIRECTIONS

**Directions are important.** If something is coming from the East it is a new opportunity. It is like the rising Sun. Each dawn it brings a new day. If it is coming from the West, it is already in the making. You could already be involved in it or know of it. If not, then you will become aware of it.

## HANDS

Throughout the cards you will see that objects are held in the hands of the people. The object itself is important, but even more important is which hand are they using.

When talking about the King, Queen, and Knights in reference to their hands, it would be as if you placed yourself in that position. Just take the card and place it on your chest with the King facing away from you. You can see that your right and left arms line up with those of the card. Now, walk straight ahead into the tree.

Your right arm is on the right pillar of the Tree and your left arm is on the left pillar. The right pillar and right arm is masculine/positive in energy and is the element of Fire. The right hand is the masculine, positive, Fire, outgoing, authoritative, active hand. When an object is in this hand the aggressive energy is being applied and the conscious mind is used.

The left pillar and left arm is feminine/receptive in energy and is the element of Water. The left hand is the feminine, receptive, Water, drawing in, sensitive, psychic and nurturing hand. When an object is in this hand the intuitive energy is being applied and the subconscious mind is used.

The middle pillar of the Tree represents the element of Air and aligns with the spinal column, kundalini or chakras.

## COLOR

Color is something to be aware of when looking at the Tarot cards. There are three primary colors. They are red, blue and yellow. They break down into 7 colors of the rainbow. These 7 colors can further divide into 12.

Since everything that we are talking about leads us to spirituality, it is only appropriate here to connect the colors as well. They relate to the elements and the Yod He' Vau He'. The three primary colors are related to the three elements and the three Hebrew letters also.

Red stands for the outgoing Fire element and the Hebrew letter Y,Yod ‎י.

Blue stands for the sensitive, nurturing Water element and the Hebrew letter H, He' ‎ה.

Yellow stands for the intellectual Air element and the Hebrew letter V, Vau ‎ו.

These three elements and letters are found in the Kabalah on Sephirah #1 (Kether) on the Tree. Kether is the Divine Light and, in throwing out this light, it creates the three pillars of the Tree. When you see them, remember that there is this connection. See Table 1: Color, page 23 for the meanings of colors.

## MUSICAL TONES FOR THE SIGNS

Every word rings a bell or has a musical vibration to it. The Zodiac signs can each correspond to a note also. See Table 1: The Musical Notes, page 23.

**Table 1:** <u>Colors and their meaning.</u>  |  <u>Musical notes for the signs.</u>

| Color Influence | Astrological Sign | Musical Note |
| --- | --- | --- |
| RED: Enthusiasm, aggressiveness, energy | Aries | DO |
| YELLOW: Intellectual, mental | Taurus | LA |
| GREEN: Growth | Gemini | MI |
| BLUE: Sensitivity | Cancer | TI |
| PURPLE: Spiritual (combines red & blue) | Leo | RE |
| GRAY: Wisdom and age | Virgo | MI |
| BROWN: Practical and earthy | Libra | LA |
| BLACK: Ignorance | Scorpio | DO |
| | Sagittarius | SOL |
| | Capricorn | FA |
| | Aquarius | FA |
| | Pisces | SOL |

# HEBREW ALPHABET

| Letter | Latin/Phonetic | # Value | Eqivalent | Word Value |
|--------|----------------|---------|-----------|------------|
| א | Aleph (Ah`leff) | 1 | A | Ox or Bull |
| ב | Beth (Bay`th) | 2 | Bh/V B | House |
| ג | Gimel (Ge mel) | 3 | GH/G | Camel |
| ד | Daleth (Dahl`eth) | 4 | DH/D | Door |
| ה | He' (Hay) | 5 | H | Window |
| ו | Vau (Vow) | 6 | V/W | Nail |
| ז | Zain (Zah` yeen) | 7 | Z | Sword |
| ח | Cheth (K a' th) | 8 | CH | Field |
| ט | Teth (Tath) | 9 | T | Serpent |
| י | Yod (Yodh) | 10 | Y | Hand |
| כ | Kaph (Kaff) | 20 (11) | KH/K | Closed Hand |
| ל | Lamed (Lahm`ed) | 30 (12) | L | Oxgoad |
| מ | Mem (Mam) | 40 (13) | M | Water |
| נ | Nun (Noon) | 50 (14) | N | Fish |
| ס | Samech (Sahm'ekh) | 60 (15) | S | A prop |
| ע | Ayin (Ah yeen') | 70 (16) | O | Eye |
| פ | Pe' (Pay) | 80 (17) | Ph=F/P | Mouth |
| צ | Tzaddi (Tzahddi) | 90 (18) | TS/X | Fish Hook |
| ק | Qoph (Quof) | 100(19) | Q | Back of Head |
| ר | Resh (Rash) | 200(20) | R | Head or Face |
| ש | Shin (Sheen) | 300(21) | SH/SCH/S | Teeth |
| ת | Tau (Tah` oo) | 400(22) | TH/T | Cross |

**Table 2: The Hebrew Alphabet**

The Hebrews used a system that combined letters and numbers. They were placed in an order to show evolution. The Kabalah is a work which describes the creation of the universe in terms of the Hebrew letters.

When talking about the Tree of Life, the Sephiroth (circles on the tree) are referred to as paths 1-10. (Sephiroth is plural and Sephirah is singular) Additionally, there are 22 more paths (they actually *are* paths) and are numbered 11-32. When the Sephiroth and paths are combined they form 32 paths. You will see that I will refer to the 11th path as #1 and the 12th path as #2 and the 13th path as #3, etc. This will be shown as follows: #11 (1), #12 (2), #13 (3), etc. The reason for this is that each path will vibrate to the number in the parenthesis, not the number of the path. Please make special note of this.

There are 22 letters in the Hebrew alphabet. They have numbers corresponding to their letters. In these 22 letters and numbers is the basis of all universal ideas. The 22 Hebrew letters and numbers go on the 22 paths #11-32 (#1-22) of the Tree of Life in the Kabalah. One of the 22 cards of the Major Arcana will be placed on each of the 22 paths. You can see this on page 42, Figure 4: Tree with Major Arcana cards on each path. In addition to each of the 22 cards of the Major Arcana being placed on one of the paths in the Tree, each path has a planet or astrological sign that relates to it. This planet and sign come from the Hebrew letters that are on that path. Even though we do not relate the numbers of the cards and paths together, we **do** relate the Hebrew letter, planet or astrological sign to the card placed there.

**There is an important difference when we talk about the numbers of the Hebrew alphabet and the number at the top of the _22 Tarot cards of the Major Arcana_ of the Rider Waite deck.** On the Tarot cards in the Rider Waite deck, the numbers on the Major Arcana cards start with 0 and end at 21. This gives us 22 cards. The cards of the Major Arcana are placed on the paths of the tree #11-32 (corresponding numbers 1-22). The cards start with the #0 but the paths of the Tree start with the #11(1). This first path can also be considered #1, since it is the first path for the Major cards as explained above.

Therefore, **when relating the numbers of the cards and paths together, they will be off by one number.** The number on the top of the card is for sequence. **We do not relate the card number on the Major Arcana to the Hebrew chronological order of letters and numbers.** If you try to do this, you will see that they do not line up. In the Rider Waite deck we start with the Fool and it is #0. The Fool is placed on the first path #11(1) of the Tree of Life. However, we do use the Hebrew letter of the first path to give us added information for the card. The first Hebrew letter is Aleph and it is a Mother letter relating to the element of Air. See the next page for explanation of the letters. Air is what we talk about that propelled the Fool on his way.

The Hebrew numbers **do** relate to the paths of the Tree and the Sephiroth in the Tree. They also relate to the numbers at the top of the cards in the **_Minor Arcana_**. The Minor Arcana are the suits of the cards. Each suit has a King, Queen, Knight, Page and cards numbered 1 through 10. The Minor Arcana are placed on the 10 Sephiroth (circles). The 10 Sephiroth are numbered 1-10 so they line up with the number of the cards. There is no problem here.

**Example**: If we look at the #5 in all the suits we see that the #5 is at the top of each card. All four of these cards that are numbered 5 will have the meaning of the #5 behind them. This #5 also relates to the #5 in the Hebrew system. These four cards will be placed on Sephirah #5.

I will try to keep this as clear as possible, by referring to each of the 10 Sephiroth (plural) as Sephirah (singular) and the 22 paths #11-32 (1-22) on the Tree as paths.

The Hebrew letters are divided into three groups. They are the Mother letters, the Double letters and the Simple letters.

## HEBREW MOTHER LETTERS

**MOTHER LETTERS** - Mother letters represent the **three elements:** Air, Water and Fire. In the Hebrew alphabet there are three mother letters. They are:

**Letter #1 Aleph א is Air.** This letter is on path #11 (1) in The Tree. The Tarot card on path #11 (1) is #0 (The Fool) which goes with Air.

**Letter #40 (also known as #13) Mem מ is Water.** This letter is on path #23 (13) in the Tree. The Tarot card on path #23 (13) is #12 (The Hanged Man) which goes with Water.

**Letter #300 (also known as #21) Shin ש is Fire.** This letter is on path #31 (21) in the Tree. The Tarot card on path #31 (21) is #20 (Judgement) which goes with Fire.

These three elements form the Trinity or the Supernal Triangle on the Tree. The three elements, when combined, form the element Earth.

# HEBREW DOUBLE LETTERS

**DOUBLE LETTERS** - They are called double because they indicate two sounds, one positive and strong, and the other negative and weak. It is a duality of hard and soft sounds. The Hebrew double letters represent the 7 **planets** which govern nature. These 7 planets were the only ones known to us at the time of the forming of the cards and religion. They also are the planets that rule each day of the week as well as the 7 directions: Above, Below, East, West, North, South and Center. See Table 3: Hebrew Double Letters, page 28.

**Example:** Notice that Hebrew double letter B ב (Beth) #2 is on path #12 (2). The planet Mercury goes with the Hebrew letter Beth. The Tarot card #1 (The Magician) is on path #12 (2). Since Mercury goes with the Hebrew letter and is on path #12 (2), the Magician, being placed on this path, is allowed to use the letter and planet. You can also see this on the following pages that have examples of the different Trees.

The planet that rules the day of the week on which you were born is important to you. The day it rules also is an eventful day for you. I have included a perpetual calendar so you can look up the day of the week on which you were born. See Table 5: The Perpetual Calendar on pages 30-31.

## HEBREW SIMPLE LETTERS

The simple Hebrew letters represent the 12 signs of the Zodiac and the 12 months. They also relate to the senses. See Table 4: Hebrew Simple Letters, page 29.

**Example:** Hebrew simple letter H, He' #5 is on path #15 (5) and brings with it the astrological sign Aries. The Emperor #4 is on path #15 (5) and is allowed to use the sign Aries.

If you understand what I have just related, then you understand the process from which the cards have evolved. I have created a sheet for each card which has explanations to help you with this understanding.

It is all right for you to mark your cards to help in remembering. Use a permanent marker, as a ball point will rub off. While marking your cards you might look at the back of the cards. If there is no way to tell if the card is upright or not, then put a mark in the upper corner to remind you if it is upright. This way, you will know before you turn your card over whether or not it is upside down. Being upside down changes the meaning of the card.

## Table 3: Hebrew Double Letters

| Hebrew Letter | Hebrew Number | Path # and Number | Planetary Connection | Day of Week | Tarot Card |
|---|---|---|---|---|---|
| ב Beth | 2 | 12 (2) | ☿ Mercury | Wednesday | The Magician (card #1) |
| ג Gimel | 3 | 13 (3) | ☽ Moon | Monday | The High Priestess (card #2) |
| ד Daleth | 4 | 14 (4) | ♀ Venus | Friday | The Empress (card #3) |
| כ Kaph | 20 | 21 (11) | ♃ Jupiter | Thursday | Wheel of Fortune (card #10) |
| פ Pe' | 80 | 27 (17) | ♂ Mars | Tuesday | The Tower (card #16) |
| ר Resh | 200 | 30 (20) | ☉ Sun | Sunday | The Sun (card #19) |
| ת Tau | 400 | 32 (22) | ♄ Saturn | Saturday | The World (card #21) |

## Table 4: Hebrew Simple Letters

| Hebrew Letter | Hebrew Number | Path # and Number | Astrology Sign | Sense/Action | Tarot Card |
|---|---|---|---|---|---|
| ה He' | 5 | 15 (5) | Aries | Sight | The Emperor (card #4) |
| ו Vau | 6 | 16 (6) | Taurus | Hearing | The Hierophant (card #5) |
| ז Zain | 7 | 17 (7) | Gemini | Smell | The Lovers (card #6) |
| ח Cheth | 8 | 18 (8) | Cancer | Speech | The Chariot (card #7) |
| ט Teth | 9 | 19 (9) | Leo | Taste | Strength (card #8)* |
| י Yod | 10 | 20 (10) | Virgo | Sexual Love | The Hermit (card #9) |
| ל Lamed | 30 | 22 (12) | Libra | Work | Justice (card #11)* |
| נ Nun(Noon) | 50 | 24 (14) | Scorpio | Movement | Death (card #13) |
| ס Samech | 60 | 25 (15) | Sagittarius | Anger | Temperance (card #14) |
| ע Ayin | 70 | 26 (16) | Capricorn | Mirth | The Devil (card #15) |
| צ Tzaddi | 90 | 28 (18) | Aquarius | Imagination | The Star (card #17) |
| ק Qoph | 100 | 29 (19) | Pisces | Sleep | The Moon (card #18) |

# PERPETUAL CALENDAR - 1776-2000

Look for the year you want in the index at left. The number opposite each year is the number of the calendar to use for that year.

Table 5: Perpetual Calendar

Table 5: Perpetual Calendar

# KABALISTIC TREE
## Queen Scale

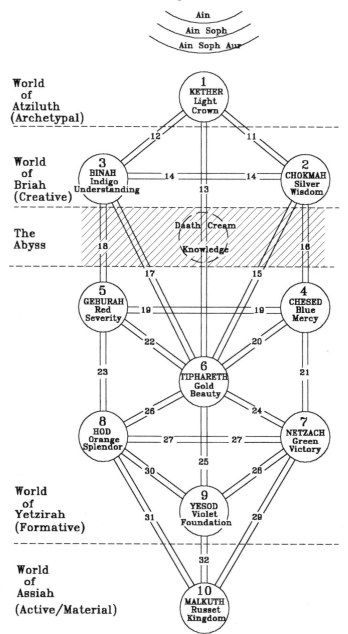

Figure 1: Kabalistic Tree

# THE KABALAH AND THE TREE OF LIFE

Let me explain that, when I talk about the Kabalah and the Tree of Life, I am **facing** the Tree. When referencing the right pillar it is the pillar on the right hand/East side of the paper. The left pillar is on the left hand/West side of the paper.

See Figure 1: Kabalistic Tree, on page 32 for reference.

## THE THREE VEILS

**Above the Tree are three veils**. They are called Ain, Ain Soph, Ain Soph Aur. The Tree is our universe, so anything outside of the Tree is the source as each individual knows it. This is the true God force or source from whence the Tree and we are created. A veil dimly hides what is there. It is veiled from understanding because it is beyond our comprehension. Energy flows constantly down to the Tree and to us.

The Ain is the pure white light of the God force. It is the highest of energies and veils. It is unmanifested, yet has the seed of positive existence.

The Ain Soph is a step below the Ain. It receives the light from Ain. It is said that it is the container to hold the light, but is also described as a container that does not allow the energy to remain there dormant. It is like a reflective piece of metal or the channel that the light of the Ain can bounce off of or flow through, in order to become the Ain Soph Aur. In other words, the Ain Soph receives, not to keep, but to be able to pass it on. When this energy-light is passed on, the Ain Soph Aur becomes the **Primordial Point** which makes the breakthrough and creates and manifests.

This Primordial Point is passed into Kether. Kether, the Divine Light and Crown is Sephirah #1. Encompassed in Kether are the three elements Fire, Water and Air. In the Minor Arcana read about how the four Aces also are in Kether and relate to the four elements. These elements are sent forward and create the three pillars of the tree. When all three elements are united the fourth element is formed, which is Earth. At the bottom of the Tree, in Sephirah #10 (Malkuth), is the Earth element. Notice how the three pillars are connected to Malkuth. Kether is at the top of the Air pillar and Malkuth is at the bottom of the Air pillar, but in its own Sephirah, which is the Earth element. Kether is #1 and Malkuth is #10 which reduces to #1 (1+0=1). So these two symbolize that old saying 'as above, so below'. This Air pillar is important because it can be a direct path to the top. It relates to the spine, kundalini and the chakras. It is the pillar of equilibrium.

Once this Tree is created and the 10 Sephiroth are put in place, the tree is then divided into worlds. There are four worlds. Each world will relate to an element also. These worlds are shown to the left of the Tree on page 32.

## THE FOUR WORLDS

**The World of Atziluth** is the Archetypal World. It represents the Primal Fire element and the Yod. Sephirah #1 (Kether) is where all divine light and the elements are found. This world is of pure spirit and from it the other worlds evolve. The Gods are placed here. This is the world of pure ideas, the God source.

As we go down the Tree it becomes more dense until it turns into matter. Each world generates the next world. This is the same with the Sephiroth.

**The World of Briah** is the Creative World and represents the Primal Water element and the He'. This world is created through Sephiroth #2 and #3 (Chokmah and Binah). Here lie the Archangels. The ideas from the Archetypal World are now being created.

**The Abyss and Daath** is between The World of Briah and Yetzirah and is a space of demarcation of varying degrees of consciousness. The World of Briah, consisting of the Supernal Triangle, is the higher states of consciousness. Sephirah #3 (Binah) represents the archetypal idea of form, Sephirah #4 (Chesed) is a Sephirah of forms. Daath, which is in the space between Binah and Chesed, represents the state where actual forms are precipitated from the interaction of supernal forces. It is different than Kether in that Kether manifests force and Daath manifests form. From Daath the Supernal forces are brought down across the Abyss to manifest in form as 'abstract knowledge.' The Abyss is the void between force and form; the place where the transmutation takes place is known as the hidden Sephirah (Daath) which means Knowledge. This Sephirah has no number allocated to it. It is behind the Air pillar. It is said to have a color of lavender, silvery gray, pure violet, and gray-flecked yellow.

Inspiration and great awareness come from this place. The word knowledge is misleading here as this is a place where different planes of being impact and there is a resultant change of state: birth, transformation/transmutation of power. It is said that this is the Sacred Mountain that Moses contacted when he received the inspiration for the Ten Commandments on Mt. Sinai.

Pause here a minute to picture this mountain. As you study the cards in the Tarot you will see that mountains appear on them. When this happens it shows that one is trying to reach the top of that mountain. Mountains represent spiritual attainment. This is the place where transmutation takes place (Daath and the Abyss). It is where one reaches Nirvana.

On the way down the Tree, one makes the transition from above to below and becomes aware of self, with the Spirit functioning in earthly matters. In evolution up the Tree is the place where the awareness of the Soul exists and one makes the transition from the earth into the Supernal Life. When one has reached the point of making the transition into the next dimension of life, and it is time to make the choice to reincarnate or to return to the source, the choice is made. This is where the human body is shed, and the Soul decides where it will go.

Daath is the highest point of awareness of the human Soul, where it is able to understand on Supernal levels. It is the gateway called Nirvana where the Soul has reached complete evolution. After the powers of Daath are fully operative in a Soul, there is no further process of 'becoming,' for that Soul 'is.' Daath is called the Mystical Sephirah as it is the correct understanding of mysticism. It is clear realization of the various potencies of life and their unity with God and with the Soul. Here, there is a balance of realization and the absorption of these potencies with the abstract mind. The mind unites with the mind of God.

**The World of Yetzirah** is the Formative World and represents the Primal Air element and the Vau. The angels reside here. This World consists of Sephiroth 4, 5, 6, 7, 8, and 9. (Chesed, Geburah, Tiphareth, Netzach, Hod, and Yesod) These six Sephiroth contain six of the planets. This is where we can grow through the understanding of Astrology. Our chart will tell us where each of these planets is placed and how we have to work through them in order to evolve. Through these we work on our earthly evolution which leads us to our Christ center, Sephirah #6 (Tiphareth). The idea from the Archetypal World now becomes an actual expression.

**The World of Assiah** is the active Material World. It is the physical world, the world of sensation. It is the unseen energies of matter. The element it represents is Primal Earth and the second He'. The cherubim reside here. This is appropriate since Sephirah #10 (Malkuth) is the Earth element and Assiah works through the Sephirah #10. Here the idea has evolved into physical existence.

## PILLARS

Sephirah #1 (Kether) contains the elements that form the three pillars on the Tree of Life. By disseminating its energy, like seeds being sown, the pillars are formed.

The **right pillar is positive or masculine or active**. It, therefore, is the element of **Fire. The Kings** are placed here.

The **left pillar is negative or feminine or receptive.** It is the element of **Water. The Queens** go here.

The **middle pillar** symbolizes the consciousness of Man balancing the positive and negative of life. It is the element of **Air. Air is the path of equilibrium. The Knights** are on Sephirah #6 (Tiphareth) on the Air Pillar.

The **base** of the Tree is **Earth. The Pages** are here on Sephirah #10 (Malkuth).

See Figure 2: Tree with Pillars and Sephiroth, on page 37.

These four elements relate to the four suits of cards:
**Fire** - Wands, **Water** - Cups, **Air** - Swords, and the **Earth** - Pentacles.

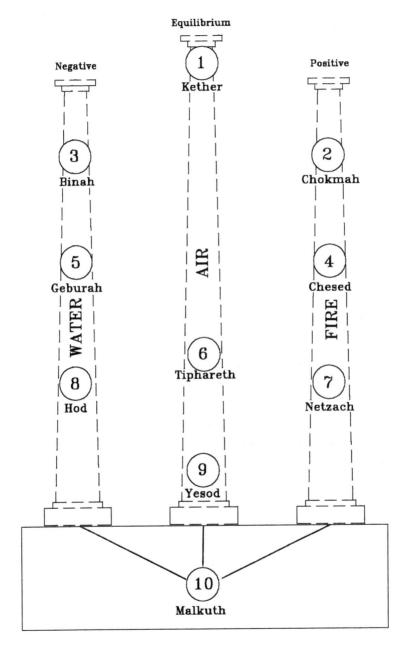

**Figure 2: Tree with Pillars and Sephiroth**

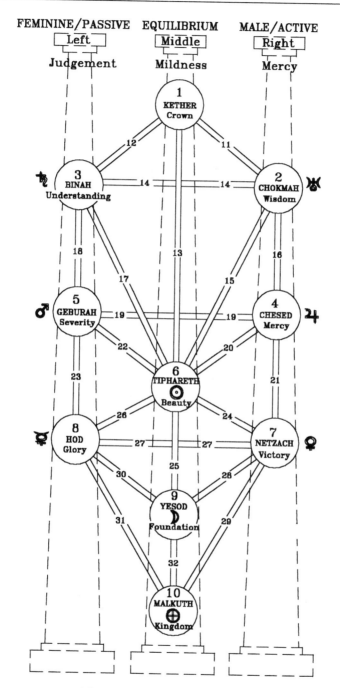

**Figure 3: Tree of Life with Sephiroth**

# THE MINOR ARCANA
## #1-10 are placed on the 10 SEPHIROTH of
## THE TREE OF LIFE

See Figure 3: Tree of Life with Sephiroth, page 38.

There are 10 Sephiroth (circles) placed on the pillars. They are numbered 1-10. Each one picks up the element of the pillar it is on. Since polarity is important to make energy and cause events, each Sephirah will alternate from + positive to - negative. The positive ones are 1, 2, 4, and 7. The negative ones are 3, 5, 8, and 10. Each Sephirah is dependent on the next one in order to grow and be fulfilled. As they increase in number, the energy becomes more dense. This goes without saying that when the numbers decrease in number, the energy is lighter. The cards 1-10 in the Minor Arcana are placed on the Sephiroth. Since there are four suits of cards, there will be four cards on each of the Sephirah.

Each Sephirah has an astrological planet that corresponds to it. At the time of the creation of the Kabalah there were only 7 known planets. The planet Uranus, later discovered, is placed on Sephirah #2. This makes a total of 8 planets used.

All #1's (Aces) are on the Sephirah #1 (**Kether**, Crown, Divine Light) and contains the masculine, positive element Air which is intellectual. Behind Kether is negative existence from which all things came. This is referred to as the Veils of Negativity: the Ain, Ain Soph and the Ain Soph Aur. Negativity is nothing and yet it is already something. It is up to Kether to disperse the energy of the elements in order to form the Tree of Life.

All the **2's** are on the **right** Fire, positive pillar on Sephirah #2 (**Chokmah,** Wisdom and the planet Uranus ♅). Since this is a Fire pillar, we start interpreting the cards by first looking at the Two of Wands (Wands are Fire).

All the **3's** are on the **left** Water, negative pillar on Sephirah #3 (**Binah,** Understanding and the planet Saturn ♄). Binah is called the Mother of Form as it completes the first triangle on the Tree. Since this is a Water pillar we start interpreting the cards by first looking at the Three of Cups. (Cups are Water).

Sephiroth #1, 2, and 3 make up the Supernal or Archetypal Triangle. They represent the super-conscious and spiritual aspects of the psyche. See page 55 for the three triangles.

Between the Supernal Triangle and Sephirah #4 (Chokmah), we find the Abyss and the hidden Sephirah Daath.

All the 4's are on the **right** Fire, positive pillar on Sephirah #4 (**Chesed,** Mercy and the planet Jupiter ♃). Another name is Greatness or Magnificence. Since this is the Fire pillar, we start interpreting the cards by first looking at the Four of Wands. Four is a square or a foundation stone upon which all further development in form is based.

All the **5's** are on the nurturing **left** Water, negative pillar on Sephirah #5 (**Geburah,** Severity, Strength or Fear and the planet Mars ♂). Since this is the Water pillar, we start interpreting the cards by first looking at the Five of Cups. Chesed and Geburah are opposite each other. Opposites work together: one is positive and assertive and one is negative or receptive to balance the structure. These two are the beginning of the World of Formation and work together with their energy to start the universe or the world as we know it.

All the **6's** are on the intellectual **middle** Air, positive pillar on Sephirah #6 (**Tiphareth,** Beauty and the Sun ☉). Since this is the Air pillar, we start interpreting the cards by first looking at the Six of Swords (Swords are Air). This pillar is the spine and refers to the chakras. The Sun is the Solar plexus and, astrologically, it rules the heart. The Tree's heartbeat is here. The middle pillar is the pillar of equilibrium. All paths lead into Tiphareth.

This pillar holds everything in balance the same way that the Sun holds all the planets in their orbits of gravitation. This is where man's religious beliefs lie.

Sephiroth #4, 5, and 6 form the Ethical or Moral Triangle with Chesed, Geburah, and Tiphareth.

All the **7's** are on the **right** Fire, positive pillar on Sephirah #7 (**Netzach,** Victory and the planet Venus ♀). Since this is the Fire pillar, we start interpreting the cards by first looking at the Seven of Wands. This Sephirah is the creative imagination. It is here that the 7 bands of the spectrum of Tiphareth divide.

All the **8's** are on the **left** Water, negative pillar on Sephirah #8 (**Hod,** Splendor and the intellectual planet Mercury ☿). Since this is the Water pillar, we start interpreting the cards by first looking at the Eight of Cups.

From Netzach the energy comes to Hod. They are opposite on the Tree. Number 8 is a double 4. Sephirah #4 (Chesed) brings Jupiter ♃, the planet of expansion, increase and philosophy. Chesed is diagonally opposite Hod on the Tree. Above Chesed is Chokmah which starts the rhythm of the Tree. Chokmah brings Uranus ♅, the planet of quickening, and Hod brings Mercury ☿, the planet of breathing. The 8 is the number of our breathing. Uranus is the planet of higher cosmic thought and Mercury is the planet of everyday common knowledge.

All the **9's** are on the **middle** Air, positive pillar on Sephirah #9 (**Yesod** Foundation and the intuitive planet the Moon). Since this is the Air pillar we start interpreting the cards by first looking at the Nine of Swords. This is the foundation of the physical form.

This completes the formation of the Astral, Psychological or Material Triangle of Netzach, Hod and Yesod. (Sephiroth 7, 8, 9)

Malkuth is on its own and is the physical Earth world.

All the **10's** are on the **bottom**. It is the feminine, receptive **Earth** ⊕ so we start with 10 of Pentacles. Sephirah #10 (**Malkuth**, Kingdom) and the Earth are here.

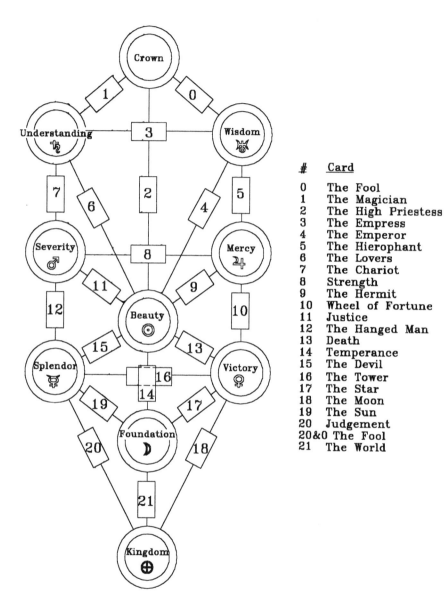

| # | Card |
|---|------|
| 0 | The Fool |
| 1 | The Magician |
| 2 | The High Priestess |
| 3 | The Empress |
| 4 | The Emperor |
| 5 | The Hierophant |
| 6 | The Lovers |
| 7 | The Chariot |
| 8 | Strength |
| 9 | The Hermit |
| 10 | Wheel of Fortune |
| 11 | Justice |
| 12 | The Hanged Man |
| 13 | Death |
| 14 | Temperance |
| 15 | The Devil |
| 16 | The Tower |
| 17 | The Star |
| 18 | The Moon |
| 19 | The Sun |
| 20 | Judgement |
| 20&0 | The Fool |
| 21 | The World |

**Figure 4: Tree with Major Arcana Cards on Each Path**

## THE MAJOR ARCANA
## 0-22 are placed on the 22 PATHS of
## THE TREE OF LIFE

See Figure 4: Tree with Major Arcana Cards on each Path, page 42

The pillars of the Tree have been formed. The ten Sephiroth are in place. Now we connect the pillars and Sephiroth by adding the 22 paths numbered 11-32 (1-22). Remember that the reason for starting with #11 is that the Sephiroth were numbered 1-10. Every path connects two Sephiroth together. The 22 Major Arcana cards are placed on the paths. Each one defines the experience needed to unite two Sephiroth together.

The paths between the 10 Sephiroth are channels that partake of the meaning of the two Sephiroth they connect and show a way of blending or working out the energy of the Sephirah. Remember, we discussed previously that the numbers for the 22 Major Arcana are different from the path numbers. Hebrew letters and numbers, and Astrological planets and signs, go with the paths.

Sephirah #6 (Tiphareth) is the vital center of the Tree. Most of the paths connect with it. The light of Kether shines directly down the middle Pillar (Air) and becomes the life light in Tiphareth (Sun/Son Christ center). Each of the 22 cards of the Major Arcana are discussed in full in Part One, The Major Arcana.

# NUMBERS

At this time we are going to study the numbers from 1-10 in detail. A thorough knowledge of each one will allow you to understand the setup on the cards.

Pythagoras got his knowledge of numbers from the Hindus. The Hindus considered numbers to be a sacred science and declared that they came from God. The Hebrews also attached this significance to numbers. They used numbers and letters together. Their numbers were placed in an order and given a form that showed the beginning of and levels of cosmic evolution. Every letter of a word that was written or spoken could be transposed into numbers and reduced to a single digit. Each number had a meaning behind it. The meaning of the number will relate to the card.

This is why they are placed on the paths and Sephiroth of the Tree of Life of the Kabalah. The numbers and paths tell us about the lessons that lead us to spiritual fulfillment.

The Zodiac is made up of a circle of 360 degrees. This circle can be divided by the numbers 1-9. Each number is called a harmonic. When a number is divided into 360, the sum will show the structure that goes with the number (such as when 4 is divided into 360 degrees the result is 90 degrees). The #4 and also 90 degrees represents the form of the square. This is called the square aspect in astrology and means that the energy between the two planets is stressful. The #4 also has this meaning. You will see this as we continue and talk about numbers.

## COMPARISON between the Tarot and regular cards

The Tarot deck is unique in that it has 78 cards. 22 of the cards are the Major Arcana and are considered spiritual abilities and lessons. The other 56 cards are the Minor Arcana and deal more with the mundane matters of life. The following is a comparison between a regular deck of 56 cards and the Tarot deck. Each deck has four suits. The Minor Arcana is similar to a regular deck of cards that have the four suits of hearts, diamonds, spades, and clubs. The four Knights are the same as the Jacks. The difference is that the Minor Arcana includes four cards called the Pages.

| REGULAR DECK | TAROT DECK | ASTROLOGICAL ELEMENT |
|---|---|---|
| Hearts | Cups | Water |

The Hearts and Cups represent Water which is sensitivity and emotions. Water is receptive and maternal. The astrological Water signs are Cancer, Scorpio and Pisces.

| Clubs | Wands | Fire |
|---|---|---|

The Clubs and Wands represent Fire. Fire is aggressive, outgoing with enthusiastic energy. The astrological Fire signs are Aries, Leo and Sagittarius.

| Spades | Swords | Air |
|---|---|---|

The Spades and the Swords are Air. Air represents intellectual knowledge, intuition and communication. When consciousness is exalted to the level of pure wisdom, spiritual intuitiveness and full realization of unity exists. The astrological Air signs are Gemini, Libra and Aquarius.

| Diamonds | Pentacles | Earth |
|---|---|---|

The Diamonds and the Pentacles are Earth. Earth represents hard work, goals, business and money. The astrological Earth signs are worldly and materialistic and are the signs Taurus, Virgo and Capricorn.

## NUMBERING THE CARDS

The first 22 cards, which are the Major Arcana, are numbered 0-22. If you were to continue numbering the cards to 78, they would fall into the pattern shown below. The 56 Minor Arcana cards are divided into suits. They follow in the same order as the creation of the pillars.

Fire=**Wands**
Water=**Cups**
Air=**Swords**
Earth=**Pentacles**

Starting with the suit of Wands and the next number in succession, 23, we have the **King of Wands** #23, **Queen of Wands** #24, **Knight of Wands** #25, **Page of Wands** #26, **Ace of Wands** #27, **2 of Wands** #28, **3 of Wands** #29, **4 of Wands** #30, **5 of Wands** #31, **6 of Wands** #32, **7 of Wands** #33, **8 of Wands** #34, **9 of Wands** #35, and **10 of Wands** #36.

The first suit, Wands, starts with #23 and ends with #36. This gives us 14 cards.

You can do this with all the suits. Take a moment now and number your Minor Arcana cards. Make sure you follow in the order listed.

The suit of Cups is next. It starts with #37 and ends with #50. This gives us 14 cards: King, Queen, Knight, Page, Ace, 2, 3, 4, 5, 6, 7, 8, 9, 10.

The next suit is that of Swords. It starts at #51 and ends with #64. This gives us 14 cards: King, Queen, Knight, Page, Ace, 2, 3, 4, 5, 6, 7, 8, 9, 10.

The last suit is the Pentacles starting with #65 and ending with #78. This gives us 14 cards: King, Queen, Knight, Page, Ace, 2, 3, 4, 5, 6, 7, 8, 9, 10.

Another interesting thing to be aware of when looking at the cards in the **Minor** Arcana is the positioning of the Cups, Wands, Swords and Pentacles in each individual card. They will be separated, forming different clusters of the objects. There is a reason for this. The number of the card has a meaning. That number can be made up by different combinations of numbers. For instance let us use card #7 for an example. The number 7 can be made from the following combinations; 1+6=7, 3+4=7, 2+5=7. Each number 1-9 has its own meaning. The combination of numbers forming the #7 would represent a specific message to be understood. As we talk about each number individually, this will be explained further.

The basic numbers are 1-9. When a number consists of two digits they are added together to get a single digit number. This tells us what vibration the number is responding to (such as #18 is 1+8=9). Number 9 and 18 have the same meaning. However, #9 would be on the lowest level and #18 would be on the second level.

The numerical value for any word will give you a clue to the energy behind that word. Once you know the meaning for each number, you can interpret the energy behind the word. Each letter can be substituted for a number. See next page for this chart.

```
1  2  3  4  5  6  7  8  9
A  B  C  D  E  F  G  H  I
J  K  L  M  N  O  P  Q  R
S  T  U  V  W  X  Y  Z
```

# NUMBERS 0-10

## NUMBER 0

**NUMBER 0** is the source before manifestation. **Number 1 is God, the one divine unity.**

**EVEN NUMBERS** are mundane and work on the physical plane. They are #2, #4, #6, #8 etc.

**ODD NUMBERS** are divine and work on the spiritual plane. When odd numbers are divided by 2, 1(one) remains. The odd numbers are #1, #3, #5, #7, etc. The 1 (one) that remains represents the God force, or the deity in the midst of his works. Number 1 can remain unchanged. If you divide it by 1 it remains 1. If you multiply it by 1 it remains 1. Number 1 (one) is like the straight path that leads to spiritual understanding. When referring to the Kabalah, consider that Sephirah #1 (Kether, on the top of the Air pillar) is connected to Sephirah #10 (Malkuth on the bottom of the Air pillar) 10=1+0=1. 'As above, so below.' The Air pillar is a direct root to that which is below (the Earth). This pillar connects Kether and Malkuth. At the end of the Fool's journey on his way home, this is the path that he spiraled upward to receive the Divine Crown of Light.

# NUMBER 1

```
( 1 )  Kether
 |\
 | \      Path 11 (1) - (The Fool)
Air\               Air
 |   \
 |    \
```

**Number 1, ꜞ YOD, Masculine, Positive, Father**
Number 1 represents individuality, that which is born from spirit. It is initiation. It is the upright geometrical line. In this #1 is all potential creative force. It is spirit descending into matter. Number 1 is male, man, the father force, positive (+) and outgoing like the Yang energy. (The Chinese use the Yin and Yang to express the receptive/negative and positive/outgoing energy). It is ever creating and expressing the function of creativeness. It is the foundation of all His love and His seeking for union with God, expressing itself in a desire to create. One is a single principle, and if it is to go forward another principle must be added or it remains forever a #1. So a whirlwind of energy starts everything moving. When Air is active, it brings about changes. When it is quiet, it is in a meditative state.

**Sephirah #1 (Kether, Crown)** is where creation merges with the veils of nonexistence. This is the place of The Most Holy Ancient One, the Creator of All. Divine light carries the energy of the #1. Kether is on the middle pillar which is the Air pillar on the Tree. Air balances Fire and Water. If you think about the bellows that one uses to get a fire going, the Air element does that also to the other elements. This makes movement. In the beginning a whirlwind of Air propelled the Souls onward. Every element can have a positive and negative side. Air being positive can also be negative when it is rushing and destructive. Even then, the destruction can bring about a positive result such as a storm removing old debris to make way for new growth. Each Sephirah has to make movement in order to reach the next Sephirah. Kether is the Sephirah that will produce the other nine Sephiroth on The Tree. It receives the descending energy from the Primordial Point and now uses this energy to create.

**The 1st Hebrew letter A (Aleph) א** is the same as #1. It is the first of the Hebrew Mother letters representing Air. It is the breath of life as manifested in man. It can be thought of as the breath of God since it is Air. For God "Breathed into his nostrils the breath of life and man became a living Soul."

Number 1 has so much creative energy that a person must decide how to use it. (Raw energy, positive, original, creative, a leader and pioneer.) Number one is always the beginning of anything. You always start anything new on a #1 year.

Aleph = 1, Alpha = 1, Omega = 10 (in Greek) is the same as the Hebrew letter Y, Yod is #10 and when reduced is a #1.

**Path #11 (1)** means the same as #1. The Hebrew letter A, Aleph is on this path. The path will carry us across to the next Sephiroth. The Tarot card #0 The Fool is also on this path. The Fool used the Air to propel himself to earth.

**1st commandment:** "I am the Lord thy God. Thou shalt have no other gods before me." Exodus, XX, 2,3 (the God force is #1)

**In reference to Astrology** #1 is like the conjunction aspect. This is powerful energy.

**The Tarot cards** relating to the energy of #1 are card #1 in the Major Arcana, (The Magician) and the four Aces in the Minor Arcana.

When using a number for a letter in the English alphabet, we can get a numerical value for a word. Substituting a number for each letter, the following words reduce to #1, which means that they have the power of what is written above. See page 47 for the letter equivalent to number table.

Heaven = 8,5,1,4,5,5=28=10=1
Spirit = 1,7,9,9,9,2=37=10=1
Man = 4,1,5=10=1
Adam = 1,4,1,4 =10=1

# NUMBER 2

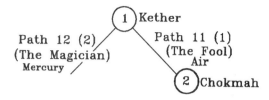

Path 12 (2)
(The Magician)
Mercury

①Kether

Path 11 (1)
(The Fool)
Air

②Chokmah

**Number 2 or II, ּ ֹ HE', Feminine, Receptive (negative), Mother**
Number 2 is a reflection of itself or the #1. It is like the Roman Numeral II.
It is duality, polarity, inner reflection, the mother principle. It is receptive
energy and can therefore be like Yin. The Moon represents the feminine
energy and reflects the light of the Sun. The Sun is like #1 and masculine.
The Moon is like #2 and feminine. It also represents the element Water and
water reflects. Number 2 separates from the father. The energy of 1 is
broken up in order to create + (positive) and - (negative), Spirit and Matter.
It is the perfect union of Man positive and Woman negative. Number 1 is the
straight line showing the descent of the Soul into matter. Matter is the
horizontal line that crosses the #1 and forms the cross of matter +. The #2
can never enclose itself. It is powerless until the #3 closes it up and makes a
triangle.

Referring to the Bible #1 is Adam, #2 is Eve. Number 2 is woman, creation,
productive forces, divine mother force, holy ghost. The foundation of
woman's love is divine mother love. Mother love is woman's divine state.
The womb is the inner shrine or secret place where we can retire.

The right pillar on the Tree is the positive, masculine, Fire pillar and the left
pillar is the negative, feminine, Water pillar.

**Sephirah #2** is (**Chokmah,** Wisdom) and carries the energy of the #2.
Chokmah is on the right pillar which is the Fire pillar on the Tree. Because
it is on the Fire pillar it works through the positive, masculine energy. It is
the seminal spark of life but not complete until it joins with Binah (mother).
The planet Uranus is placed here. Just as Chokmah is Wisdom, Uranus is
cosmic knowledge. It is the knowing beyond our everyday concept. It is our
intuition that allows us to always know that we are connected to something
greater than us.

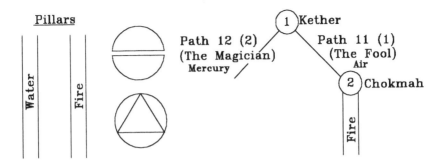

Pillars

Path 12 (2)
(The Magician)
Mercury

1 Kether

Path 11 (1)
(The Fool)
Air

2 Chokmah

Water

Fire

Fire

**The 2nd Hebrew letter is B (Beth)** ב and the same as #2. It is one of the 7 Hebrew double letters and brings with it the planet Mercury. Mercury is the planet that rules our intellect. It means house or sanctuary and therefore can be a birthplace. Beth-el is the house of God, Eliz-a-beth is house of Eliza, Beth-lehem is house of bread. A house is like a container because it can house our studies and any knowledge. The hieroglyphic for Beth looks like a wide open mouth. It is also thought of as the womb. All of these expressions show a container. The #2 is on Sephirah #2 and thinking of 2 as a house one can relate to the word Wisdom for this Sephirah. Sephirah #2 houses our knowledge.

**Path #12 (2)** is the 2nd path. It, therefore, represents #2. The Hebrew letter B, Beth and the intellectual planet Mercury are on this path. The Tarot card #1, The Magician, is on this path. The Magician uses the planet Mercury (the intelligence) to know that his power comes from above.

**The 2nd commandment:** "Thou shalt not make unto thee any graven image, or any likeness of *any thing* that *is* in heaven above, or that *is* in the earth beneath, or that *is* in the water under the earth. Thou shalt not bow down thyself to them, nor serve them." Exodus, XX,4, 5.

**Astrology:** Since #1 remains stagnant nothing can manifest without duality. Number 2 is the contrasts and the pair of opposites. In Astrology the #2 is like the opposition aspect. Opposition cuts the circle of 360 degrees into two halves. It is reflective, balancing or pulling apart. Since it is duality, it is balancing the positive and negative. It is good and evil, truth and error, day and night, hot and cold, pleasure and pain, health and sickness, joy and sorrow, male and female. The astrological glyph for the sign of Gemini is II.

It is thought of as the twin. Gemini is the sign that goes with the intellectual planet Mercury.

The #2 has to do with joining or pulling apart. If you take the 2 and apply it to the same spot, balance occurs. It is the same as when two people want the same thing. They work toward a common goal. Two opposite forces pull apart which is the negative energy of the #2. The opposing force makes something happen: action and counter action.

**The Tarot cards** relating to the energy of #2 are card #2 in the Major Arcana (The High Priestess), and the four 2's in the Minor Arcana.

Ecclesiastes, XXX, 1,2,4,6,8 tells us about the polarity of the positive and negative.

1. "To every thing there is a season, and a time for every purpose under the heaven:

2. "A time to be born, and a time to die; A time to plant, and a time to pluck up that which is planted;

4. "A time to weep and a time to laugh; A time to mourn, and a time to dance;

6. "A time to get, and a time to lose; A time to keep, and a time to cast away;

8. "A time to love, and a time to hate; A time of war, and a time of peace."

# NUMBER 3

**Number 3, )VAU is Completion, the forming of the trine.**

Trine
1+2=3

The #3 completes and brings form. Form can only be produced when the active principle of #1 and the receptive principle of #2 are blended together to form #3. This forms the trinity or triangle. Any act of creativity produces a product. Man who is positive and masculine, plus Woman who is negative and feminine, when put together are able to produce, and that can be a child or any object of their desires. Man the conscious mind, woman the subconscious mind, join together and form the child, the super-conscious mind.

Number 3 symbolizes the evolution of the pairs (II) of opposites to a point of perfect balance as at-one-ment with their source. All Souls are pre-existent in the world of emanations and are in their original state androgynous, but when they descend upon the earth they become separated into male and female and inhabit different bodies. If in this mortal life the male half encounters the female half, a strong attachment springs up between them. Therefore, it is said that in marriage the separated halves are again conjoined and the hidden forms of the Soul are akin to the cherubim. Since #1, #2, and #3 form the Supernal Triangle, our soul mate really is God or you may call it Universal spirit. Number 3 is a symbol of satisfaction and completion.

A triangle has a solid base and is pointing up. When anything is pointed up it means that the Supernal energy is involved. Think of it as pointing towards the heavens.

**Sephirah #3** is **Binah** (Understanding) and is feminine. It is on the Water pillar which is also feminine or receptive (negative). The Trine is now formed by the three Sephiroth on the Tree. They are the Sephirah #1 (**Kether,** Divine light), Sephirah #2 (**Chokmah,** Wisdom), and Sephirah #3 (**Binah,** Understanding). Chokmah the father and Binah the mother are the key to sex as the biological opposites male and female. Binah is like the divine mother who by *understanding* divine light and wisdom can bring them forth in our lives. Divine light and Wisdom are not complete until understanding has been accomplished. Before understanding is added there are only two single lines. When understanding is added, it is complete and forms the triangle. This is the **Supernal Triangle.** Kether is on the middle

Air pillar, Chokmah is on the right Fire pillar, and Binah is on the left Water pillar. The elements of Air, Fire and Water joined together create matter which will then be the next number, which is 4. These three Sephiroth pull the Tree together and radiate their energy below.

The #1 Sephirah is Air and establishes a force that can flow around and back to the starting point. Sephirah #2 is Fire which has leadership qualities and always activates and starts. Sephirah #3 is Water and allows a flow of polarity where, when transformed as force, can travel back and forth. These three form the triangle or trinity (doc-TRINE or TRIN-ity).

Saturn is the planet on Sephirah #3. Saturn is the task master and stands for structure and stability. The placement of Saturn in the astrological chart tells what the Karma for this life time is. It is said that Saturn ate his children. What this means is that he gave them birth and he also gave them death. In #3 the birth takes place. On path #32 (22) the Hebrew double letter T, Tau also represents Saturn. When we come to the end we also have to deal with Saturn as we make our transition. It is then the time to see if we have fulfilled our Karma.

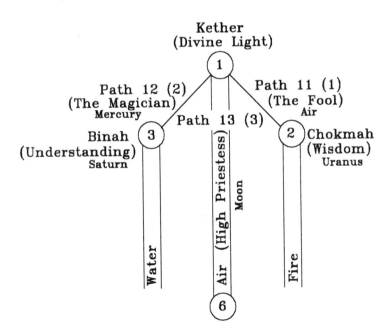

There are three triangles that are formed on the Tree of Life. They are the Supernal Triangle, the Ethical Triangle and the Material Triangle.

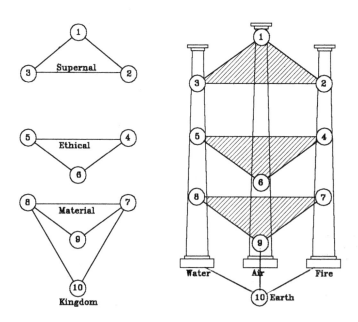

**The 3rd Hebrew letter is G (Gimel)** ‎ג‎. Gimel is the 2nd of the 7 double letters and brings with it the planet the Moon. It is called Camel or Gamal in Hebrew. A camel holds water. Water represents life.

**Path #13 (3)** is the 3rd path and, therefore, represents #3. Hebrew letter G, Gimel on path #13 (3) is on the Air pillar of the Tree. It connects Sephirah #1 (Kether, Divine Light) with Sephirah #6 (Tiphareth, Beauty). The divine light from Kether shines all the way down the Air pillar to Tiphareth.

Tiphareth represents the planet the Sun. In the olden days the Sun and the planets were worshipped for the power that was behind them. The Sun was very important and it was always adorned. The Sun is the center of our galaxy and became the Son (Christ consciousness), center of The Tree. His light and the light of Kether from the father above shines out for us. In the Tarot cards you will often see the Sun off in the distance showing that we are trying to travel the path to higher consciousness. Sephirah #6 is the life force for the Tree. The High Priestess sits on this path between Kether and Tiphareth.

She faces the Sun and draws in its power and adds to it the perception and psychic ability given to her by the Moon which Gimel represents. Being between the two great lights makes her very powerful.

She sits between the right Fire pillar and left Water pillar. Again we are balancing the elements of Fire and Water. The right pillar is Jachin which means yes and the left is Boaz which means no. She is connected to these two pillars and Kether. She has all the knowledge that is possible.

**3rd commandment:** "Thou shalt not take the name of the Lord (Law) thy God in vain; for the Lord (Law) will not hold him guiltless that taketh his name in vain." Exodus, XX,7

To pronounce a word is to evoke a thought and make it present. Air represents speech. We are responsible and will be made responsible for every wrong word or deed we put into being. When we speak we put form to what is being said. In the alphabet there are 26 numbers. These 26 sum up to 8 (2+6=8). Eight is infinity when turned on its side. The numerical value for God is: G is 7, O is 15 and D is 4. 7+15+4=26  26=8  God is present in all words. When we manifest on any plane (physical, mental, or spiritual) we experience ecstasy from the conscious union with the higher self. Examples are when we perform an unselfish deed, say a kind word, or express generous forgiveness.

**Astrology:** In Astrology the Trine aspect is formed by dividing the circle of 360 degrees by 3 and getting 120 degrees. A trine is the angle of 120 degrees. The trine involves three signs that are of the same element. Since we have four elements there are four trines formed from the twelve signs of the Zodiac. The three Fire signs that trine are Aries, Leo and Sagittarius. The three Earth signs that trine are Taurus, Virgo, and Capricorn. The three Air signs that trine are Gemini, Libra and Aquarius. The three Water signs that trine are Cancer, Scorpio and Pisces. Sign #3 in the zodiac is the intellectual sign Gemini.

**The Tarot** cards relating to the number 3 are the Major Arcana #3 The Empress and the four 3's in the Minor Arcana. **There is a hidden message in each of the cards from 1-10 in the Minor Arcana. This hidden message is known only to those who have studied numerology.** The position that the objects (Wands, Cups, Swords, or Pentacles) form will tell you about this mystery. Look now at the 3 of Wands, Cups, Swords and Pentacles and notice the way each has been grouped together.

The 3 of Wands is 1+2=3   In this card you see that the Wands are separated as a single Wand and two grouped together. This shows that the process of the Divine will (1), or light with reflection (2), brings completion.

The 3 of Cups is 3 or 1+1+1=3
The 3 of Swords is 1+1+1=3  or 3
The 3 of Pentacles is 3 or 1+1+1=3

The above 3's can be thought of as a Trine which is completion. All the 3's can have a triangle drawn between the objects. You may draw this on your cards if you wish.

When using the Divine word Jehovah which is formed by the Hebrew letters **Yod ' He' ה Vau ו He' ה,** we have used the Yod He' and Vau with the #1-3. Number 1, the Divine, came down into manifestation and is the Yod +, in #2 it was met by the inertia of matter which is He' -, but in #3 it penetrated into matter which is Vau +, and manifested the "only begotten Son." Spirit penetrates matter, thereby evolving many living forms, all different depending on how much positive or negative energy they have in them. In the Tarot cards you will see man, woman and child both together and separate. They also represent the 3 states of consciousness: the conscious, subconscious, and super-conscious. The #1, 2, and 3 form the Supernal Triangle. To continue in motion, the second He' in the name of Yod He' Vau He' has to be used. This draws us to the next beginning and completes the square which is the base of life. See #4 for more explanation.

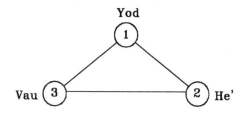

# NUMBER 4

**Number 4** ה **HE' is receptive and starts a new cycle. Form and foundation.** 4 is a double 2

When the Trinity or Supernal Triangle descends and manifests upon the physical plane, creation is complete and takes form. The last He' is added. The great name Yehovah is complete. Yod He' Vau He' is the Tetragrammaton. This He' draws to itself and starts a new cycle. One cycle gives rise to produce another. It forms the square.

**Example A:**

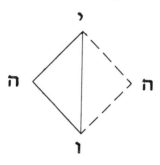

A cross is formed when lines are drawn from the four corners. This is called the cosmic cross. All arms are equal.

**Example B:**          **Example C:**

Imagine yourself with your back facing this page. If you back into the cross and place yourself in the cross and draw a line from the horizontal arm of the cross to the apex, it symbolizes man standing upright and holding in his right hand the trine of divinity. This also looks like the #4. See Example C. Look at The Hanged Man card #12 in the Major Arcana. His legs form the number 4.

The cross is an excellent symbol for the fusion of the dual consciousness. The horizontal line represents the subconscious (Water). The perpendicular line represents the active (Fire) consciousness. This is active and passive joined harmoniously.  The square is two triangles reflecting, as above, so below.  #4 is the reflection of the Trinity.

**Example D:**

Number 4 is the stable, enduring cubic stone.  Each side is a perfect square. It is the perfect square that goes with the #4, perfect form.  The cube which has 6 sides forms the cubic seat.  (see #6).  If you unfold the cube, you have a cross.  The spirit of man, when unfolded, forms the cross.  You will see throughout the Major Arcana and in the court cards that people are sitting on a solid piece of concrete or throne.  That represents the meaning behind the square and cube.

**Example E:**

 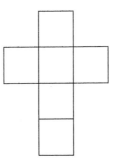

There are four geometrical figures.

**Example F:**

Most of the great buildings of the world were also designed based on a system of proportions.  The balance of the pyramid is the square base or the building of a strong foundation.  It is a well organized system.  Planning and practicality is the #4.  There is a determined attitude and self-discipline, a need to define and make things orderly.

The cross represents the four corners of the earth (North, South, East and West) as well as the four seasons (Spring, Summer, Fall and Winter) the four elements (Fire, Earth, Air, Water) the four phases of matter which are the roots and source of all things, both above and below. There are four Hebrew letters in the name of God, four suits in a deck of cards. On the fourth day God created the earth.

The four brightest stars of the first magnitude marked the cardinal points in the heavens when the cards were created. They were Aldebaran and the direction North and Fomalhaut, South, and Antares, East, and Regulus, West. At that time the cardinal points according to sidereal astrology were Taurus, Leo, Scorpio and Aquarius. They are no longer the cardinal points. Through the precession of the equinoxes, they have retrograded and are now in different signs. These four fixed astrological signs are still important when one looks to the declinations. The declinations represent a space in the heavens that measures the path of the Sun.

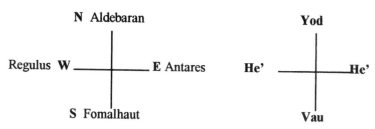

The above mentioned fixed signs formed the sphinx during the Age of Leo. You will see the sphinx in many of the cards.

"There are 4," according to the old saying, which take the first place in this world: Man ♒ (Aquarius)  among creatures, eagle ♏ (Scorpio)  among birds, ox ♉ (Taurus) among cattle and lion ♌ (Leo)  among wild beasts.

The sphinx asked King Oedipus, "Who in the morning goes on 4 legs, at midday on 2, and in the evening on 3?" The answer was Man. As a child he crawls on all four, at maturity he walks on two, and in old age he adds a cane. The numbers 4, 2, and 3 = 9  Number 9 is the completion of the numbers. The 4 represents the ignorant man, the 2 the intellectual man, and the 3 the spiritual man. The beginner on the spiritual path crawls on 4 legs, evolving humanity on 2, the illuminated man adds the staff of wisdom 3.

Number 4 completes the first series or group of numbers from which all others are derived. There are three numbers that are considered complete. They are #4, #7 and #10. Each will have within itself all energy that resorts back to the #1 of the Divine will. If you add all numbers before and including the number, the final reduction will be #1.

$$1+2+3+4=10=1$$
$$1+2+3+4+5+6+7=28=10=1 \quad 1+2+3+4+5+6+7+8+9+10=55=10=1$$

**Sephirah #4** is (**Chesed,** Mercy). In the #4 (square) everything stabilizes. Chesed teaches us our spiritual lessons, values and ethics. It is ruled by the astrological planet Jupiter which also looks like a 4 ♃. Jupiter expands our visions and philosophies. It shows that you should be able to work spiritually on your life. It is a turning point. It is a time to accomplish what is wanted.

We talked about the Supernal Triangle and that Kether was the Divine Light that shone through it. When we get to the #4 and Chesed we have left the Supernal Triangle. Although still connected by a path, we now enter a new dimension called the World of Formation. The World of Formation on the Tree of Life in the Kabalah consists of the planets that are the closest to the Sun. The Sun is the center gravitational force. Notice the square that is formed in Example G. The Sun is in the center of the tree on the Air pillar and on Sephirah #6 (Tiphareth). The #4 is the cube or square that teaches us our earthly lessons. Squares are stumbling blocks until they become building blocks.

Just as Kether was the light for the Supernal Triangle, the Sun is the light for the World of Formation. Since the Sun is on the same pillar of the Tree as Kether, it can also draw energy from that above. In the olden days the Sun and the planets were worshipped for the power that was behind them. The Sun was very important and it was always adorned. The front door of temples and teepees were built facing the rising Sun. In the Roman days, 600 AD during the reign of Justinian, it was decreed that there would be a new religion (not really new, but the players would be changed). The Sun was changed to the Son of God and the 12 signs of the Zodiac became the 12 disciples. On the Tree, the Sun represents the Son of God. His light, and the light of Kether from the father above, shines out for us. In the Tarot cards you will often see the Sun. Now you know its symbology. Most paths of the tree are connected to Sephirah #6. It is a life force for the tree. Interestingly enough, the Sun in astrology represents the heart. This Sephirah is the heart of the Tree.

The Sun in your astrological chart is your center and represents the God-given talents bestowed on you at birth. The planets in your chart are also there to help you. Your astrological chart along with the Tree will give you an understanding of your reason for being in this incarnation.

Notice that this part of the Tree forms a square.

**Example G:**

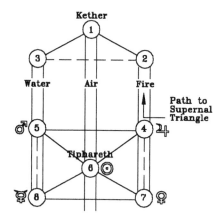

**The 4th commandment:** "Remember the Sabbath Day, to keep it holy. Six days shalt thou labor, and do all thy work: But the seventh day *is* the Sabbath of the LORD thy God." Exodus, XX,8,9,10

**Astrology:** A square has four 90 degree angles. The signs that create the square aspect are signs of different elements. When the elements are not alike, friction occurs. This friction is what causes people to move on in their lives. It creates enough agitation for one to act on it and make a change.

**The 4th Hebrew letter D (Daleth)** ヿ is the third of the 7 double letters and means womb or door. It is on path #14 (4) Daleth and represents the planet Venus. The womb and Venus ties in with the tarot card The Empress.

**Path #14 (4)** means the same thing as #4. This path has the Major Arcana card The Empress on it. She is very strong in using the planet Venus. More of this is discussed on the card page for The Empress. Path #14 connects the right Fire pillar and left Water pillar together. This path forms a bridge over the top, which makes it look like a porch. This also symbolizes Solomon's porch. In the Bible it was said that they gathered at Solomon's porch and is an expression of where knowledge is learned: the door where man enters the holy of holies. If you look at the diagram on the next page, you will see how path #14 creates that bridge or porch. Path #14 (4) also closes the triangle.

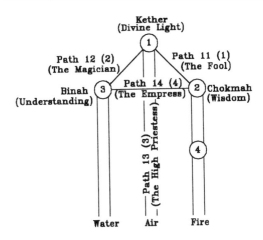

The Tarot cards relating to the #4 in the Major Arcana is The Emperor. The Emperor is ready to battle whatever is put before him. Also the four #4's in the Minor Arcana.

The 4 of Wands is the combination of 2+2=4. Balance of 2 elements: one active and one passive. The object is to remain as it is. It is a stable form of creation. On the 4 of Wands you will see that the Wands are separated into groups of two. Two of them are completed and two are still being worked on.

The 4 of Cups and Swords are a combination of 3+1=4, meaning a new cycle of creation. 4 appears when a new impulse 1 is added to the already existing 3. Notice, in the 4 of Cups and Swords, how one is separated from the other three.

The 4 of Pentacles is a combination of 1+1+2=4. (could also be a 3+1=4) In the 4 of Pentacles you will see that there are 2 pentacles secured on the floor, one in the man's arms and one on his head. The two ones mean new beginnings or points of activity (masculine) joined with the reflection of 2, which is both masculine (positive) and feminine (negative). However, #2 is female and receptive.

**ATTENTION: If you can understand the concept that we have talked about in the #1, #2, #3, and #4, you will be able to form all additional numbers and see that these four numbers are represented in them in one form or another. When you read the combinations in the cards, you will be able to understand the meaning behind that number.**

# NUMBER 5

**Number 5:** The number 5 is the half way breaking point between #1 and #9. 1, 2, 3, 4, **(5)** 6, 7, 8, 9  Five is the middle ground.  It represents both male and female and is said to be the number of the soul and man. We also have 5 senses: to see, to hear, to touch, to taste and to smell.

There are 5 fingers on each hand and 5 toes on each foot.  We hold our hands palm up to receive the blessings from above.  We emerge from the depths at the beginning of every cycle.  We use our hands and feet to swim to these depths and we use them to climb to the highest peak within the cycle.  When we reach the peak we then return to the depths to start another new cycle. Peaks and mountains that are seen in the cards pertain to just this process. When they are seen, it means attainment.

**Astrology:** The constellation of Capricorn has 28 stars in it.  Number 28 when added together equals 10.  Capricorn is the 10th sign of the Zodiac. Number 10 is also equal to #1 when reduced.  Therefore, both #10 and #1 refer to Capricorn.  It is seen as a goat with the tail of a fish.  This is symbolic of swimming to the depths and climbing to the top of the mountain. 10=1+0=1 Kether is #1 and Malkuth is #10.  Kether is the mountain and Malkuth is the depth of matter.  They are both on the Air pillar, one on each end.

This #5 is very much like that.  It forms the pentagram.  Man's hands held up are shown in the upright pentagram.  We have the choice to climb to the heights (upright pentagram) or to swim to the depths (inverted pentagram). The goat's head, which is the symbol for Capricorn, is seen in the inverted pentagram.  This goat head is called the "Goat of Mendes," the fall of the morning star.

When the pentagram is upside down and looks like the head of a goat, it represents black magic and the devil, the father of lies.  This symbol is seen in the Tarot card The Devil.  This is man immersed in himself. The upside down pentagram is a combination of 2+3=5.  Two points up and 3 down. There is another way to look at the inverted pentagram.  If we place it into the Tree of Life, one can see that it is man going down.  This can also be thought of as man descending in his involution through life before he is aware of his reason for being here.  This is man caught up in matter.  When he becomes AWARE of spirit, he can then turn the pentagram around and use it to ascend in his evolution.

| **UPRIGHT PENTAGRAM**<br>**Man standing upright** | **INVERTED PENTAGRAM**<br>**Man upside down**<br>Head of Goat<br>"Goat of Mendes" |
|:---:|:---:|

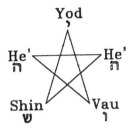

| **EVOLUTION**<br>**Man ascending** | **INVOLUTION**<br>**Man descending** |
|:---:|:---:|

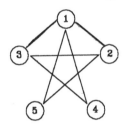

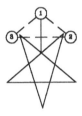

The Mystic Wand said to have been used by Moses and Aaron and all Initiates is described as a rod with a 5 pointed star (pentagram). Man can stand erect in the pentagram. It is the God force when the point is up. Man has attained power over the elements and astral currents. He is endowed with super-physical abilities which makes him a magician. By means of the pentagram in each Soul, man can master and govern all creatures inferior to himself. This is considered white magic. It is reaching or ascending up to the higher realms of divinity. The upright pentagram is a combination of 3+2=5. The three points up (trine/trinity) and two down.

Notice that around the 5 points of the star there are configurations that look like flames. These are the hieroglyphics for the Hebrew letters. Four of them spell the word for Jehovah: Yod He' Vau He'. The other symbol is the Hebrew letter Shin. Shin is the holy spirit. Everything has the four elements Air, Fire, Water and Earth. These are activated by the fifth which adds Shin, the Holy Spirit and the second element of Fire to them. These flames are the powers inherent in the perfect body. They are divine Fire. They are the spiritual powers which allow man to perform all miracles of life.

## MYSTIC WAND

## PENTAGON

**Sephirah #5** is **Geburah** (Severity and Justice) and carries the energy of the #5. Geburah is on the left negative, Water pillar, with the aggressive planet Mars. The sign Aries (which Mars rules) is represented by the Hebrew letter H, He'. This is the most forceful and disciplined of the Sephiroth. Mars is like Fire, constructive or destructive, having a purging or cleansing effect. Sephirah #3 (Binah and Saturn) above brings the discipline or control.

The #5 is a number worth taking time to understand. If we use the occult way of addition #5 equals 1+2+3+4+5=15. Number 15 is sometimes called the number of the devil. The Tarot card The Devil *is* card #15. When you reduce the 15 it is 1+5=6. 6 is the Christ force. As previously said everything has a positive and negative side to it. The Sephirah #6 (Tiphareth) that we talked about earlier has the planet the Sun in it. This Sun was changed to the Son of God. Sephirah #5 (Geburah) brings with it the planet Mars. Mars is the aggressive war lord. The energy of Mars is used here for man to do his battle. Is his battle between the Devil and Christ? Mars brings unrelenting effort which pushes on and overcomes all obstacles and difficulties. Number 5 is the place where man can choose how he wants to respond to life. Does he wear his pentagram with the point up or the point down?

**The 5th Hebrew letter is H (He')** ה and means Window. The eyes are the windows of the soul. There is a great saying: when a door closes, God opens up a window. A window lets light in and allows us to look out. H, He', is a simple letter representing the zodiac sign of Aries. Aries is ruled by the planet Mars. Aries is the sign that stands for the self, self esteem. It is the astrological sign #1. Number 1 is the renewal of life. Number 5 starts a new cycle. This Hebrew letter is on path #15 which is also path #5.

**Path #15 (5)** has the letter H, He', on it and the Major Arcana card The Emperor. If you notice, The Emperor has the symbology for Aries (head of the ram) on his throne and clothing. He has the courage to conquer whatever is required.

**The 5th commandment:** "Honor thy father and mother, that thy days may be long upon the land which the Lord thy God giveth thee," Exodus, XX, 12.

To just honor man and woman because they supplied us with a physical vehicle is not enough. When looking at the Tree of Life, one sees that there is a masculine, Fire pillar on the right, representing the father. There is a feminine, Water pillar on the left, representing the mother. To be initiated, one must sit between these two pillars and understand the knowledge and wisdom that comes from them. There must be perfect balance here and the ability to rule life in a spiritual way by choosing to obey. These pillars are seen in many of the Tarot cards, such as The High Priestess, The Hierophant, Justice, The Chariot, and the two towers in The Moon and Death.

**The Tarot cards #5** in the Major Arcana is The Hierophant and the four #5's in the Minor Arcana. They stand for trial, choice, cooperation, reciprocal action.

**The 5 of Wands** is the combination of 1+4=5. Number 1 is the divine essence and the #4 is the basic necessity of a form. This can be seen in the 5 of Wands. One Wand enters where 4 have assembled in confusion. Man is master of the elements, or it could be an impulsive man whose manifestations depend upon the outer influences of his physical nature.

**The 5 of Cups** is a combination of 2+3=5. Three Cups are down and two are still standing. However, the figure in the card only sees the three that are down. This is like the inverted pentagram. He only sees the negative. If there were 3 up and 2 down than it would be the upright pentagram. So 3+2=5 is better than 2+3=5. The trine up is better than the trine down.

**The 5 of Swords** is the combination of 2+1+2=5, as seen in the 5 of Swords. Two are on the ground and finished and two remain to be completed or duplicated. One he points to the ground and is still holding onto, showing that it was just finished.

**The 5 of Pentacles** is the same as the Swords. One Pentacle is on the top showing the divine essence, and the double two below show reflection/duplication.

# NUMBER 6

Number 5 is man and #6 is his Soul. Number 6 forms the 6 sided cube which when unfolded forms the cross. It is an important decision, harmonic equilibrium: 2x3 3+3 5+1 4+2; intelligence awakened and ready to receive it. Six is two triangles put together. They are actually interlaced. These form as above so below, as well as the Star of David. The Star of David is also thought to be the Seal of Solomon. However, there is a difference. There is a dot in the center of the Seal of Solomon and is discussed more completely under Number 7. This dot makes the Seal of Solomon a #7 instead of a #6. Six is the number of dependability, honesty, responsibility and protectiveness toward others.

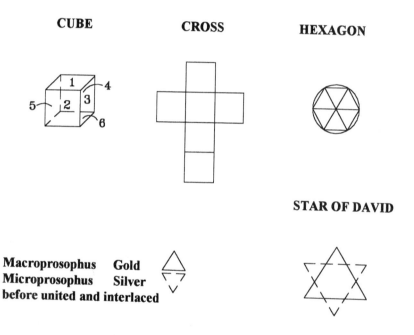

| CUBE | CROSS | HEXAGON |
| --- | --- | --- |

**STAR OF DAVID**

**Macroprosophus**  Gold
**Microprosophus**  Silver
**before united and interlaced**

The Star of David came into being when David wore this symbol on his shield. In the astrological chart for David, his planets formed two triangles. When David went into battle and his shield was seen, one knew that these two triangles meant that he was powerful. They showed that he had great courage, luck and strength.

The two interlaced triangles represent the Macroprosophus and the Microprosophus. The Macroprosophus triangle pointing up is the Supernal Triangle. It points to the heavenly light. It is what we are working hard to attain. It is our aspiration. The Microprosophus triangle pointing down is the one that absorbs the brilliant light from above and reflects it back. This reciprocal relationship is like the Sun and the Moon. The Sun is the Supernal, Macroprosophus Triangle; the Moon, having no light of its own, reflects the light from the Sun. We also have the Divine Light within us. When it is recognized in our consciousness, we shine as beacons. Our aura beams. This attracts those to us that want to bask in our knowledge and at that time we can share it with them. It is said that the Macroprosophus is the figure of a Radiant Old Man with a white beard and a long face. The Microprosophus is a black-bearded God with a short face.

**Sephirah #6 (Tiphareth,** Beauty) is on the masculine, Air pillar where the Sun is placed. As we previously said, this Sephirah brings back to mind the place of Christ. Most paths lead into Sephirah #6. All religions lead to the same place. As the Sun pours out its radiance and warmth, it keeps us alive. As we read and learn of the ways of Christ, we are also warmed and enlightened. Sephirah #6 completes the two trinities or triangles.

The lower triangle is lifted up until it becomes interlaced with the Supernal Triangle above. At that time, man has united his consciousness with the super-conscious. (See number 3.)

**The 6th Hebrew letter is W (Vau) ו** and means nail or is sometimes called the eye. It is on the 16th path which is actually the 6th path. Vau is a simple letter standing for the astrological Earth sign Taurus. Man is always tackling earthly matters. The bull is the symbol for Taurus. The eye of the Bull is the fixed star Aldebaran. This brilliant star is the leader of this constellation. The eye of the bull shines to lead man's Soul upward. Taurus also has two very difficult fixed stars in its constellation. One is Algol and the other the Pleiades. There is great sorrow connected to these stars. It was believed that, when the Sun moved through the constellation of Taurus and made contact with the eye of the bull, there was a turning point in the affairs of the individual. In like manner when we make this same contact it is said that we leave the era of darkness. Taurus is also ruled by the planet Venus, which is the planet of love.

**Path #16 (6)** means the same as #6. It has the Hebrew letter V, Vau on it and the sign Taurus. The Tarot card that is on this path is The Hierophant. This is trial, choice, cooperation and reciprocal action.

**The 6th commandment:** "Thou shalt not kill." Exodus, XX, 13.
**Astrology:** If you take the circle of 360 degrees and divide it by 6 you get 60 degrees. When using the subject of Astrology, 60 degrees represents the

sextile aspect. This is an aspect formed by signs of the zodiac that are in harmony by element. This is a positive aspect and gives the individual an opportunity to develop whatever the sextile shows by the signs and planets involved.

**The Tarot cards** represented by the #6 are The Lovers in the Major Arcana and the four 6's in the Minor Arcana.

**The 6 of Wands** is the combination of 1+2+3=6. One is the divine energy, two is the duplicate and three is the completion.

**The 6 of Cups** is a combination of 1+1+4=6. The 4 Cups show the hard work that was successful. The two ones show new beginnings by sharing.

**The 6 of Swords** is the combination of 2+4=6. Two is reflective and the four was the difficulty overcome.

**The 6 of Pentacles** is a combination of 3+1+2=6. The #1 divine energy is in between the #3 and #2. The #3 is form that has been productive. The #2 is reflective and still being worked on.

# NUMBER 7

The #7 is the sacred number and number of completion and perfection. It is the crown of attainment. Number 7 represents action and reflects consequences. It is a combination of 3+4, 1+6, 5+2, or 4+3. It is the stage of intellectual and moral perception with victory. It is the number for intuition, silent wisdom, mysticism and spirituality.

1 is positive + husband.
2 is receptive - wife.
3 is neutral or child and birth.
4 is form and attains sufficient authority to manifest itself on the astral plane.
5 is in the name of the whole family but there meets the choice of good and evil.
6 is good and gains victory.
7 is victory.

## HEPTAGON

## SOLOMON'S SEAL
The dot in the middle makes it different from the Star of David.

## SEVEN POINTED STAR
A point for each of the 7 planets. They are the creative forces.

## SPIRIT OVER FORM
The trine (3) is the trinity, God and spiritual light. This is combined with the Square (4) which is man, matter and physical human life.

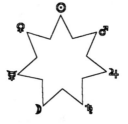

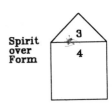

Spirit over Form

7 is perfection. If you take the 22 cards of the Major Arcana or the number 22 and divide it by 7 you get 3.142857. This is the value of Pi, the logarithmic number that means infinity. 7 is very powerful because it brings with it every available knowledge to be used for the spiritual development of man. It is The Chariot in the Major Arcana which also shows all knowledge available to man.

**The 7th commandment:** "Thou shalt not commit adultery." Exodus, XX,14. To adulterate something is to add a foreign substance which makes it no longer pure. Our task is to keep our white light pure and shining. It is up to us to allow only the knowledge which leads us upward to be part of our lives.

## THE 7 PLANETS

At the time when the cards were created there were 7 planets. These 7 planets relate to the 7 base metals, 7 chakras of the body, 7 days of the week (named after the Goth deities) and 7 color rays. The 7 colors are violet, indigo, blue, green, yellow, orange and red. The perfect white light from the Absolute comes from the blending of the 7 colors. When they are placed on a disc and rapidly revolved they will blend into a white light. When a light passes through a prism it shows 7 colors. See Table 6: Associations With Number 7, on page 74.

There were 7 angels that stood before God (one for each planet), 7 spirits sent forth and 7 churches. There are **7 musical notes:** Do re me fa sol la ti. 7 is the master number for the **phases of the Moon.** Every 7 days there is a new quarter of the Moon. It is said that a baby born in the 7th or 9th month of gestation can have a good chance for survival. The 8th month is not a good month for the child. The reason for this is that the even numbers are of only one polarity and when divided by two there is no remainder. When you divide the odd numbers by two, there is always a 1 left over. This 1 is the will of God and also shows that there is a polarity of male and female involved.

Every 7 years our lives go through a change of cycle.

**Sephirah #7 (Netzach,** Victory) is on the masculine, Fire pillar where the planet Venus is placed. Venus, the goddess of love (spiritual passion) also represents instincts and emotions. It is a creative planet. True Victory is to express oneself, through love.

**The 7th Hebrew letter is Z (Zain) ז.** The letter Z looks like two 7's one up and one down. Z or Zain is the first part of man's unfoldment where man understands these underlying principles of life and by the power of his manhood grasps them as a weapon with which to carve his destiny. Z means sword, weapon or arrow. Many of you can remember a television program called Zorro. Whenever he left his mark it was a Z. Z is a simple Hebrew letter standing for the astrological sign of Gemini. Gemini is an intellectual sign representing the mind and communication. Our mind, speech and learning ability are our greatest assets. Number 7, like #5, is one of the special numbers that by occult reduction becomes a #1. Add all the previous numbers and the number together. 1,2,3,4,5,6,7=28=10=1 Number 1 is the will and the will of God. It is the beginning. It is connected with all forms of life and force. So, #7 and #1 have the base of the same meaning behind them. The Bible is full of stories that relate to the number 7.

**Path #17 (7)** has the Hebrew letter Z Zain on it and the astrological sign Gemini. The card in the Major Arcana that is on this path is The Lovers. In The Lovers card the three stages of consciousness are being used: (woman) sub-conscious, (man) conscious, and (angel) super-conscious.

**TheTarot cards** represented by the #7 are The Chariot in the Major Arcana, and the four 7's in the Minor Arcana.

**The 7 of Wands** is a combination of 1+6=7. Will and experience brings victory. It could be 3+1+3=7 The divine will between the two completed trinities. The divine three's perfected.
**The 7 of Cups** is a combination of 4+1+1+1=7 or 4 +3=7: form and spirit combined.
**The 7 of Swords** is a combination of 2+3+2=7: the Trinity unfolded in the midst of the pair of opposites.
**The 7 of Pentacles** is a combination of 1+6=7 (same as 7 Wands).

When I was in Ireland, I visited the town of Knowth. This is an intriguing place. There were six mounds of dirt, each supported by a base of stones. All six of these were chambers at one time. They all surrounded a very large mound which was considered the temple. This is like the combination of #1 and #6. At this sacred place there were hieroglyphics and carvings on rocks that showed that the civilization living at that time knew about all of the sciences of the cosmos.

# Table 6: Associations With Number 7

| 7 Planets | | Angels | Goth | Days of Week | 7 Metals | 7 Chakras |
|---|---|---|---|---|---|---|
| ♄ | Saturn | Oriphiel | Seatur's | Saturday | Lead | Sacral Plexus (base of spine) |
| ♃ | Jupiter | Zadkiel | Thor's | Thursday | Tin | Suadistthana Chakra (Solar Plexus) |
| ♂ | Mars | Samael | Teusco's | Tuesday | Iron | Prostatic Ganglion (below navel) |
| ☉ | Sun | Michael | ---- | Sunday | Gold | Anahata Chakra (Cardiac Plexus) |
| ♀ | Venus | Anael | Friga's | Friday | Copper | Visuddhi Chakra (Pharyngeal Plexus) |
| ☿ | Mercury | Raphael | Wotan's | Wednesday | Mercury | Sahasrara Chakra (Pineal Gland) |
| ☽ | Moon | Gabriel | ---- | Monday | Silver | Ajna Chakra (Pituitary or Post Nasal Ganglion) |

## NUMBER 8

The #8 is the symbol of justice and construction as well as a balance between the spiritual and the material. It is mental conception of the transgression committed by one's neighbors or life. The #8 on its side is the symbol for infinity. However, there is an interesting study for the figure 8. It looks like the fly belt in a car joining two forces together that are dependent on each other for survival. This is like the currents of life. It is evolution, transmission of the force of one cycle into the next. It is like trying to pass through the eye of a needle. In the circle or zero we go round and round. In the 8 we cross over and try to balance with the new.

Look at the symbol 8 and picture one side as a circle being complete and full. Visualize there being a very thin space in the middle where the two lines cross each other. This point is where one can squeeze through to create a perfect balance by filling up the other half of the 8. This can be considered a crossover point. When we finished #7, we thought we had it all. In a sense we did, because one side of the 8 was filled to capacity. When we reach the number 8 we realize that there is still more needed in our growth pattern. What we have achieved we now need to release and share.

If one stops at the #7 and considers that it is all there is, it is unfortunate. Having everything and not using it creates inertia. In order to use the power of the #7 we must add #1 to it. Remember that 1 is the new beginning of a cycle. When we have 'filled our cup' we are required to be there to help those who have not yet achieved this knowledge. This allows us to have the other half of the 8 filled. We have balanced ourselves to receive and give of life.

It also reminds me of the art structure that is called the Wave. As it teeter-todders up and down, the water flows back and forth.

**THE WAVE**

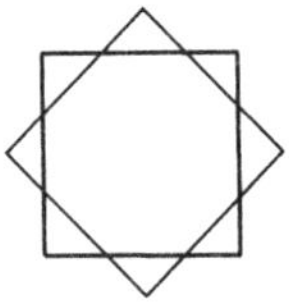

**OCTAGON** **2 SQUARES**

The 8 is like the lungs as they are used to breathe in and out. As we take in, we raise our ideals higher. The reflex action is to then let the breath out. In and out, in and out is what it is all about. The ability to control the breath raises the kundalini energy up the chakras, which brings enlightenment. To have abilities and not use them would be a waste. In #7 one recognized the abilities. In #8 they are put to use. In Egypt the Soul was weighed. Man was put on one side of the scale and the heart on the other. Also a feather was on one side and the heart or Soul on the other. Both sides had to balance.

**Sephirah #8 (Hod,** Splendor) is on the Water pillar where the intellectual planet Mercury is placed. Mercury is the rational mind and the intellectual communicable powers in man. Hod and Netzach (Sephirah #7) have to function together. Express words through the understanding of Love.

**The 8th Hebrew letter is Ch (Cheah) ח.** It means field. In a field a crop is ready for harvest. In order to harvest it, we have to put forth labor and effort. What we have grown comes to another use. This is seen in the card the Eight of Pentacles. Ch (Cheth), a Hebrew simple letter, represents the astrological sign Cancer. Cancer rules nurturing and the breast, a container of nourishment.

The #7 is a combination of #3 and #4. The Major Arcana card #3 (The High Priestess) and card #4 (The Empress) show that both of these ladies have an abundance to give out. Add to it card #1, (The Magician), 3+4+1=8. The Magician has the sign for infinity over his head. He knows that he has power that comes from above and works through him. He sees energy as a flowing process, not one to be attained and kept stagnant. The combination of all the knowledge and power of card #7 (The Chariot) with card #1 (The Magician) releases the flow of this energy. By taking #1, the will of man, and adding it to the #7 of complete knowledge, we have #8. The Chariot #7 is on path #8.

**Path #18 (8)** has the Hebrew letter Ch, Cheth on it and the sign of Cancer. It also has the card of the Major Arcana The Chariot (#7) on it.

**The 8th commandment:** "Thou shalt not steal." Exodus, XX, 15.
We cannot steal from others what we need to develop in ourselves in order to raise our consciousness. To not allow the self to grow to a higher evolution or to deny it the opportunity to learn, meditate, or unfold is stealing from the self.

**Astrology:** When the circle of 360 degrees is divided by 8, the result is 45 degrees. The 45 degree aspect is called a semi-square. This is interesting because #8 is made up of two 4's which represent the square. The semi-square is awareness of a difficulty and working with it before it manifests.

**The Tarot cards** represented by #8 are Strength in the Major Arcana. With Strength we see that the figure is using her psychic powers to tune in to the power of the inner beast. She has the sign of infinity over her head. Strength can also be interchanged with card #11 called Justice. In Justice the weighing of the use of knowledge is applied. See both of these cards for more information. The four 8's in the Minor Arcana also come under the energy of the #8.

**The 8 of Wands** is a combination of 3+1+2+2=8 or 4+2+2=8. Number 3 is the completion and #1 the will applied. Number 2 is double reflection. Number 4 is the obstacles requiring energy and the double reflection is #2.

**The 8 of Cups.** Here we can see the true meaning of #8. Man has laid aside old thoughts and ways and ventured on to get more. What has fulfilled its cycle of manifestation must give way to something higher. This is a combination of 1+2+5=8. Like the Eight of Swords, the Will of man #1, reflecting on life #2 connects with the powers above like the Pentagram.

**The 8 of Swords** is a combination of 1+2+5=8. #1 the Will is being reflected upon by #2 and #5. Man is connected with the powers above as in the Pentagram. He sees only what he has been deprived of. He has a limited conception of understanding and has failed to conquer fears.

**The 8 of Pentacles** is a combination of 1+1+1+5=8. The working man is concentrating on his work. Will #1, and the #5 man is connected with the powers above as in the Pentagram. He is moving swiftly ahead by using what he has acquired. One reaps what one has sown.

# NUMBER 9

Number 9 is getting ready for change, either because one has completed what has happened or has the maturity to recognize it needs an ending. The #9 is the square of 3, 3x3. The #9 represents the completion or perfection of what a person has done represented by the #3. Number 9 is a finishing and completing number. This is seen in the Nine of Cups and Swords. When man has gone the 9 steps, he has acquired the knowledge that is needed to make him a Master Initiate. His Initiation is being completed. He has worked through three planes of consciousness. He has gone through the 1st, 2nd, and 3rd degrees.

The #9 never changes. No matter how you multiply or add it, the sum always returns or reduces to the 9.

9+9=18=9   9x9=81=9   1+2+3+4+5+6+7+8+9=45=9   2x9=18=9   3x9=27=9
4x9=36=9   5x9=45=9   6x9=54=9   7x9=63=9   8x9=72=9   9x9=81=9
10x9=90=9

Each step or number that we go through brings its own initiation. Every three numbers brings a completion and a closing. Therefore, we have the three degrees listed below.

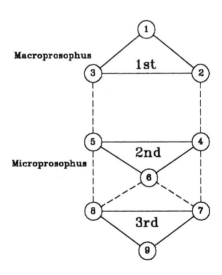

**1st degree** and upper triangle on the tree of life is the Supernal Triangle representing God, the Divine Light.

**2nd degree** is the Ethical Triangle. It is the middle triangle. As above so below. That which is the most powerful is transferred and worked on. This is man and woman.

**3rd degree** is the Astral Triangle of matter. This brings us to the #9 completion that unites the above two triangles together. They become the interlaced Star of David. This is seen in the lantern on the Hermit card.

If one is found lacking in the development of one of the numbers, he must wait and grow stronger before he is allowed the final initiation. The #9 brings things to an end. In 9 months the baby is ready to be born.

Number 1 starts and #9 finishes.
10=1+0=1 A new beginning.

**Sephirah #9** (**Yesod,** Foundation) is on the Air pillar where the planet the Moon is placed. The Moon rules the brain where all memory is contained. It is one's perception. It is the inner self and has rule over our habits and emotions. When one goes within to meditate there is a connection with all powers. Yesod does this also. It channels the energies of the higher power (Kether) down to Malkuth (Earth) and then back up again. The Moon also reflects the light of the Sun (Son) Tiphareth #6. The Sun is the masculine part of us and the Moon is the feminine part of us.

**The 9th Hebrew letter is T (Teth) ט.** It is a Hebrew simple letter relating to the astrological sign of Leo. This is on path 19 which is also #9. Teth means serpent. A snake loses its skin, we also lose our skin when we leave and become reincarnated. Each life brings us higher on our path of evolution.

**Path #19 (9)** has the Hebrew simple letter Teth on it and the sign Leo. The card in the Major Arcana that is placed on this path is Strength or Justice. There is a controversy as to which belongs here.

**The 9th commandment is:** "Thou shalt not bear false witness against thy neighbor." Exodus, XX, 16.

Not everyone is on the same path in evolution. Those that we meet become our neighbors. Instead of talking about their shortcomings let us take them by the hand and share what we have with them. We all need to become brothers and sisters.

**The Tarot cards** represented by the #9 are The Hermit in the Major Arcana and the four 9's in the Minor Arcana. The Hermit represents spiritual thirst and how its fulfillment can lead to personal wisdom and enlightenment through more understanding of the spiritual needs within us. The Cosmic Self (Leo and the Sun) searches through life for its identity: identity with that above, a perfect state of higher consciousness. This is performed as we go up our spiral or channel the energy in the Kundalini. The Hermit on a mountain top says he has, through devotion to spiritual practice (Star of David and staff), reached supreme consciousness and unity of the self with that above. As a result, he can hold the light of consciousness as a beacon that others might see and make their way up the mountain. Solitude many times can help us to reach this state. Take time to be alone with yourself. As said in the Bible, "go into your closet and when all is quiet pray (meditate)." This action will bring your own concept of God and spiritual enlightenment.

**The 9 of Wands** is the combination of 5+3+1=9.  #5 (Man) #3 (completion) and #1 (thinking through the will) for what is next.

**The 9 of Cups is 9.** This shows completion and pride in its accomplishment.

**The 9 of Swords is 9.** Time to let go of the past memories.

**The 9 of Pentacles** is the combination of 6+3=9  Number 6 is unity of the forces through the power of the two triangles. Notice how the two triangles are formed by the pentacles. The last three also represent completion.

# NUMBER 10

From 0 all numbers proceed and into 0 they all are resolved again. The #10 begins a new cycle.

10=1+0=1   10=1+9   10=9+1   10=2+8   10=3+7   10=7+3
10=4+6   10=6+4   10=5+5   10=1+2+3+4

10 is the number of completion and perfection. It brings us back to 0 and a new beginning. 10 contains all numbers of creation and returns to unity.

1+2+3+4+5+6+7+8+9+10=55  55=5+5=10  10=1+0=1

10 = Decad = Greek deka =10

Number 10 is a decagon.

## MAN'S UNFOLDMENT

#1 Crown-Spirit descends into matter and offers man a Crown of Life. He can attain this crown only as he unfolds and manifests the qualities expressed in each of the numbers. You will see Crowns in the cards of the Major and Minor Arcana.
#2 Wisdom
#3 Understanding
#4 Mercy
#5 Severity
#6 Beauty
#7 Victory
#8 Splendor
#9 Foundation
#10 Kingdom      Completion of Man's unfoldment
When we express all these qualities we are a #10. We can now reach the Kingdom. While the Father has crowned us his heirs, we are not gods in our present, undeveloped state. Only as we grow, unfold and express these powers of the 9 digits can we rule over our Kingdom in #10.

Upon completion of the first 10 numbers or lessons, man can start a new cycle in his evolution. Each #1 starts a new cycle and each #9 brings it to completion. Each #10 allows us to start anew on a different level. Since man now has in his consciousness the knowledge acquired, the next step or cycle will be different. Man was given the rod, which the Fool had when he entered. This rod guided him along the paths. It was a hollow rod which allowed the energy of the power above to flow through to man below. The next cycle will have the experiences already known as its base. This is like going to grammar school, high school, Jr. college and then college. Each segment prepares one for the next level and allows one the ability to utilize the previous knowledge. You cannot skip a level since each is needed for you to have as a base when starting the next level.

After #0-9 has been completed, man found out what it was like to travel the path and find the Light. Man is now responsible for helping those that are just starting their first cycle. At the same time, Man is starting the next cycle.

In the 2nd cycle #10-18 man is learning to use the polarities on all levels. He will complete #10 for the second time.

In 3rd cycle #19-27 man is applying the knowledge of the Trinity to each experience. He is reaching down, expressing, and bringing forth into completion. This is the third time of completion.

In the 4th cycle #28-36 allows man to use the knowledge of the square and the foundation. He learns how to use the knowledge of form in everything he does. This is the fourth time of completion.

In the 5th cycle #37-45 man recognizes his power as a Man. This is the fifth time of completion.

In the 6th cycle #46-54 man realizes that the power of the universe is at his disposal. This is the sixth time of completion.

In the 7th cycle #55-63 man can take a sabbatical or apply the knowledge to meditation and inner growth. This is the seventh time of completion.

In the 8th cycle #64-72 it is time to allow the energy to get to the other side of the 8 (or infinity) to balance. A time to grow by giving instead of just going round and round. This is the eighth time of completion.

In the 9th cycle #73-81 is the ninth time around. This creates the final judgment and the return to the source. When all is completed and known, man returns to God and becomes one with Him. The Fool returns to the Garden of Eden. As God said when they left the garden, man will become all knowing and be as God. The cherubim with the flaming sword at the gate is a welcomed sight.

**Sephirah #10** (**Malkuth,** Kingdom) has the planet Earth (manifested earth). It is also what would be called the Earth pillar. However, this is not a pillar. It is the realm of matter which is made up of the four elements. Here is where the other three pillars connect. It is the root of the Tree. It is where man deals with the earthly realm.

**The 10th Hebrew letter is Y (Yod) ʼ.** It means hand and is a simple letter representing the astrological sign of Virgo. The hieroglyphic for the Yod is in all Hebrew letters.

**Path #20 (10)** has the Hebrew letter Yod and the astrological sign of Virgo on it. The card in the Major Arcana that is placed on this path is The Hermit.

**The 10th commandment:** "Thou shalt not covet thy neighbor's house, thou shalt not covet they neighbor's wife nor manservant nor his maidservant, nor his ox or his ass or anything that is thy neighbor's." Exodus, XX,17.

Once you have been enlightened and have completed the 10 lessons there is no need to covet anything. You have what you need. You may not have everything in life, but you will have what is needed in order for you to live out what is expected for your life experience.

**The Tarot cards** represented by the #10 are Wheel of Fortune in the Major Arcana and the four 10's in the Minor Arcana.

**The 10 of Wands is** 10 but here there seems to be a heavy burden. He has chosen the material side of life.

**The 10 of Cups is** 10. Success and achievement fulfilled. Celebration time!

**The 10 of Swords is** 9+1=10 One Sword is deeper than the rest and it is in the place of the Heart. #9 is completion. #1 leaves it up to the Will, to raise man up to start a new beginning.

**The 10 of Pentacles is** The Tree of Life, the Kabalah. All experiences are complete and Man has all he needs.

## MASTER NUMBERS

There are four master numbers: 11, 22, 33, and 44. All master numbers are powerful because they stand in their own right, but when reduced, they make the reduced number powerful also. Remember that 1, 2, 3, and 4 are the base of all numbers. They also stand for Yod He' Vau He'. When you look at 11, 22, 33, and 44 one can see that these numbers have special vibrations. They are double numbers bringing a double amount of energy relating to each number.

### NUMBER 11
Once the numbers 1-9 have been completed, the next number is 10. Ten is the completion of the nine numbers and now raises the vibratory energy of the number one. Remember that we talked about #1 representing the Hebrew letter Y, Yod which is part of the Tetragrammaton Yod He' Vau He', the word for God, or Jehovah. The Hebrew letter Yod is really #10 but when reduced is #1. Behind it is the element of Fire, aggressive energy. This #11 allows one to tap into the creative sources with an inspirational touch. The Will power is important here, and #11 shows that the inner energy can be used to the betterment of self and humanity: a leader in a humanitarian service, such as a minister, reformer, teacher, or charity worker.

### NUMBER 22
The #2 is the Hebrew letter He' and there are two He's in the Tetragrammaton. The same as two 2's in #22. It is a reflective energy. He' is #5 and two of them make #10 which reduces to #1. #2 and He' relate to the element of Water. Number 22 is also 2+2=4 which shows us that the cubic base is included with #22. Remember that we talked earlier about this (1,2,3,4=10). 11x2=22. This is #11 as a double. Through the 2 of duplication and the 4 of structure this number brings with it the ability of accomplishment on a high level. The #22 has within it the 22 paths and the 22 cards of the Major Arcana. This is a number of illumination and controls the inner planes of force.

It is important that this number be understood with respect to the power that it carries with it. Look at the combinations that #22 forms. It incorporates all numbers.    1+21    2+20    3+19    4+18    5+17   6+16   7+15   8+14    9+13   10+12    11+11.

### NUMBER 33
The #3 is the Hebrew letter W, Vau.  #3 and Vau brings with it the element of Air. Three also stands for completion as it forms the trine or the trinity. It includes the three elements when the Air unites them together.  3+3=6. Six

is the number for Tiphareth where the Sun is placed. This center of the Tree connects all the paths together. The Sun became the Son of God and the central form of gravity to draw to it. #33 is 11x3. This is #11 trined.

**NUMBER 44**

The #4 is the cubic base or square. It becomes matter when #1, 2, and 3 join together. This brings into play the Earth and matter. A double #4 or double square brings with it form and discipline and perseverance to be able to handle any difficult situation. The 4+4=8 shows that the energy continues. The #8 is the sign for infinity when placed on its side. The three words Yod He' Vau He' add up to a #8. 10+5+6+5=26=8.    #44 is 11x4. This is #11 as a square or cube.

To continue through the rest of the cards in the Major Arcana, consider the number of the card. Take that number and reduce it to a single digit number. This will tell you the meaning behind the card. Refer back to the ones previously discussed.

In the remaining 12 cards and paths of the Major Arcana there will be different Hebrew letters than mentioned before. Each path has its own letter, and these will be listed under the interpretation of each of the cards. The 22 Major Arcana cards are on a higher spiritual level and therefore, relate to the 22 Hebrew letters.

The Minor Arcana does not refer to the Hebrew letters. However, as you have seen the numbers from 1-10, do relate to these cards. Notice how the symbols are grouped together to get a better understanding of the number and card.

I have prepared an information sheet for each of the cards. On the sheets please notice that everything is listed for you. When I talk about the **NUMBER,** it is the # on the card.

When I talk about the **HEBREW LETTER,** it is the letter for the path. The Hebrew letter has a number that corresponds to it. That is the number of the path on the Tree of Life in the Kabalah.

The **ASTROLOGICAL SIGN OR PLANET** for the card comes from the division of the Hebrew letters according to Mother letters, Double letters and Simple letters. They relate to the elements, astrological planets and signs. Please refer to pages 26-29.

There is a lot of mental confusion when studying and trying to incorporate many things together. Each stands in its own right and they are not mixed.

For years I have tried to figure out the numbering system of the cards, paths, and Hebrew numbers. I have tried to make them all the same such as if it is card #1 it should be on path #1 and the 1st Hebrew letter should also be there. Well, this is not possible because we are talking about different things here.

# YOUR INDIVIDUAL NUMBER, PATH, TAROT CARD

## WHAT IS YOUR BIRTH NAME AND BIRTH DATE???????

Before we get into looking at the Tarot cards, I want you to figure out what path or paths and what card or cards are important to you in this incarnation. Then as you are learning the cards and paths, you can relate to how this affects you.

There are only 9 basic numbers. Number 10 is a two digit number and can be reduced to 1 by adding 1+0=1. When there is a double number, write this down. It will relate to the card in the Tarot deck that is that number. Then reduce the two numbers to a single number. This number will also relate to a Tarot card. Find which path or Sephiroth these cards belong to. Number 11 and #22 are spiritual numbers and are usually left as is.

### BIRTH DATE

Your birth date is very special to you. Astrology can tell you what sign your planets were in when you were born. Numerology will tell the number or numbers that are important to you.

Change the month you were born into a number. The months start with January as #1 and ends with December as #12. Add this number to the number for the day and year.

**EXAMPLE:** May 5, 1952: May becomes the 5th month + 5th day +1+ 9+5+2 for the year =27. Number 27 is a two digit number so add the two digits together: 2+7 and it is reduced to #9, a single number.

**YOUR LIFE LESSON:** The life lesson is why one is incarnated and what one must learn or overcome. Your birth date gives you the number for your life lesson. In this case it is #9. Look back and see what the #9 means. It is a number of completion. One who has experienced all 9 steps.

**CURRENT LIFE LESSON:** To see what number you have for this year just change the year you were born to the current year. Note that the year does not begin until the time of the birthday.

**EXAMPLE:** May 5,1997: May is 5th month + 5th day + 1+9+9+7=36 Reduce 36  3+6=9  This happened to come out to be the same. If it was 1996 it would have been a #8. This would show that the current lesson would be a #8.

# ESOTERIC MEANING OF THE NAME

Your birth date and name are special to you. Your name is the musical rhythm picked out just for you. The name that you use is the one that you started with. It is the name that was given to you at birth. If you have an assortment of names, such as those given at baptism or a name change for any reason, including marriage, you can investigate them one by one. Look to see the different vibrations that each one brings with it. Some people have had multiple marriages. Each one brings with it its own story to tell. Each one will give you a different card and path.

A man usually never changes his name. A woman often changes her name at marriage. The change in name will result in a number change, as well as a card change. After all, we do take on a different vibration when we include another in our life. Investigate each number to see which one you want to use.

Your name has a special vibration to which you are also tuned. Use your birth or baptismal name. The letters in your name can be changed to numbers. Use your full name. For added information if you are married, drop your maiden name and use your married name. This number will tell you what effect the marriage has on you. Using the chart below, place a number over each letter in your name. Place the numbers over the consonants first. Place these above the name. Place the numbers under the letters for the vowels.

## THE ENGLISH ALPHABET

The alphabet that we know of as the English alphabet has 26 letters in it. If we numbered each letter they would be numbered 1-26. However, we are only using single digit numbers 1-9. Therefore, each letter is reduced to one of these single digits. J would be normally be #10 but it is reduced to #1. S would be #19 but is reduced to #10 which is further reduced to #1.

| 1 | 2 | 3 | 4 | 5 | 6 | 7 | 8 | 9 |
|---|---|---|---|---|---|---|---|---|
| A | B | C | D | E | F | G | H | I |
| J | K | L | M | N | O | P | Q | R |
| S | T | U | V | W | X | Y | Z |   |

**Example:**

| Consonants | 4 | 5 | 4 | 9 7 | 1 4 | 2 8 | =44 | 4+4=8 |
|---|---|---|---|---|---|---|---|---|
|  | D I A N E | M A R Y | S M I T H |  |  |  |  |  |
| Vowels | 9 1 | 5 | 1 |  | 9 |  | =25 | 2+5=7 |

When you come up with 11, 22, 33, or 44, they are not usually reduced. These are master numbers and function on a higher vibration. The above name has the total consonants 44. This can be left as is and interpreted. For curiosity's sake, one can also reduce the double numbers.

**YOUR OUTER SELF**: Your personality and what others see in you. Add together only the numbers for the consonants. What Tarot cards have this number? What path or Sephirah on the Tree of Life is this number?

In the example, #44 is card #44 which is the 4 of Cups. 44 reduces to 8. In this case #8 is the Major Arcana card Strength or you might favor Justice. It is also the four #8's in the Minor Arcana. It is path #18 which is #8 and has the Chariot on it. It is Sephirah #8 (Hod and the planet Mercury). Diane's outer self is working on these numbers and lessons.

**YOUR INNER SELF**: This is your Soul number. It is what you really are inside. Add together only the numbers for the vowels and reduce it. What Tarot cards have this number? What path or Sephirah on the Tree of Life is this number?

In the example, #25 is card #25 which is the Knight of Wands. In this case #7 is the Major Arcana card The Chariot. It is also the four #7's in the Minor Arcana. It is path #17 which is #7 and has the card The Lovers on it. It is Sephirah #7 Netzach and the planet Venus. Diane's inner self is working on these numbers and lessons.

**YOUR DESTINY OF LIFE**: This is what one must manifest or carry out. Add together the numbers for both the consonants and vowels. What Tarot Card is this? What path or Sephirah on the Tree of Life is this number?

Adding the vowels and consonants together in the example, we get 44+25=69 and 69 further reduced is 6+9=15 & 1+5=6.

Card #69 is the Ace of Pentacles. Card #6 in the Major Arcana is The Lovers. Sephirah #6 is Tiphareth and the planet Sun. Diane's destiny of life is working on these numbers and lessons and expressing the planets.

If the *Outer self* is more than twice the *Inner self*, then the personality is greater than the Soul or what one feels within.

If the *Inner self* is more than twice the *Outer self*, then there is more in you than can be expressed.

If the *Inner and Outer self* is the same, then you never meet any situation in life that you cannot control. One is well balanced.

If the *Path of Destiny* is more than three times that of the *Inner self,* then you take on more than you can produce.

There are no accidents in life. Everything happens the way it is meant to. As you know by now, every word has a vibration or meaning that goes with it. The title of this book, "The Spiritual Study of the Tarot," becomes a #33 (6) in Numerology. Each word can be considered on its own, and you can see in the information below that they all individually add up to the following: 6, 8, 8, 3, 6, 2. The total of these numbers is 33, a master number, which is usually left as it is. This means that the book is placed on the third level of numbers. The third level of numbers is on the vibration of the Supernal Triangle. The number 33 is a double 3 which is a double Trinity. If we were to reduce 33, it would become a #6. Sephirah #6 (Tiphareth) is the Christ center and the heart of The Tree of Life. Note also that the word SPIRITUAL adds up to a #44 which is on the 4th level of numbers and involves the Yod He' Vau He', the four elements, and the name Jehovah.

| 2 8 5=15=6 | 1 7 9 9 9 2 3 1 3=44=8 | 1 2 3 4 7=17=8 | 6 6=12=3 |
|---|---|---|---|
| **T H E** | **S P I R I T U A L** | **S T U D Y** | **O F** |


| 2 8 5=15=6 | 2 1 9 6 2=20=2 |
|---|---|
| **T H E** | **T A R O T** |

# PART
# ONE

# THE
# MAJOR
# ARCANA

# KEYWORDS FOR THE MAJOR ARCANA

**0 & 20** **THE FOOL**
New beginning, faith in being guided

**1** **THE MAGICIAN**
Everything at your disposal, power from above works through you

**2** **THE HIGH PRIESTESS**
Understanding positive Vs negative

**3** **THE EMPRESS**
Fertility, material abundance, growth

**4** **THE EMPEROR**
Leadership, order, control

**5** **THE HIEROPHANT**
All knowledge is within, blessing

**6** **THE LOVERS**
Discrimination, choice between two, love

**7** **THE CHARIOT**
Intellect and higher consciousness over emotions

**8** **STRENGTH**
Handling a difficult situation with intuition and love

**9** **THE HERMIT**
Guided by wisdom offered

**10** **WHEEL OF FORTUNE**
Ups and downs of life, good luck, turn for the better

**11** **JUSTICE**
Decision, judgement and legal matters

**12** **THE HANGED MAN**
Enlightenment brings a complete change of ways

**13** **DEATH**
Transformation, death, can no longer continue as is

**14** **TEMPERANCE**
Balancing emotions and practicality

**15** **THE DEVIL**
Deception, escapism, mistaken ideas and negative thinking keep you in bondage

**16** **THE TOWER**
Turmoil, unexpected change

**17** **THE STAR**
Past experience allows emotional control

**18** **THE MOON**
A crisis

**19**    **THE SUN**
Attainment
**20**    **JUDGEMENT**
Spiritual awakening, completion, time for a decision,
reincarnation
**20 & 0**    **THE FOOL**
The need to be reincarnated and repeat or speed home
**21**    **THE WORLD**
Feeling balanced, centered, completed evolution

# THE PATTERN OF THE TRESTLEBOARD

0. All the **POWER** that ever was or ever Will be is here now.

1. I am a center of expression for the **PRIMAL-WILL-TO-GOOD** which eternally creates and sustains the universe.

2. Through me its unfailing **WISDOM** takes form in thought and word.

3. Filled with **UNDERSTANDING** of its perfect law, I am guided moment by moment along the path of liberation.

4. From the exhaustless riches of its limitless **SUBSTANCE**, I draw all things needful both spiritual and material.

5. I recognize the manifestation of the undeviating **JUSTICE** in all the circumstances of my life.

6. In all things both great and small I see the **BEAUTY** of the Divine expression.

7. Living from that Will, supported by its unfailing wisdom and understanding, mine is a **VICTORIOUS** life.

8. I look forward with confidence to the perfect realization of the eternal **SPLENDOR** of the Limitless life.

9. In thought, word and deed, I rest my life, from day to day, upon the sure **FOUNDATION** of eternal being.

10. The **KINGDOM** of spirit is embodied in my flesh.

This can be recited before you shuffle the cards or do a reading.

# PART ONE: THE MAJOR ARCANA

## INTERPRETATION OF THE CARDS

By including the Kabalah we have included the ability to look at the cards as a spiritual growth pattern. Man's highest aim is the realization of the Spirit in Man. Through the learning of the Metaphysical subjects, this can be accomplished. You now have the background knowledge of the Kabalah which includes the 10 Sephiroth and the 22 paths on The Tree of Life. When this is combined with the understanding of the basic numbers, the next process is to apply this knowledge to interpreting the 78 cards in the Rider Waite Tarot deck.

The discussion of the cards will be done in two parts. Part one will be the 22 cards in the Major Arcana and part two will be the 56 cards in the Minor Arcana. Take your cards and separate them into these two sections.

Some of the new Waite decks being reproduced may not have the vivid colors that the original did. Also some of the writing of the name Yod He' Vau' He' was not made clear. I will tell you when this happens so that you may mark your deck.

As we look at each of the cards you will come to the awareness that everything that is seen on each card has a special meaning. It is like interpreting a dream. When one is not aware of this and quickly looks at the cards, they overlook many of the details. Again, it is all right for you to mark your cards with a permanent pen, as any information that you wish to have before you will help while you are learning the cards.

Say an affirmation, prayer, or recite the 'Pattern On The Trestleboard' as you shuffle the cards. Try to place yourself in the card and feel intuitively what the story of the card has to say. In this way you will acquire your own interpretation of the card and will not have to rely on authors to explain them to you.

The following pages will list everything that is on each card with a brief description as to its meaning. As you study each card make it the card for the day. Keep it in your consciousness and before you go to sleep at night let it be the last thing that you look at. During the night it will register in your subconscious and, you will find that when you awaken, there will be a complete understanding of that card.

A black and white card will be displayed for each of the Tarot cards. It would be good reinforcement for your learning if you colored the card for each of the Tarot.

## 22 HIGH SPIRITUAL LESSONS
## TREE OF LIFE AND THE 22 (12) PATHS

In everything that we do we are always brought back to the concept of spirituality. It does not matter what religion you are since many roads lead to the same place.

In the Christian religion they talk about the Garden of Eden. This was a place of joy with no problems or unhappiness. Just BLISS existed.

In the Garden there were two trees, the Tree of Life and the Tree of Knowledge (good and evil). The Kabalah also shows this Tree of Life.

The Serpent, whom many of us are afraid of, or look down on, we have to thank. Without the push that he gave Eve to take that apple, we would still be in the garden and know nothing of the many parts of life. It was the serpent that said: "You will not die if you eat the apple. God knows that when you do, you will be as God knowing good and evil."

God said, "Behold man has become as one of us to know good and evil. **Now he must put forth *energy* to seek and eat of the Tree of Life to live forever.**" Energy whirled around. The seeds of Souls were scattered to grow and evolve through life experiences, the final goal being the return to the Source.

To make sure that this happened, God placed a cherub with a flaming Sword at the East gate of the garden to show the way back to the Tree of Life. The Sword placed at the gate is the same Swords in the Tarot. They stand for the Air element and knowledge. As we study the Tarot and the Kabalah (Tree of Life) we are also led back. It goes without saying that *any* study of a metaphysical subject leads in that direction. Placing the cherub at the East gate reminds us that everything rises in the East. Anything that is new comes from the East.

The Fool is the first card and represents the descent of the Soul and its arrival on the earth plane.

# THE JOURNEY OF THE FOOL

The Soul of man, pure and unblemished by the material world, looked down upon the animals. He saw that they were capable of experiencing many pleasures that he was denied. He was created in the likeness of his creator which was pure spirit. There were no bodies or coverings. Animals had a body. He also wanted a body, so he set off to get one!

The Fool packed his knapsack with only those things that he knew he could take. He chose a Sword knowing that it would give him the power of communication. He chose a Cup which symbolized feelings. He chose a Pentacle to help him attain material gain. He chose a Wand to give him future endeavors.

He attached his bag to a stick and placed it over his shoulder. Off he went! The wind propelled him. He landed on path #11 (1) where he met Hebrew letter A, (Aleph) the mother letter which stands for the Air element. He was quite certain that what was ahead of him was good. He put his head up and believed that he would be guided along the way. Jumping into the new world he landed close to a precipice. He could fall! But, even if he had, he would have experienced something new and learned from it. He landed on path #11 (1) on The Tree of Life which is between Sephirah #1 (Kether) and Sephirah #2 (Chokmah). He came from Kether (pure Spirit) and will always have with him an all-knowing of the Source. He knows that one day he will return.

Chokmah, on the masculine, positive, Fire pillar, gives him energy or fires him up, so to say. Fire was the first substance that he needed for the body. It gave him nitrogen. While on this path he bumps into the planet Uranus. Knowing that Uranus is the planet responsible for the quickening of the fetus, he asks Uranus to turn on his electrical system. By doing so it produced his aura.

On path #12-(2) his first endeavor was to unpack his wares and see what he had to help him in this new life. He sees the Sword which is the intellectual Air element, a Pentacle representing the Earth element, a Cup the emotional Water element, and a Wand which gave him the enthusiastic Fire element. He does not know just what to do with them yet. He has to stimulate this energy and get charged up before he can get on with his work. This is the path where he meets The Magician. He learns that a strong, determined will and belief that the power above will work through him, will sustain him through life. He knows as above, so below. He was comfortable when above and still feels that connection now that he is below. The Magician tells him that he will need to travel to get the Fire, Water and Air substances that he needs to form the physical body.

The Hebrew double letter B (Beth) is on this path and represents the intellectual planet Mercury. He joins up with Mercury and now has intelligence to lead him. This path leads to Sephirah #3 (Binah and the Water, negative pillar and the planet Saturn). The Fool acquired his masculine power through the right pillar and now he adds his feminine power by contacting the left pillar. He remembers what The Magician told him and asks the Water pillar to give him the hydrogen that he needs to form his body. He meets up with the planet Saturn who gives him his Karma for this lifetime. Saturn tells him that whatever he works for can never be taken away from him. Saturn tells him that he will again meet up with him on path #32 (22) at the end of his life. The Fool knows that this is no longer a life of bliss but that it will be a life of hard work.

By using all of his thoughts, power, perception and remembrance from whence he came, he experiences the knowing of The High Priestess. She resides on the 13th (3) path on the Air pillar which holds the Hebrew double letter G, (Gimel) and represents the astrological planet the Moon. He has already attained Fire for energy and nitrogen, Water for emotions and hydrogen, and now he gathers Air for the intellect and oxygen. The planet, the Moon, gives him psychic ability and perception. He now has the three elements. The High Priestess teaches him understanding of polarity, the positive and negative.

He searches for The Empress (Mother Nature) and finds her on path #14 (4). She gives birth to his body. He now realizes that he is imprisoned in the darkness of this physical body. He remembers that there is something greater where he came from and tries to find his way back to it. He realizes that he is a combination of a Soul in a physical body. She gives to him the loving planet Venus, the Hebrew double letter D (Daleth) and sends him on his way. He is now ready to give birth to the beginning of his life. He leaves the Supernal Triangle and the World of Atziluth and ventures on.

On path #15 (5) he meets up with The Emperor. The Emperor represents the Hebrew simple letter H (He'), which stands for the sign of Aries. Now he prepares himself for battle with the Material World. He takes on his coat of armor. The Emperor is on the path that connects with Tiphareth and the planet, the Sun, which now gives to The Fool an ego and a will. He also acquires his God given talents through the sign that his Sun is in according to his birthday.

He decides to return to the masculine, Fire pillar to visit The Hierophant on path #16 (6). He waits for his blessing and is given the two keys to open the trunk of knowledge. Through the Hebrew simple letter V (Vau), he picks up the sign of Taurus and the qualities of structure and practicality.

He decides to be a little different and jumps back onto the Water pillar and Binah and path #17 (7). He sees The Lovers and realizes that there are three states of consciousness. Before he leaves Binah she introduces him to The Chariot and path #18 (8). He learns about spirituality from the subjects of Astrology and Alchemy. He learns the power of the mind. He experiences the sign of Cancer through the Hebrew simple letter Ch (Cheth). He remembers what The High Priestess taught him about psychic power and perception. Before he can leave the Water pillar he has to pass through Sephirah #5 Geburah and the planet Mars. Mars gives him aggressiveness and energy. This reminds him of The Emperor.

He decides to go back to the Fire pillar but, in order to do this, he has to pass through Justice on path #19 (9). He learns to balance his actions. He notices that there are two cards here doing battle to own this position on the tree. Justice is competing with Strength. Strength wants to teach him to handle a difficult situation with intuition and love. He also realizes that he has entered the World of Formation, Yetzirath. Life begins to unveil itself to him.

He arrives at Sephirah #4 (Chesed) and he finds Jupiter there. Jupiter represents freedom, philosophies, and the understanding of all of the above. At this point he could go back. Chesed says "I have a path connecting me to the Supernal Triangle. What do you say? Do you want to return or go deeper into life?"

As he looks toward Tiphareth and remembers the talents given to him, he sees a wise old man called The Hermit. He is on path #20 (10). He looks interesting! The Hermit is holding a lantern to light his way and gives to him the spiritual and astrological knowledge that he can use. He teaches him to be discriminating and analytical through the sign of Virgo, represented by the simple Hebrew simple letter Y (Yod).

He goes back to Chesed and thanks him for his offer but decides to move on. He leaves on path #21 (11). Here he finds the Hebrew double letter K, (Kaph), the planet Jupiter and the Wheel of Fortune. He remembers his involution when he came down and he knows he can turn around and go back up. He also knows that he can go around and around in reincarnation. He knows that he will be judged for what he does and he wants to attain a higher spiritual life.

He decides to go back over to the Water pillar again and Sephirah #5 (Geburah) to get more strength from the planet Mars. He sees The Hanged Man suspended on path #23 (13) with the Hebrew mother letter M (Mem). He see the bright glow around his head. The Hanged Man reminds him to keep his feet attached to heaven and make the oath to bind himself there. The Hanged Man tells him that Scorpio will help him make this transition. On path #24 (14) he meets up with Death. By sheer luck he knew about Scorpio first. Death tells him that all these earthly attachments are not what they appear to be. He points to the East and shows him what is coming. The Fool asks, as all humans do, "Why is this happening to me?" He realizes that this is part of the plan. This is what he asked for as a Soul. These experiences will help him return back to where he came from. He realizes that man makes his own happiness or unhappiness through obeying not only the physical laws made by man but also through obeying or not obeying the Natural or Spiritual Laws as well. The Fool, having experienced this knowledge from Death, is now transformed. He creates a new set of spiritual laws to live by.

The Fool realizes that he hasn't visited the Air pillar for awhile. He finds Temperance there on path #25 (15). The path of Temperance is connected to Sephirah #6 (Tiphareth and the Sun) and Sephirah #9 (Yesod and the Moon). Temperance seems to be passing water from one cup to another. She has one foot in the water and one on land. He learns that moderation and balance in all things is important. Temperance tries to expand his knowledge as he introduces The Fool to Sagittarius and Samech, the Hebrew simple letter S.

The Fool gets charged up, says farewell, moves on to path #26 (16) and discovers a dark cave. Curious he enters the cave and finds The Devil. Boy, is it dark in there! He is not sure what is here. The Devil hands him a set of beliefs. The Fool was much happier when he was outside in the light. He leaves quickly! He starts to read the paper given to him by The Devil and reaches path #27 (17), The Tower. He notices that Pe', the Hebrew double letter P, is here in the form of Mars. He remembers what Geburah taught him about Mars. He uses the power of Mars to destroy and knock all those false beliefs that The Devil gave him to pieces.

He notices that he is caught between Sephirah #7 (Netzach) on the Fire pillar and Sephirah #8 (Hod) on the Water pillar. Netzach lets him borrow Venus, the goddess of love, and Hod gives him Mercury, the intellectual god. The Fool realizes here that, when he communicates with love, he gets back on track.

This happens just in time as he finds himself with a delightful person surrounded by stars on path #28 (18). She says her name is Tzaddi/Aquarius (Hebrew simple letter Ts). She is an intriguing lady with knowledge of the stars. He pauses here and finds that he can use this information to help him stay on top of his emotions. She shows him the mysteries of life and his own mandala.

Just as The Fool is getting closer to enlightenment, he is set back by an emotional crisis. He is now in the Material World. He is tested again on how he absorbs or handles this problem. He sees a path that leads through the boundaries to the mountains. He decides to follow the path rather than wallow with The Moon on path #29 (19). The Hebrew simple letter Q (Qoph) and Pisces tells him to use his psychic ability to guide him. The path into the mountains puts him back on track. By using and developing his mind and his perception and psychic powers, he becomes an all-knowing teacher.

He finds, that once he breaks through the barriers, The Sun is there waiting for him. Path #30 (20) certainly is bright! He'll need sun glasses! He likes this much better than that dark cave. The Fool realizes that he has come a long way. He has gone through many battles and has persevered and won. He is very proud of himself!

Judgement day comes when he arrives on path #31 (21) and meets up with the Hebrew mother letter Sh (Shin). He is not only judged, but judges himself. There's Gabriel playing that heavenly music. He is reminded of home..... He misses the heavenly music.......

Hebrew double letter T (Tau) and Saturn beckons to him from path #32 (22). Where did he see him before???? Oh yes, he was the one that gave The Fool his Karma. He sure hopes his papers are in order! If not he will have to stay here or come back. Saturn looks over The Fool's papers and awards him the Universe. The Fool, proud of what he has accomplished, now decides to take a short cut home. Propelling himself into a spiral, he spins himself up the Air pillar and waves to Temperance and The High Priestess as he passes by. They are smiling and happy that he is headed home. He throws off the earthly body as he arrives at Kether and is given the Crown of Glory!!!!!

# THE FOOL AND NUMBER 0

O   A boundless circle of pulsating, vibrant life force proceeding from the center of all life forms the "waters of the great deep." They are deep in that they are unfathomable and incomprehensible to undeveloped man. Only when the Spirit of God moves upon these waters and the Son of God is sent down into manifestation are the waves of this Great Deep stilled. The vibrations are slowed down so that what we understand as life begins to manifest. Neither beginning nor ending is the zero. The zero is called naught or nothing because nothing has been differentiated or manifested. It is the Silence of Non-being. It is the "Secret habitation of the ever invisible deity."

All of nature's shapes can be traced back to and analyzed as simple geometrical figures: the line, trine, square, and circle.

We are all the center O of the life force. Until our forces are made concrete and directed towards definite ends, this circle is an invisible and unknown O circle of darkness, yet vibrant with potencies - our vague and unformed desires, longings and ideals. The Christ within is asleep and Spiritual Darkness is upon the face of the waters. "Lord save us or we perish." **We start our evolution. The wind propels us to begin.**

A circle formed by a serpent - symbol of Life and Wisdom-swallowing its tail, symbolizes unending life or immortality. The snake swallowing his tail symbolizes the source of all creation. It is the womb of nature from which the universe comes forth and also the womb from which future man proceeds. Even the fetus in the womb is curved upon itself in a circular fashion. Biting his own tail symbolizes that wisdom must be able to feed upon itself. This means that one must create his own circuit so that the high quality of the Life Force can flow through one's being. The conscious mind needs to feed on the subconscious mind.

However, in the circle one goes around and around. The following story may be of interest to you.

The circle is the symbol of the fall of man after Eve succumbed to the serpent's temptation. It is said that, after the earth was created, that the circle of movement of the world was not closed, but remained open. The 7th day was sanctified and blessed as the open part of the circle of movement of the world, in such a way that the beings of the world had access to the Father and the Father had access to them.

The serpent wanted it believed that there is no freedom for the world if the circle of the world is not closed. Because, he said, freedom is to be found in oneself, without interference from the outside, especially from above. The serpent took his tail in his mouth and thus formed a closed circle. He turned with great force and created in the world the great swirl which caught hold of Adam and Eve and the Fool. Remember that the Fool is 0. He kept the beings of the world moving on the inside of the closed circle which he formed by taking his tail in his mouth. He wanted them to believe that they would be free if they stayed in the circle.

**Figure 5: Serpent**

Ah, but woman, bless her soul, remembered that the world opened towards the Father and the holy Sabbath. As long as the Sabbath exists there is an opening in the circle of the world. So she offered herself for the rending of the closed circle in herself in order to give birth to children issuing from the world beyond, from the world where there is a Sabbath. The serpent and the woman became enemies. And it is said this is why woman receives pain when giving birth.

**An open circle can create a spiral which allows unlimited growth and advancement. A closed circle is only a prison. It is a wheel which turns on itself and, therefore, suggests no advancement. This is eternal repetition.**

When you start to open your consciousness and realize that you do not want to be in a closed circle and go around and around, Jupiter the expansion planet, is waiting to enlarge your circle and make it into a spiral so you can go up as high as you want, to reach your evolution. If one studies metaphysical subjects, one starts to ascend to the higher plane. You already have within you what you are searching for. It just has to be awakened.

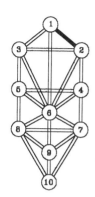

A - Aleph

## CARD #0 THE FOOL ON PATH #11 (1)

**FOOL**
Fool is Latin and means "bag of wind," life breath. The soul has just entered life. The only thing that he was able to bring with him was what is in his knapsack: that is, knowledge (Sword) from before, sensitivity (Cup), and ambition (Wand and Pentacle). The fire of Spirit descending into matter demands AIR first. The Air element is intelligence and oxygen. The Fool is headed toward a precipice as he leaps into the unknown. He looks up, which shows that he puts his trust in heaven as he jumps into life's experiences. He can fall and that would be okay. The main thing is to keep going. There will be both good and difficult times.

**KEYWORDS** - new beginning, faith in being guided
**PLANET & SIGN** - Uranus ♅ is the planet relating to this card and the ruler of the Zodiac sign Aquarius ♒. Uranus is Greek for Heaven. The Fool is neither male nor female. It represents the Soul being reborn, a carefree spirit beginning its journey along the spiritual path. You are a fool if you do not accomplish as much as you can in one lifetime. Uranus is the planet that is responsible for the quickening of the fetus. It is the planet that turns on one's electrical system. It is also the planet that gives us our intuition and cosmic knowledge, the remembrance that we are connected to something higher than ourselves.
**CARD NUMBER** - 0 represents the one force, universal intelligence, life breath, prana which is yellow. 0 like the egg, is the symbol of fertilization. The basis of all life springs from 0 (nothing). 0 is pure beginning, God reflecting on self - "just is." (Reread about the #0.)
**HEBREW LETTER #1** - A (Aleph) is a Hebrew mother letter standing for the element Air which is the life breath. This letter is on path #11 (1) of the Tree of Life. (Reread about the #1.)
**PATH #11 (1)** - Path 11 *Scintillating Intelligence.* **Sephirah #1 is called** *Admirable or Hidden Intelligence.* **"The Crown."** It is the light giving the power of that first principle which has no beginning and it is the Primal Glory, for no created being can attain its essence. The path that the Fool is on in the Tree is #11 (1). It connects Sephirah #1 Kether, (The Crown or Divine Light) and Sephirah #2 Chokmah, (Wisdom). The planet that Chokmah represents is Uranus ♅. Kether is on the Air pillar and Chokmah is on the Fire pillar. The Fool connects these two elements and adds the planet Uranus and propels itself into motion. The Fire gives him the positive masculine energy. While on this path, The Fool uses the intellectual element Air, which is represented by the Hebrew Letter #1 also on this path. The Fool came from Kether and needs a body. Therefore, he must receive the

elements. The element Air gives him oxygen and intelligence and the element Fire gives him nitrogen and enthusiasm. When quickening takes place in a body, the planet Uranus is responsible. It represents the electrical system. The planet Uranus also gives him the intuition and remembrance of his spiritual background which is always in his consciousness while on earth. This is one of the three most important paths that come from Kether. Kether is complete in the three elements Air, Fire and Water, which sends down this energy to form the Tree.

**PATH COLOR** - yellow, pale sky blue, blue emerald, gold. Yellow represents Air and Air represents the intellect. The astrological Air signs are Gemini, Libra and Aquarius.

**MUSICAL TONE** - Uranus/Aquarius is Fa

**THE FOOL LOOKS UP** -This shows faith in GOD that he will be guided every step of the way as he enters into this new life.

**HE IS COMING FROM THE EAST** - New beginnings always come from the East. Churches are built with their doors facing the East to see the rising Sun and the beginning of a new day.

**HE IS STANDING ON A PLATEAU** - Everyone is on a different one. He overlooks the valley, a field of experience.

**MOUNTAINS** - represent spiritual attainment. He has come from high attainment.

**SNOW** - on the top of the mountain will melt and fertilize the valley below. As we attain the peak of our mountains, we grow.

**GREEN WREATH** - Green represents the vegetable kingdom. A wreath shows success.

**RED FEATHER** - is like a feather in his cap. Red represents desire and passion. In Egypt the "Feather of Truth" was weighed in the balancing scales opposite the heart, when the Soul was judged.

**BLACK WAND** - (hidden power) is said to be hollow so the energy of the above can flow through. The wand will be seen in other cards as we continue. The wand can also be referred to as a rod. The rod is a symbol of the protective power of God. "Yea, though I walk through the valley of the shadow of death, I will fear no evil: for thou art with me; thy rod and thy staff they comfort me." Psalm 23.

**WALLET** - or sack has the third eye on it. Sack carries the memories of the sub-conscious that knows all of the past lives and experiences. That is all you are allowed to bring into this life. In the sack is a Sword, Wand, Cup and Pentacle. These are the four elements Air, Fire, Water and Earth. The eagle on the wallet represents the sign of Scorpio which is the memories of the soul.

**TEN STITCHES** - on the wallet or flap represent 10 types of visions on higher developed perception. 10 is the next level of numbers once you have competed 9. Ten also reduces to 1. (1+0=1) The Fool is starting a new beginning on a higher level.

**WAIST** - 7 ornaments encircling the waist represents the 7 major planets and the chakras.

**UNDER GARMENT** - is white and means that he has underlying purity.

**OUTER GARMENT** - has a black background. Black represents ignorance. By going through the lessons of the 7 planets found on the belt around the waist, and then removing the belt, he will be able to remove the black robe of ignorance so that the white robe is exposed. We spend a whole lifetime searching in order to awaken what we already have.

**TEN WHEELS** - on the robe is like the 10 Sephiroth on the Tree of Life.

**EIGHT YELLOW SPOKES** - Yellow is the life breath and stands for intelligence. Eight is the rhythm of our breathing. There are 8 pointed stars and lunar crescents on the robe representing the solar magnetic currents. Around each wheel are 7 green leaves representing Sephirah #7 (Netzach and the planet Venus) to show activation of the Venus ray in vegetation.

**LEFT SHOULDER** -Gold Sun and Silver Moon. The Sun is the outer self and the Moon is the inner self.

**CORNER OF ROBE** - As you face the card, on the bottom right corner of the robe is the symbol for Shin ש . It is the symbol of the Holy Spirit.

**WORDS ON THE UNDER SHIRT** - is the name of God. The hieroglyphics for the Hebrew letter Yod He' Vau He' י ה ו ה used to be clearly seen there. You can draw them in. In reproducing the cards they became lines. Looking on the page for the Hebrew letters, you will see that the Yod is #10, He #5, Vau #6, He #5. 10+5+6+5=26. There are 26 numbers in the alphabet. God is in all words formed or spoken. 26 is also the 8 which, when placed on its side, is the sign of infinity.

**WHITE SUN** - one force, central sun, the God power behind all things. It is in the East. The Sun is the protector and represents Sephirah #6 Tiphareth where the Sun resides.

**DOG** - was the Jackal or wolf but through evolution is now man's best friend. Everything improves, even the lower forms of life.

**ROSE** - The Christmas rose is the symbol of the birth of Jesus. It blooms just at Christmas. It withstands the coldest winters and is bursting forth with the most fragrant of blossoms even in the midst of snow and storms.

SUMMARY

+ When this card shows up, it indicates that the person you are reading for is starting a whole new beginning. They are not concerned with the pitfalls that may lie ahead, only the excitement of the new venture. Before anything is manifested, one must accept its outcome on faith and take the plunge however **Foolish** it may appear. When the spirit beckons one must follow. Have faith that you will be guided.  There is a higher position than this present one. Look up, not down.  The outcome will bring you to the level of your vision. Every new endeavor  is like the experiences that the Fool goes through. *Remember YOU'RE A FOOL IF YOU DO NOT GET THE MOST OUT OF LIFE THAT YOU CAN.*

- If this card is upside down, it can show a delay in the new venture and that the person is not taking advantage of the new changes available to him.  He is looking down instead of up and does not have faith.
*1 Cor. 3:18, "If any man among you seemeth to be wise in this world, let him become a FOOL, that he may become wise."*

There are always new ventures to bring us more growth.

ב

B - Beth

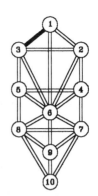

THE MAGICIAN.

## CARD #1 THE MAGICIAN ON PATH #12 (2)

**THE MAGICIAN**
This card represents the conscious mind ruled by Air and the planet Mercury ☿ . This is pure intellect. Every action must begin with thought and the energy to transfer that thought into action. He also called the Alchemist or the Minstrel. The Fool looked up and determined the goal. The Magician took that goal and put it into the mind to start the process. There is a realization that what is above will work through us here below. By blocking the flow between God and the goal, man has cut off the source of life from his efforts.

**KEYWORDS** - Everything is at your disposal and the power from above works through you.
**PLANET & SIGN** - Mercury ☿ is the planet that rules the sign of Gemini ♊. They are both intellectual. Messages and knowledge are represented here.
**CARD NUMBER** - 1 is masculine and outgoing and means to begin. (Reread about #1 under numbers.)
**HEBREW LETTER #2** - B (Beth) means house. House is our body and our soul dwells within. Your thoughts are the real houses that we live in. It is a Hebrew double letter symbolizing the planet Mercury. This letter is on path #12 (2) of the Tree. (Reread #2 under numbers.)
**PATH #12 (2)** - Path #12 (2) is called the *Intelligence of Transparency*. Sephirah #2 is called *Illuminating Intelligence*. The path that The Magician is on in the Tree, is Path #12 (2) connecting Sephirah #1 (Kether, Divine Light and the Crown and the Air pillar) to Sephirah #3 (Binah, Understanding and the Water pillar and the planet Saturn). The Magician here brings form and beginnings. The Magician uses the intellectual planet Mercury placed here by the Hebrew letter B (Beth) to know that "as above, so below." Connecting to the Water pillar, The Fool now adds hydrogen to form his body. He also adds the negative feminine qualities represented by the element Water. Having already achieved the positive energy of the Fire and the negative energy of the Water, the lesson of polarity is understood.

The Magician knows that his power comes from above (Kether). Kether (Divine Light) and Chokmah (Wisdom) is now joined with Binah (Understanding). Until understanding was added there was no comprehension what the Divine Light and wisdom meant. The planet Saturn puts everything into form. Saturn also tells of the karma of this lifetime. It tells why the soul chose to be incarnated into this life. What one works hard for is never lost. This is the second of the three most important paths on the Tree. Coming from Kether, this path sets up the Water pillar on the Tree.
**PATH COLOR** -yellow, gray, indigo violet, purple

**MUSICAL TONE** - Mi for Mercury

**ONE HAND UP** - One hand points upward, the other hand points down. Let the power from above work through us to help us handle that which is here.

**WAND** - is directing the forces from above to below. The white Wand represents purified will. It is hollow and the higher power flows through.

∞ - Symbol is for infinity. Symbol of life and evolution. The Fool was 0 and the Magician has the sign for infinity. (Reread the explanation for #8 under numbers.)

**BELT** - like the sign of infinity, the snake biting his tail makes the enclosed circle. We go around and around until the circle (belt) is taken off or opened up. We feed off of our knowledge.

**RED ROBE** - shows his aggressive will and desires. When he removes the red robe, there is a white one underneath. He can flip this robe off and on whenever he needs the energy. This is unlike The Fool who had to work through lessons before he could remove his robe.

**WHITE UNDER ROBE** - is exposed and you can see that under his desires is his purity of motive. The light of truth enables him to achieve his desired results.

**WHITE BAND** - on black hair. Black is ignorance. Through knowledge we overcome ignorance.

**TABLE** - give your attention to your abilities

**EDGE OF TABLE** - has the four astrological fixed signs on the edge. The Lion is Leo, Bull is Taurus, the glyph ♒ is Aquarius, Eagle is Scorpio. These four you will see throughout the cards. They also represent the four apostles (evangelists) and the four gospels. You see them as statues on the altar in the Episcopal Church holding the Lion, Bull etc. There is a description about them on page 113. These four signs also represent the four elements - Fire, Earth, Air and Water. The four symbols are on the table and are at the disposal of the Magician. They also represent the four elements and the four suits of the cards.

**FIRE ELEMENT - THE SUIT OF WANDS** - is will and energy to start new ventures. Fire is the right pillar on the Tree of Life. All magic is in your will. The Wand is the staff of wisdom that man can lean on, as he climbs the path of spiritual attainment.

**EARTH ELEMENT - THE SUIT OF PENTACLES** - is silence and materialization. Earth rules the base of the Tree of Life (Sephirah #10 Malkuth). The two circles around the pentagram symbolize cycles as well as the enclosed space holding matter and representing worldly wealth. Within the two circles is a pentagram. The Pentacle also represents the Host or the bread which is given at communion. (Reread #5 for explanation of the pentagram.)

**AIR ELEMENT - THE SUIT OF SWORDS** - is daring ideas and craftsmanship. They bring the most difficult lessons. Air is illuminated intelligence. God helps those that help themselves. Air is the middle pillar of the Tree of Life.

**WATER ELEMENT- THE SUIT OF CUPS** - is knowing, imagination, emotions and perception. Water rules the left pillar on the Tree of Life. A Cup is a container which holds all of life's experiences for the soul to drink. All this is at the disposal of the individual.

**ARBOR WAY** - Whenever you see an arbor, be aware that it takes a long time for this to grow and develop. It is something that the person has had for a long time. All the abilities are there at the disposal of The Magician to use.

**RED ROSES & LILIES**- 49 red petals or roses just on the top. Man has 49 centers in his body and there are 7 main centers. 7 usually refers to the chakras and the 7 planets. Below there are 5 roses representing the 5 senses; 4 lilies representing the primary aspects of truth, Fire, Earth, Air, Water; 4 primary colors. 5+4=9, the completion of numbers. He has accomplished the work of the red roses (arbor) and now is directing more attention to the unfolding of the white lilies. You will see roses and lilies throughout the cards. The Easter Lily is the symbol for Mary because she was the mother of the one whose resurrection brought victory over death to mankind. The seemingly lifeless lily bulb, springing into beautiful bloom, symbolizes the process of resurrection when Jesus arose from the dead on the third day after being sealed in the tomb.

Your body belongs to the Lord, it must serve a long time. Therefore, take good care of it, strengthen it with physical labor and eat pure food. A sound mind cannot exist in a sick body. If the body fails, the Lord cannot be served. The body is the house of the Soul given to you to be able to exist on this plane.

SUMMARY
+ When this card shows up in a spread, it shows that the client has at his disposal enthusiasm, intelligence, sensitivity and practicality. He is using these abilities, unless the cards around this say differently. He is looking at this and believing that the higher forces will work through him, when he makes the effort.

- In the reverse it shows that the client is not seeing that these abilities are there and that he is not seeing that the power above is working through him. Woe is me attitude! God did not promise a rose garden and the roses have thorns. He did, however, give one talents, the ability to learn, and energy to carry through. It is up to us to put this to use.

# SYMBOLS OF THE FOUR EVANGELISTS

The first four books of the New Testament were written by the Evangelists Matthew, Mark, Luke and John. These books tell the story of the life and meaning of Christ. Each of the writers is identified by a symbol. The basis for the symbolic imagery comes from Ezekiel 1: 5-10; Ezekiel 10: 19-22; and Revelations 4:7. "And the first beast was like a lion, and the second beast like a calf, and the third beast had a face as a man, and the fourth beast was like a flying eagle. And the four beasts had each of them wings....." (wings show being spiritually elevated).

## MATTHEW
Matthew is symbolized by a winged man with a book, because the content of Matthew's gospel is considered to deal more with the human side of Jesus' life than the other gospels.

## MARK
Mark is symbolized by a winged lion, because he emphasizes the royalty or kingship of Jesus in his gospel. The lion is known as the "king of the beasts," thus the image of the lion is a reflection of the kingly nature of Jesus.

## LUKE
Luke is symbolized by a winged ox with a book. The ox was a common beast of sacrifice, and Luke seems to emphasize the sacrificial nature of Christ in his gospel. The book of Luke opens with the story of the sacrifice of Zacharias. "There was in the days of Herod, the king of Judaea, a certain priest named Zacharias...and the angel said unto him, I am Gabriel, that stand in the presence of God...and behold, thou shalt be dumb, and not speak until the day that these things shall be performed." Luke 1:5-20. The book of Luke closes with a detailed account of the sacrificial death of Christ.

## JOHN
John is symbolized by a winged eagle. Just as the eagle soars to the heights of heaven in his daily flight, so did the gospel written by John soar to the heavens unto the throne of Grace. The spirit of Christ caught by the writing of John lifts the Soul and mind of the reader like an eagle in flight!

# SYMBOLS OF THE FOUR EVANGELISTS

MATTHEW

MARK

LUKE

JOHN

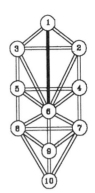

G - Gimel

THE HIGH PRIESTESS

**THE HIGH PRIESTESS**

She represents all goddesses who were mothers, for example, Isis, Hecate and the mother Mary. She is a highly spiritual, psychic, intuitive person with the wisdom and perception of blending the positive and negative forces of life to form wisdom and understanding. The wise person no longer looks upon good and evil, but sees all as one. In order to do this, she sits on the Air pillar between the positive Fire pillar on the right and the negative Water pillar on the left. The Air pillar is the intellectual pillar. Her spiritual knowledge flows without help. This is path #13 (3), one of the three most important coming from Kether. This completes the paths coming down. These three pillars form the sides of a triangle. See example in section on number 3.

**KEYWORDS** - understanding polarity, duality and opposites such as positive VS. the negative, sub-conscious duality and reflection.

**PLANET & SIGN** - The Hebrew letter G, Gimel rules path #13 (3) therefore, the Moon ☽ is the planet which rules this card and the sign of Cancer ♋. Both relate to the feelings and perception which bring messages to the sub-conscious. The Moon represents the memories carried from one incarnation to another by the sub-conscious mind. Timing using the phases of the Moon is understood. The Moon is the brain where all information is stored.

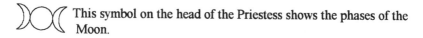 This symbol on the head of the Priestess shows the phases of the Moon.

The New Moon is waxing (growing) in light. Always start anything new right after the New Moon. Also plant crops that grow above the ground.

The Full Moon which is the fulfillment of that which was started at the New Moon.

The Old Moon is waning (decreasing) in light. It is time for inner awareness or to do that which comes from within. Plant crops that grow beneath the ground.

As you look into a pool of water, it reflects and reverses the image, the same way as a negative does.

**ELEMENT** - Two elements are used here. The Moon is Water which is perception, feelings and intuition. Water reflects that which is above, in this case, Spirit. She is on path #13 (3) which is on the intellectual Air pillar.

When intellect (Air-Mercury) and perception (Water-Moon) are used together, it gives one a powerful mind.

**CARD NUMBER** - 2 II  duality and reflection which relates to memory. (Reread #2 and #3 under numbers.)

**HEBREW LETTER #3** - G (Gimel) symbolizes a camel. A camel can store a lot of water. Gimel is the Hebrew double letter representing the planet Moon. It is on path #13 (3). The Sun and Moon are referred to as planets, but they are really called lights.

**PATH #13 (3)** - Path #13 (3) is called *Uniting Intelligence*. Sephirah #3 is called *Sanctifying Intelligence*. It is the foundation of Wisdom. The High Priestess sits between two pillars, one white + and one black -. She is the mediator between light and darkness and unites these two opposites. This is why it is called the path of Uniting Intelligence. It is the parent of Faith from which faith emanates; the path of memory and subconscious knowledge. This path joins Sephirah #1 **Kether (Divine Light and complete knowledge)** to Sephirah #6 **Tiphareth (Beauty, intuition and the Christ center).**

Between these two Sephiroth are two very dark places called Daath and the Abyss. We are reminded of Darth Vadar in Star Wars who knew all wisdom. One has to cross **Daath the center of knowledge and the Abyss** to get to Tiphareth. It is the center of the Tree and has the most paths connected to it. Tiphareth represents the planet Sun. The Sun represents the Son of God. The High Priestess sits on this powerful path between Kether and Tiphareth. **Tiphareth is illuminated consciousness.** This is the highest illumination one can attain. Behind Tiphareth is the **veil Paroketh**-all knowledge. In one of the other decks of cards, The High Priestess has a veil over her. The High Priestess faces the Sun and draws in its power and adds to it the perception and psychic ability given to her by the Moon which the Hebrew letter G (Gimel) represents.

Included on this Air pillar is **Yesod, Sephirah #6, which is also the Moon and called the psychic consciousness.** The inclusion of Kether the Divine Light and The High Priestess position with the two great lights makes her very powerful. This is the longest path on the Tree. It links the Supernal Triangle of spirit and the World of Atziluth with the World of Briah and Yetzirah or the World of Formation. This path joins paths #25 (15) and #32 (22) and continues until it reaches **Malkuth which is sensory consciousness.** Malkuth is the Earth element. The three elements Fire, Water and Air are now forming matter which is Earth.

This is the path that The Fool traveled when he came to the end of his journey and spiraled up to return home. On its way back to its spiritual home, the

Soul meets its darkest moment as it leaves the Material World of Formation and spirals upward to see the vision of God. As it travels through the Abyss and Daath, it purges everything that is of any conflict and makes the transgression into a new spiritual body to be clothed in the cloth of heaven.

**PATH COLOR** - blue, silver. Blue always represents emotions or perception. The paths from Kether to Malkuth are all in shades of blue. Blue is the color of Binah and Saturn on Sephirah #3 and also Chesed & Jupiter on Sephirah #4.

**MUSICAL TONE** - Cancer/Moon is Ti

**B-BLACK PILLAR** - B-Boaz means no. Black is negative.

**J-WHITE PILLAR** - J-Jachin means yes. White is positive. The High Priestess sits on the Air pillar between two pillars on the Tree, the pillar of Fire + and the pillar of Water -. She can use all of this knowledge. This shows that she has the wisdom to balance the two energies and reflect with wisdom (gray). The two pillars are like 'Solomon's Porch' in the Bible. Pillars hold up the porch. The porch is the entrance where one gathers to enter the house. They gathered on Solomon's porch to hear the wisdom that he had, so that they may enter into the house (new dimension).

**TORAH** - She holds the book of knowledge of the cosmos.

**SCROLL** - records like the Akashic records. Part of it is concealed and one hand is covered. She holds all knowledge until ready to use it. She does not give of it freely, only piece by piece, as the inquirer is ready for it. A true teacher knows that the best way to teach is to plant seeds in the pupils' minds and let them search for the understanding of them. Don't tell all you know. Silent wisdom knows when to release it, and only when needed. This card represents three laws: the association of things similar, things near together in space or time, things sharply contrasted.

**BLUE GOWN** - flows and looks like water flowing to manifestation. It turns into a river and flows throughout the Major and Minor Arcana. Wherever you see a river, it tells you that the wisdom of the High Priestess is there. Water is the subconscious flow. Notice the water in the background.

**METAL** - Silver

**STONE** - reflective ones like the pearl, moonstone or crystal

**LILIES** - White-purity

**YELLOW** - intellect

**CROSS** - is of equal length. It is used for measurement. It is called the Greek cross and the builder's square. It also represents the union of the positive (Fire) and negative (Water) forces.

**POMEGRANATE** - has many seeds. When cut open, it burst forth in a joyous, abundant fashion. It is a symbol of Christ and His resurrection. The pomegranate was the fruit fed to Persephone.

**CUBE** - She is sitting on a square stone, a cube. This rests on a yellow (intellect) floor. There are 6 sides to a cube. The 6 sides when unfolded form a cross. (Reread #6.) There are 8 points or corners and 12 boundary lines. 6+8+12=26, the number for Yod He' Va He' (name for perfection and God). You will see many figures sitting on a cube, which means they have dimension and that they are grounded on a solid spiritual foundation. (See Figure #6-8.) Each of the Major Arcana holds a position on the cube.

The wise man no longer looks upon Good and Evil but sees this all as one. He realizes that through one's tribulations one actually becomes wiser and has more wisdom. Realize this and use your wisdom to work through difficulties. Life gives us problems, but we create the stress in handling them by not having the wisdom to work through balance. Next time you get into a situation that makes you feel stressed, try the method of reflection and deal with it with wisdom, not the negative method of creating stress.

SUMMARY
+ When this card shows up in a spread, it represents a person in the client's life who has the wisdom from above to heal the body or soul such as a Nurse, Psychologist, Astrologer or Spiritual leader. This could also be the client's occupation or how the life is handled.

- If it is reversed, it shows that the client is functioning more in the negative and has not learned the wisdom of balancing the positive and negative.

**THE CUBE**

The cube has a location for each of the Tarot cards. Look at Figure #8.

**The three lines represent the three coordinates shown by dotted lines.** They are from A (Above) to B (Below), from E (East) to W (West), and from N (North) to S (South).

**The Hebrew mother letters are these three lines.** The Tarot card that goes with the Hebrew letter is placed there.

The Hebrew mother letters are:
A, Aleph, (Coordinate connecting Above with Below) and is **The Fool**.
M, Mem, (Coordinate connecting East with West) and is **The Hanged Man**.
S, Shin, (Coordinate connecting North with South) and is **Judgement**.

The six Hebrew double letters represent the directions Above, Below, East, West, North and South.

B, Beth      is Above and **The Magician.**
G, Gimel     is Below and **The High Priestess.**
D, Daleth     is East and **The Empress.**
K, Kaph     is West and **Wheel of Fortune**.
P, Pe'     is North and **The Tower.**
R, Resh     is South and **The Sun.**

Where these three lines cross is the 7th Hebrew double letter Tau and the Tarot card The World. See Figure #8.

The 12 Hebrew simple letters are the 12 edges of the cube. See Figures #6 and 7. The cards that they represent are:

H, He'     is Northeast and the card **The Emperor.**
V, Vau     is Southeast and the card **The Hierophant.**
Z, Zain     is East Above and **The Lovers.**
Ch, Cheth     is East Below and **The Chariot.**
T, Teth     is North Above and **Strength.**
Y, Yod     is North Below and **The Hermit.**
L, Lamed     is North West and **Justice.**
N, Nun     is South West and **Death.**
S, Samech     is West Above and **Temperance.**
O, Ayin     is West Below and **The Devil.**
Ts, Tzaddi     is South Above and **The Star.**
Q, Qoph     is South Below and **The Moon.**

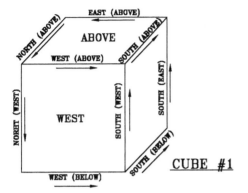

**CUBE #1**

Cube #1 represents the Cube of Space viewed from the west, showing the top, west and south faces. The boundary lines are named and arrows show the direction of the current flowing in each line.

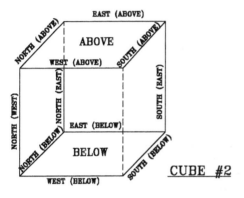

**CUBE #2**

Cube #2 shows the top, bottom, north and east faces, together with the boundary lines: North (below), East (below), and North (East) which are omitted from Cube #1.

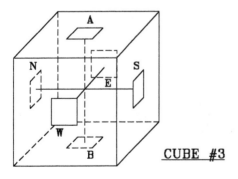

**CUBE #3**

Cube #3 represents the three coordinates by dotted lines from A (above) to B (below), from E (east) to W (west), and from N (north) to S (south). To these three lines the Hebrew mother letters are assigned. To the twelve edges the twelve Hebrew simple letters are assigned. To the inner central point, (where the three lines cross), the 7th Hebrew double letter, Tau, is assigned.

D - Daleth

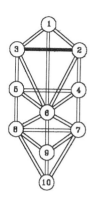

**THE EMPRESS**
The Empress's job is to bring completion by closing the Supernal Triangle with path #14 (4). She is the conveyor of the Life Force and symbolizes the ultimate triumph of the generative force, when balanced. She is the place of the birth of light, the subconscious and the womb of those ideas which enlighten the world, which comes to mind with no effort. The female needs to do nothing but be feminine. She is Mother Earth.

**KEYWORDS** - Fertility, abundance, growth, time for harvest and creative imagination
**PLANET** - The Hebrew letter D, Daleth, rules path #14 (4) and brings with it the planet Venus. Venus ♀ is the principle of growth and rules the throat. The brain perceives and thought is disclosed and the throat utters sound. Venus stands for the female power--mother nature. It can represent a person pregnant with child or pregnant with product, anything about to give birth. The blending of #1 the positive male energy with #2 the negative female energy produces a product or child. It influences the creative nature and desire. Venus shows how we share of ourselves socially. Venus is the planet for love and attraction. The color for Venus is green.
**CARD NUMBER** - 3 is a number of satisfaction and completion. It forms the trine or trinity. Since this number is the number of completion and giving birth, it brings to mind what we talked about regarding a child being born in the 8th month. There must be the three energies to produce anything. The #1 is the masculine positive energy which has behind it the Yod, which is the God power; the #2 is the negative feminine energy with the energy of He'. Vau is masculine and is joined here in reference to the #3. Therefore, the **odd numbers** when divided by 2 always leaves a remainder of 1. This #1, the masculine, Yod and God power must exist as well as He', the feminine, in formation. We must have the polarity in order to start form. A child born in the 7th or 9th month has this #1. The 8th month child does not. It is appropriate that The Empress is #3, because it shows that what has been worked on is now ready to be born. (Reread #3, & #8 under numbers.)
**HEBREW LETTER #4** - D (Daleth) means door and also breast. Breast is appropriate since it has to do with nurturing. In the Empress the birth is ready. The Soul descends into incarnation or ascends into initiation. When you have the key to open the door, it opens upon an ever expanding vista of spiritual glories. This letter on path #14 is the door that closes off the Supernal Triangle from the world below. This is the Hebrew double letter representing the planet Venus.
**PATH #14 (4)** - The 14th path is called *Illuminating Intelligence.* Sephirah #4 is called *Cohesive or Receptive Intelligence.* Passive and loving control

over growth and formation (pregnant with growth) in the unseen realm of things. One has to develop within before it can show externally. On the Tree Sephirah #1 (Chokmah, the planet Uranus and the Fire pillar) connects with Sephirah #3 (Binah, the planet Saturn and the Water pillar). Saturn is the planet of form and structure. This is the path of love, beauty, fertility and growth. This path is completion and closes the upper triangle, which is the Supernal Triangle connecting Sephirah #1(Kether, Divine Light), Sephirah #2 (Chokmah) and Sephirah #3 (Binah). It connects the male and female, the positive and the negative pillars. It is one of the three paths that connect the two sides of the tree. Kether is Air, Chokmah is Fire, and Binah is Water. All three combined produce matter, Earth. The Christ child must be born within. Kether is the Yod, Chokmah He', and Binah Vau. It is at this place that The Fool is given his physical body. He has the elements that create it. He came in as a Soul and, in completing the first four paths, now has a physical body, a combination of a Soul in a physical body. This is what the Supernal Triangle reminds us of. The Fool knows, as we do also, that we have a connection with the Divine Light from above.

**PATH COLOR** - emerald green, sky blue, early spring green

**MUSICAL TONE** - La-Venus Libra

**STREAM** - represents the one source and the subconscious mind. It starts from the High Priestess's gown and brings with it her knowledge. Ideas are manifesting.

**WATERFALL** - The underlying stream of consciousness is now in active operation.

**YELLOW HAIR** - means one thinks with intelligence. Also, yellow background symbolizes that intelligence is behind her.

**CYPRESS TREES** - are evergreen and never go dormant. They have been growing for a long time and have gone through many seasons. They are everlasting.

**CROWN** - 12 stars on the crown are the celestial influence representing the 12 signs. One's day of birth gives them a horoscope of the 12 signs and planets. Through this horoscope, one is able to see why the Soul chose to be incarnated into this life. It tells of the lessons that one goes through in the same way that the Tree has the paths to be learned.

**GREEN WREATH** - success

**STARS** - are 6 pointed like the Star of David. It shows that she has dominion over the laws of the macrocosm. 6 is a double 3.

**PEARLS** - 7 pearls around the neck. The neck and throat are ruled by Venus. 7 pearls are the 7 planets and the 7 chakras.

**SHIELD** - is heart shaped. The heart represents the heart chakra and should be copper in color. Copper is the metal for Venus.

**SCEPTER** - globe of the world on the top. In some cards the ball on the top of the scepter is the planet Venus ♀. She reigns through love and the female intuitive principal which uplifts the generative force. The scepter is in her masculine right hand, which shows that the masculine power is combined with love.

**WHEAT** - shows growth of that planted, ready now for harvest. The Empress carries the kind of consciousness that can influence planets to grow.

**RED PILLOW** - She is sitting on her desires.

**STONE SEAT** - She sits on a solid foundation. Note the symbol for Venus on the pillow and also her dress.

**KNEES** - Her knees are open to show openness or giving birth. These are also the gates of life from which all bounty flows. Women are considered to be highly evolved because their subconscious (Water) contains a wealth of knowledge.

SUMMARY
+ When this card shows up in a spread, it means that what the person has been working hard for is just about ready to be completed and born. It can represent a pregnancy.

- If the card is reversed, then there is a delay and the person has to work a little harder or longer to bring it to completion.

This completes the upper triangle on the Tree. It is called the Supernal Triangle.

ה

H- He'

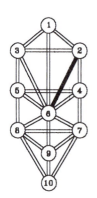

IV

THE EMPEROR.

## Card #4 THE EMPEROR ON PATH #15 (5)

**THE EMPEROR**

This card represents authority, a leader in charge. Dressed in armor, he is ready to battle the material world. The Emperor is all Fire and action. He brings energy, will and aggressiveness and is able to jump in and become involved. He has plenty of red clothing for activity and the armor is there, if needed. He is acting upon form. He stimulates. The Empress presented him with a project, idea (child). Now he can act and take responsibility (as a father).

**KEYWORDS** - leadership, order, control

**SIGN & PLANET** - Mars ♂ is the aggressive planet that rules Aries. The Hebrew letter He' rules path #15 (5) and brings with it the sign Aries ♈. Aries is a cardinal (active) Fire (enthusiastic, aggressive) sign. Notice the rams' heads on his throne and on the shoulder of his cape. Aries people are courageous and not afraid to fight for what they want. Notice the armor that is under his clothing. He is prepared for anything.

**CARD NUMBER** - 4 represents a struggle. It is a square, cube or cross. Think of it like stumbling blocks that change into building blocks, once worked through. Stress brings us our challenges. Number 4 is the beginning of the square. On the Tree of Life the 4th Sephirah Chesed, on the right hand side of the Tree, starts the World of Formation. Chesed represents the planet Jupiter ♃. Notice that Jupiter is made from a cross with the Moon on the side. The cross of matter is elevated by the perception of spirit. Jupiter is philosophies and expansion. We must grow. If you look at Sephiroth 4, 5, 7, and 8, they form the square. This is the World of Formation. Leaving the Supernal Triangle and the life of bliss, we now enter what we know of as the real world. This square brings with it the planets Jupiter, Mars, Mercury, and Venus, with the Sun in the middle. On the earth we need (Mars) energy to work on our goals (Mercury), intelligence to be able to understand and comprehend, (Venus) love to draw to us what we need and the Sun to give us our individual talents which is shown through our Sun sign. We have left the upper triangle or trinity and now begin our growth. (Reread #4 in numbers.)

**HEBREW LETTER #5** - H (He') is a window. A window admits light into the house. Light represents knowledge or enlightenment, also life breath and the spirit. H, (He') is a Hebrew simple letter and stands for the sign of Aries. The letter H (He') is important. It occurs twice in the name for God, HVHY (Hebrew is read right to left). He' has the numerical value of 5. There are two 5's in the name which add up to 10, the number of completion. Number 3 was the Door we entered through. After the three was completed in order to keep the energy going, the additional He' was needed. Once inside #4 we see the window we look out of, and that lets in light. Number 5 is what we see, like the awareness of the Soul looking out the eyes of the body. This second He' is the start of a new beginning.

**PATH #15 (5)** - on the Tree. The 15th path is called *Constituting Intelligence*. Sephirah #5 is called *Radical Intelligence*. Path #15 connects Sephirah #2 (Chokmah, Wisdom, Fire and Uranus) to Sephirah #6 (Tiphareth, Beauty, Air and the Sun). This path uses the energy of the astrological sign Aries which is here because of the Hebrew Letter He'. The Supernal Triangle is connected to Tiphareth through this path. Tiphareth is the powerful center of the Tree with the most paths connected to it. The Sun which is the gravitational pull for all the planets is there. Remember that the Sun was changed to the Son of God (The Christ). Christ is the center of all of the World of Formation as well as the whole Tree. Even though we leave the Supernal Triangle, we still are connected to what we know is the center of our lives. That power from above is there for us to tap into when needed.

**PATH COLOR** - scarlet, red, brilliant flame, glowing red. Red is the color of the planet Mars and the sign Aries. His cape and gown is red showing his aggressive nature.

**MUSICAL TONE** - Do- for Mars and Aries

**SOLID CONCRETE THRONE** - He sits on a very solid concrete throne showing strength for his convictions. A perfect square, symbol of truth and order.

**MOUNTAINS** - High mountains show a lot of accomplishments.

**RIVER** - left hand corner-showing emotions and the subconscious and comes from the original High Priestess gown.

**BEARD** - shows wisdom. Usually it is on old men who have been through a lot in life and should have experience. White shows purity.

**BALL** - represents the earth. It is in his left hand, the feminine (Water) hand. The balance of spirit and matter through the feminine power of love.

**GOLDEN ANKH** - Gold is the metal of the Sun. It is held in his right hand, the masculine side of the body, to show from where he draws his power and light. Solar conscious mind. He rules with strength as well as sensitivity since the arm is blue. The ankh is an Egyptian cross. It is the symbol of eternal life. The T symbolizes being forced downward to our darkest part to understand who we are. The ball on top is the Spirit.

**T-TAU CROSS** - oldest cross used by the first Christians. This is the one Moses used to lift up the Brazen serpent in the wilderness (Numbers 21:8). It is also called the prophetic cross. It was worn as a symbol of death or of human sacrifice. It was a protecting talisman which focused a power that would help the wearer to unfold his godlike nature through the crucifixion of the human and the balancing of the pairs of opposites. It was laid upon the breast of the neophyte when, during his initiation, he was placed in a mystic sleep and laid in a crypt, or tomb, for three days. It was also placed upon the breast of the dead, after being embalmed. Spirit cannot penetrate matter or manifest in creation without forming the cross, which is the two polarities. Solar Fire energy integrated with the Water thereby enlarges the potential of the unity of the conscious and subconscious mind. (See also card #22.)

**HAT** - gold, little circles around it are like the Sun. The Sun is exalted in the sign of Aries. The symbol on the top of the hat, $\Upsilon$, is the hieroglyphic for the sign of Aries.

**ORANGE** - is the blending of the colors, yellow (intellect) and red (desire or activity).

SUMMARY

+ This card either shows a client or someone around the client who is in authority and has leadership ability. He is not afraid to take a chance and to be an aggressive person. He has courage to start his descent or ascent. It can also be a man who is like an Aries or a self-made man.

- Reversed, this card represents a person who is not living up to his abilities and does not realize his strength, one who is dependent on others.

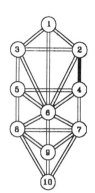

V - Vau

# CARD #5 THE HIEROPHANT ON PATH #16 (6)

## THE HIEROPHANT

In the ancient Egyptian Temple ceremonies, the aspirant was brought into the presence of the great god Osiris to receive his blessing. As he listened to the triumphant chants of the Temple choirs, he perceived that he had indeed achieved that high estate in which **neither feminine nor masculine was predominant over the other, but both functioned in harmonious equality. Such as the blending of pillars Fire and Water, + and -.** This is shown by the two figures in front of the Hierophant, awaiting his blessing. Many times this card can be a marriage. It is a high religious card, the working out of an ideal, the union of linking together, like using yoga and meditation to get the body into the universal consciousness. It is a person who has a good religious background that they can fall back on. He reveals sacred things. Two fingers down means not revealing all, much to learn.

**KEYWORDS** - Yoking together the super-conscious mind with the human mind. Notice the yokes on the back of the men and also on the front of The Hierophant. Yokes symbolize taking a challenge.

**SIGN** - Taurus. The Hebrew simple letter V (Vau) rules path #16 (6) and goes with Taurus, a sign of values and ability to attain high ideals. Taurus makes something solid. The Hierophant/Pope on path #16 (6) shows that religion is fixed and formed. Sephirah #6 also is a point where this is so.

**CARD NUMBER** - 5 is the half way point between 1 and 9. It is also the half way point between nature and God. Train the human will to be one with the Divine will. The ability to achieve high goals. The blending of the elements and spirit with man. This is the meaning of the 5 pointed star or pentagram and considered the number of man himself. (Reread #5 in numbers.)

**HEBREW LETTER #6** - V (Vau) means nail or hook. Something that joins together. The Hebrew letter looks like it is being driven down with dynamic force as a nail. (Reread #6 in numbers.) It is a Hebrew simple letter standing for the astrological sign Taurus. This is on path #16 (6).

**PATH #16 (6)** - Path #16 (6) is called *Triumphal or Eternal Intelligence.* The Sephirah #6 is called *Mediating Intelligence.* Path #16 (6) connects Sephirah #2 (Chokmah, Wisdom, Fire, Uranus) and Sephirah #4 (Chesed, Mercy, Fire and Jupiter). On this path is Vau and the astrological sign Taurus. The Hierophant is on this path. This path connects the lower World of Formation with the Supernal Triangle. The planet Uranus, which is cosmic knowledge, and the planet Jupiter, which is philosophical, is combined by this path. Both Chokmah and Chesed are connected to Tiphareth (Sephirah #6) by paths #15 (5) and #20 (10). This connection gives power, and since path #16 (6) is on the masculine Fire pillar, it also activates all this energy.

**PATH COLOR** - red orange, deep indigo, deep warm olive, rich brown

**MUSICAL TONE** -La-Venus, Taurus

**SENSES** - speech

**PILLARS** - On the card, he is sitting between two pillars as is the High Priestess. The Hierophant expresses formal religion but the High Priestess is spirituality. The pillars are gray, showing wisdom in the balance of the positive and negative energy. These are the same as the two columns on The Tree of Life. The left one, Water -, and the right one, Fire +. The union of two things. The blending of black + and white - makes gray. Gray shows wisdom. To become an initiate, one must know and find a balance of the polarities and obey the law.

**THRONE** - He sits on a firm solid foundation.

**ROBE** - Under garment is white showing the spiritual nature. It is under a robe of red. Red represents desire and action. A blue robe also shows underneath revealing compassion, feelings and intuition. On his robe is the white trimming that holds crosses.

**CROSSES** - The cross signifies the ideal blending of the male/female, +/-, Fire/Water, the two levels of consciousness. Look at the crosses on this trimming. They are all different. The top one has equal arms. On the second one down, the horizontal line is moved up to form the Calgary cross. The bottom one is even higher. A square is on the bottom of the trimming. A square has within it a cross when lines are drawn from the corners.

**CROWN** - triple tiara like the Pope's crown. It is gold or yellow showing he has intelligence. The bottom has 5 designs, which are the 5 senses. The middle has 7 representing the 7 planets, and the top has 3, which are the 3 states of consciousness. 5+7+3=15  15 represents JAH-Adam or God. On the top of his crown is a W which is the Hebrew letter for Shin שׁ, which stands for the Holy Ghost and the element Fire.

**FEET** - white with crosses on each. His feet are on a box, preventing you from opening it. Knowledge is there, if you search for it. It is not given and you must have the DESIRE and the Keys to open the box. On the box are circles with crosses inside. Pull down the cross and you have the symbol for Venus, ♀.

**TWO KEYS** - There are two keys symbolizing the Tarot and Astrology. One key is silver (Tarot) and the other gold (Astrology). When you have the knowledge of these two subjects, you will be able to unlock the box and understand the knowledge of the higher powers. It is also the symbol for Peter. They represent the power to bind and the power to loose. Christ said to Peter ,"I will give unto thee the keys of the kingdom of heaven" (Matthew

16:19). One is silver to represent Earth and one is gold to represent Heaven. Notice that both keys have a cross in the circle.

**STRAPS** – around box are black and white representing positive and negative.

**SCEPTER** - holds it in his left hand. He is using his sensitivity and his psychic abilities. (The left side of the body is the feminine side showing that he is using his instincts.) He is placed on path #16 (6) on the right Fire-masculine pillar of the Tree. This unites the masculine and feminine (+ & -) energy. This is a three tiered cross, called the Papal Cross. There is a place for the 7 planets on the cross. This cross was designed to be used only in processions when the Pope participates. It shows that he functions on three planes, the physical, mental and spiritual. This is also seen on the three tiered crown.

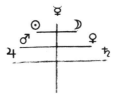

**HAND** - His right hand gives the blessing. Note the fingers. It forms the sign of Esotericism. "Thy right hand O Lord glorious in power" (Exodus 15:6). This position of the fingers is the Latin form of the hand of God. The thumb and the first two fingers straight, the remaining two fingers bent back to the heel of the hand. You see his hand raised over the heads of the two men, in a blessing. This symbolizes that when one has the wisdom and position that he has achieved, they can bless both the masculine and feminine nature of humanity and have them bow before him in recognition.

**MEN** - 2 men in front of Hierophant. On their garments are yokes. One has red roses showing desire and the other has lilies showing purity. These represent the yoking of the desires and spirit as well as Fire and Water, + and -.

SUMMARY
+ When this card shows in a spread, it shows that the client is using his inner powers of intuition to help with his decision. It is also like receiving a blessing, as in a marriage ceremony. Some say it is the official act of making the marriage legal. A blessing is being bestowed on what one is doing.

Z - Zain

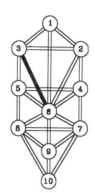

## LOVERS

The Lovers card represents the act of choice. Cupid in another deck aims his arrow not to the heart, but to the head and the pineal gland. When the pineal gland force center is aroused into activity, the whole body becomes full of life and light. Life is dedicated to loving selflessly with service for uplifting and blessing all. Follow the heart as it will lead you to the path that will bring transformation and happiness. Man looks at woman and woman looks up to the angel or spirituality. Again male and female, Fire and Water represent the conscious and subconscious mind. The angel is the Super-conscious mind. The blending of the conscious and subconscious mind creates the Super-conscious mind. Cosmic or universal love can be attained.

**KEYWORDS** - Discrimination, cooperation, reciprocal action

**SIGN** - The Lovers is sometimes thought of as Taurus since Taurus goes with #6. The planet Venus ♀ is its ruler. It represents our social and love nature. However, the sign for the card comes from the Hebrew letter that falls on the path that the card is on. In this case, since The Lovers card is on path #17 (7) which holds the Hebrew simple letter Z (Zain), and the astrological sign Gemini ♊; therefore, the sign is Gemini. The sign of Gemini always gives choices. It is a curious sign and always asks WHY?

**CARD NUMBER** - 6 is a lucky number, good for money and ruled by Taurus and Venus. 6 represents the hexagram-6 pointed star which represents the Star or shield of David. Notice that it is made up of two triangles which represent the #3 and completion. The triangle on the bottom is silver and reflects the light of the triangle above which is gold, as the Moon reflects the light of the Sun. The upper triangle represents the spiritual, Fire side and the lower one the emotional, Water side of life. These symbols relate to two polar opposites which are complimentary and equal.

**HEBREW LETTER #7** - Z (Zain) is sword. This is on path #17 (7). The Swords in the Tarot represent intelligence and communication. This Hebrew simple letter stands for the astrological sign of Gemini. Gemini, a dual sign, is the sign that has the intellectual planet Mercury for its ruler. Our thought process gives us the awareness to be able to choose between two things. Swords represent the Air element. Gemini, an Air sign, is also the sign for The Lovers. With Gemini there are always two things to choose from. This is a card of duality and making a decision.

**PATH #17 (7)** - Path #17 (7) is called *Disposing Intelligence.* The 7th Sephirah is called *Occult Intelligence.* Path #17 (7) connects Sephirah #3 (Binah, Understanding, on the Water pillar and the planet Saturn) to Sephirah #6 (Tiphareth, Beauty, on the Air pillar and the planet the Sun). Structure, form and understanding come with Binah. Binah is part of the

135

spiritual (Supernal Triangle), Super-consciousness. In The Lovers card, the woman is looking up as The Fool did. This shows she realizes that the power of the Super-conscious mind will help her to make decisions. The Lovers on path #17 (7) makes a connection with the Christ within through the attachment to Sephirah #6 Tiphareth. This path provides faith to the righteous.

**PATH COLOR** - pale mauve, reddish gray, orange.

**MUSICAL NOTE** - La-Taurus; Mi-Gemini

**ANGEL** - Raphael is the angel of the Air and means God the healer. Michael is the angel of the Sun. He represents the Super-conscious. His garment is purple. Purple is the blending of the red and blue. Red is desire and blue is emotions. Wings are red showing desire and action. The head piece is red and green representing desire and growth.

**SUN** - is yellow representing intellectual power, one's illuminated rays

**CLOUDS** - are white representing purity.

**MOUNTAINS** - are attainment, climbing to your highest aspiration, or goal.

**MAN** - is the conscious mind. Adam.

**WOMAN** - is the subconscious mind. Eve.

**12 FLAMES ON TREE** - represent the 12 signs of the zodiac and the Tree of Life. Through this knowledge we evolve. Each flame has three parts which represents the three decans of each Zodiac sign, as well as our three states of consciousness and the three triangles on the Tree and the 3 elements Fire, Air and Water.

**TREE OF GOOD AND EVIL** - 5 Fruits represent the 5 senses.

**SNAKE** - represents temptation, which arises as we become inquisitive, and causes a choice. Man looks to woman and woman looks up to the Angel. This is the conscious mind, subconscious mind, and Super-conscious mind. Woman has always been the one responsible for the spiritual development in the family. She is more intuitive since she is female and is negative (Water).

SUMMARY

\+ This card shows that the client has a choice to make and has two paths to choose from. It can also be that there are two loves in the life of the individual. Look to the positive and above for guidance. There is an inner marriage of the male and female polarity, a true spiritual union. Can also represent a marriage.

\- There can be delusions in making a choice resulting in much difficulty and delay when this card is reversed.

Ch - Cheth

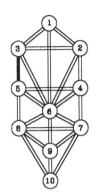

## CARD #7 THE CHARIOT ON PATH #18 (8)

**THE CHARIOT**

A chariot carries us from one place to another as well as from one subject to another. All magic is in the will. Ideas are carried into the field of consciousness by the mind. Notice that there are no reins. The reins are invisible as they are the power of the mind (Gemini). There is no need for physical reins, because the mind is developed to such a degree that it directs the path of the chariot by *will* alone. By keeping in tune with this Force our progress is unlimited. His chariot is in a cubic form. The cube becomes the philosophers' stone. He rises out of the cube, like in the ascension of the 3 over the 4. 3+4=7. (Reread #7.) He travels the path of understanding, the one path that goes between the forces of good and evil. In so doing, he causes both to succumb to his will.

A person with Chariot energy developed within himself or herself will have risen above all personal aspects of *will*. They are driven by their true self, which desire only the expression of the cosmic solar principle, the Sun (Christ power) within. This person has thus opened a path that leads to his or her cosmic self within.

A true driver of the Chariot knows cosmic truth and is able to let it manifest in life. He or she would be one with *Primal Will*, knowing that the aspect and function of the God head within is omnipotent and supreme. All mundane and lowly things would have no importance to a developed Chariot person unless they had use for the correspondence of cosmic will. The personal needs would be fulfilled by the very belief and recognition of God or Spirit as a force, the force in nature that he or she taps into.

The Chariot rides the waves of Primal Will, travels the path that he or she is shown, pursues the vision that is perceived. The vision of the Primal Will is the vision of the Chariot. This level of knowledge comes to those who seek. Therefore, Gemini, the intellectual, is co-ruler of this card. Cancer/Moon also rules since the Moon represents the brain and stores all knowledge and is represented by the Hebrew letter Cheth that rules path #18 (8), which this card is on. The right directive influences or the spiritual will represent the arms which Gemini rules, 2 projections of power.

**KEYWORDS** - Using the intellect and higher consciousness over the emotions. The conqueror (of self), supreme spiritual achievement.

**SIGN** - Since the Hebrew simple letter Ch (Cheth) stands for the astrological sign Cancer ♋, this is the sign for this card. Cancer's ruling planet is the Moon ☽. The subconscious (Moon) is at all times in control of every subhuman manifestation of cosmic energy. By directing it, we have control over every situation. The Moon is the perception that allows you to understand whatever situation you are dealing with. People come to those who have this ability. The mothering, healing principle is channeled and directed to lead the individual to know the cosmic will of the universe.

**CARD NUMBER** - 7 is spiritual and sacred. There are seven planes/rays and 7 steps to illumination. God favored the #7. On the 7th day God rested. At-one-ment. After every 7 years there is a change. (Reread #7 in numbers.)

**HEBREW LETTER #8** - Ch (Cheth) is a Hebrew simple letter which means field. It suggests space with no bounds or limits. No blockage: on and on and on. The psychic intuitive power is limitless. The sign Cancer goes with Cheth and path #18 (8).

**PATH #18 (8)**-Path #18 (8) is called the *Intelligence of the House of Influences*. Sephirah #8 is called *Absolute or Perfect Intelligence*. Path #18 (8) connects Sephirah #3 (Binah, Understanding, Water and Saturn) with Sephirah #5 (Geburah, Severity, Water and Mars). Both of these Sephiroth are on the Water pillar. Saturn and Mars are direct opposites in nature. Mars initiates and becomes action, then Saturn stabilizes the energy to make it productive. If Mars did not propel the will to move onward, we would still be in the Supernal Triangle where Saturn resides. This is similar to the Emperor who was ruled by Aries, the sign that Mars rules. This indicates applying action in order to accomplish. To have all knowledge shown by The Chariot is useless if one does not put it to use.

**PATH COLOR** - red-orange, maroon

**MUSICAL TONE** - Mi-Gemini; Ti-Cancer

The right directive influences or the spiritual will represent arms (Gemini), 2 projections of power.

**WALL** - in the background. A fence or wall holds in. He has crossed over the river and now puts worldly objects behind him.

**HOUSES** - represent Beth, The Magician and Air (Gemini).

**WINDOWS** - represent He', The Hierophant--some clear, some not. We are limited by our knowledge. We only see according to what we know.

**TREES** - Cypress-evergreen/everlasting like on card #3, The Empress.

**WATER** - is the subconscious mind of The High Priestess.

**PILLARS** - The 4 pillars in the canopy are the 4 elements-Fire, Earth, Air, and Water.

**CANOPY** - The heaven is his canopy. It includes the stars, which represents the celestial forces.

**STARS** - show the influence of the planets of the Zodiac on human forces.

**SHIELD** - is on the front of the chariot and shields against the negative and positive forces. It represents union between the two. The two wings with the circle in the middle is called a 'lungam,' a sphere named by the Egyptians. It is like the number 8. It is a winged globe rushing onward in time.

**RED** - represents desire, activity. Wings over shield--flying to higher consciousness. The god Mercury had wings on his hat and shoes to make him go faster.

**SCEPTER** - He holds it in his right hand (masculine) and rules with authority. Action is required. The glove shows this hand is protected. Other hand reveals the compassionate, feminine side.

**MOONS** - on shoulders. One waxing and smiling and one waning and sad. Knowledge of the phases of the Moon, which is used in timing events in one's life. Also represents conscious and subconscious.

**SQUARE** - on the chest represents purity and order. Some cards have a black T in the square which is the limiting power of Saturn or Saturn stabilizing and making secure the knowledge. Learn discrimination, take your lessons in order.

**BELT** - is the circle of the Ecliptic. It has the Zodiac signs on it.

**SKIRT** - has the symbols for Alchemy (salt, sulfur, etc.).

**CROWN** - is yellow and represents the intellect.

**SPHINX** -The sphinx is made up of the combination of the astrological four fixed signs. The head of Man is Aquarius. The body of the Lion is Leo. The Bull is Taurus. The Bird is Scorpio. Notice, their tails are in a submissive position. One is white and one black representing the balance of life, positive and negative.

**WHEELS** - are yellow, the color for Gemini and the intellect. The chariot moves with the power of intelligence. There is also a yellow background.

**RED TOP**- Jewish toy called "Dreidel," a Symbol of God.

SUMMARY
+ This card shows that the client is using all of his or her powers: intuition, psyche, religious, common sense, astrology, alchemy, phases of the Moon to be in control of his life. One has self control. See introduction above.

- Reversed, this scard shows that one is not ready to use his powers. He must further develop them. There is loss of control, failure or defeat.

T - Teth

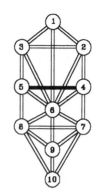

VIII

STRENGTH.

XI

JUSTICE .

# CARD #8 STRENGTH ON PATH #19 (9)

**STRENGTH**
The law states that the subconscious is at all times in control of every sub-human manifestation of cosmic energy. Man too often hopes to claim his heritage through physical powers and personal will, instead of the sword of the spirit. Those with spiritual courage, strength and love are worthy to open the Lion's mouth or to keep it closed. Here Strength, which is female, tunes in with her intuition to know that which is within and to keep it calm and under control, the controlling of the beast within us. Take the courage to let the Life Force flow through until it automatically becomes one's core.

**KEYWORDS** - Handling a difficult situation with intuition and love.
**SIGN** - Leo - The Hebrew simple letter T (Teth) represents the astrological sign of Leo ♌. Leo is known for leadership ability. He is able to stand up, be proud and share that which he has. Leo signifies the royal house of Judaea, especially David and Solomon (Star of David). The King is called "the Lion of the House of Judaea." The Queen is Cancer, a sign which is sometimes called "the mouth of the Lion." Sheba is the Wisdom Queen, humanity collectively.
**CARD NUMBER** - 8 is the Life Force, unending, unbreakable force. It is the rhythm of our breathing. It is the sign of infinity when turned on its side. It also calls for balance. (Reread #8 in the numbers.)
**HEBREW LETTER #9** - is T (Teth) and is on path #19 (9) and means snake, serpent power, (kundalini) cosmic electricity, universal life principle, conscious energy, which takes form in all things and builds everything from within. The control of this energy is by intellectual means and is the secret of practical occultism. The Serpent also symbolizes wisdom. When you overcome the temptation of the snake, it becomes instrumental in your salvation. The shedding of the snake's skin is like our shedding of our body at the end of each incarnation. The snake shedding his skin is a type of reincarnation or regeneration or immortality. The snake started us on our search for knowledge and now has brought us to completion.

Moses raised up the serpent upon his staff in the wilderness. The Serpent relates to Initiation, which is the supreme lesson awaiting humanity. The most ancient form of Teth was the cross, referring to the serpentine fire force which wreathes itself about and through the staff of Hermes. Through the misuse of this fire force, mankind took upon itself "coats of skin," which must be acquired at birth and repeatedly cast off in death, until at last the disciple is the Initiate over whom death has no power. He then embodies within himself all the powers of Teth. The Master Initiate has ascended the 9 steps of the Lesser Mysteries to the fullness of knowledge. The Hermit in

142

card #9 is like the Egyptian god Osiris who sits at the top of the staircase. Teth is a Hebrew simple letter standing for the astrological sign of Leo. Strength has a garland of roses, which is like a snake wrapping around her.

**PATH #19 (9)** - Path #19 (9) is called the *Intelligence of the secret of all the activities of the spiritual beings*. Sephirah #9 is called *Pure Intelligence*. Path #19 (9) connects Sephirah #5 (Geburah, Severity, Water pillar and Mars) to Sephirah #4 (Chesed, Mercy, Fire pillar and Jupiter). This is one of the three paths that cross the Tree and connect the two sides. There is a controversy as to which card should be on this path. It is between Strength and Justice. Both will be discussed and you can make up your mind. **If you do switch them, then the Hebrew letter Teth, the sign of Leo and the musical note Re for Leo should go wherever Strength goes.**

**PATH COLOR** - greenish yellow, deep purple, gray, reddened yellow

**MUSICAL TONE** - Re-Leo

**GIRL** - closing the jaws of the lion. Some say closing the mouth and some say opening the mouth. If you look at the position of her left hand you see that it is pushing down on his mouth. This shows she is in control of her energy and the lion (notice that his tail is in a submissive position). Look at the card. It is as though she was using her psychic ability to tune into the mind of the lion in order to control him. By taming this great power and lifting it above the animal level and making it submissive, one can call it forth willingly through love.

**WHITE ROBE** - is purity and spiritual consciousness, showing she has accomplished her spiritual growth.

**MOUNTAIN** - is spiritual attainment.

**CHAIN OF ROSES** - twines around the waist like the snake or twisted like the figure 8. When we learn to weave our desires together into a chain, reflecting all desires which are compatible with our main purpose, we shall be able to make wonderful applications of creative imagination to the control and direction of the serpent power.

**SIGN OF INFINITY** - This is the same as on the card The Magician. It means eternal life, and the blending of consciousness.

SUMMARY

+ This card shows the client is using his strength, intuition, and psychic ability to perceive and understand, in order to be in control of any situation that may seem too powerful to handle.

- The situation is out of control when this card is reversed. The situation is taking over and one's power is not being applied. There can be uncontrolled fears. **At times some switch this card with #11 Justice. Read the following and make your decision.**

## CARD #11   JUSTICE  ON  PATH #19 (9)

**JUSTICE**
Justice is form through balance.  For every action there is an equal and opposite reaction.  We must learn to eliminate useless worn-out forms.  This includes people, situations and things.  Education is completed by action or work.  Just hearing the word or reading it is not true education.  You have to act or apply it.  A balanced personality is faithful, constant and confident, because the right use of reason has been established and ensures certainty as to the just outcome of all activities.  You really learn when you have to act (Mars), judge (Jupiter) and balance a decision.

**KEYWORDS** - balance, decision, judgement, legal matters

**See page 143 for explanation for Path #19 (9), Path color, and Card #. The Hebrew letter Lamed, the sign of Libra and musical note La should remain with Justice.  See page 158.**
**PILLARS** - He sits between the two gray pillars of wisdom.  These are the two pillars of Fire and Water on the Tree.  The purple cloth draped between them symbolizes spirituality.  Purple is the blending of red and blue.  The desires and emotions are balanced.  He is not blindfolded.
**RED ROBE** - is active desires and the green cape is growth.
**SQUARE** - is white with a red center.  Shows activity (red) of spirit manifested in form (square).
**YELLOW** - hair shows one thinks with intelligence.  This is the same as the crown, background and scales.
**SWORD** - in up position shows that she has not finished, hasn't made a decision.
**SCALES**-are the symbol of justice.  The two sides of the balance has been dealt with by man.  The balancing of the conscious and the subconscious.  It was the belief of early Christians that there would be a day when all the activity of their lives would be judged as if it were laid on the scales.  St. John Chrysostom, one of the early writers, recorded, "In that day our actions, our words, our thoughts will be placed on the scales, and the dip of the balance on either side will carry with it the irrevocable sentence."  The balance scales was a symbol associated with the archangel Michael, who was considered to be the judgement angel.
**WHITE SHOE** - a peek of purity

SUMMARY
+ There can be a court decision pending.  Card upright shows a positive outcome.  The client is using his intelligence, weighing and balancing to come to the right decision about a matter.

- With a reversed card, the decision is delayed or not favorable. One must contemplate longer before a decision can be made. Maybe he/she does not have all the facts.

### #11 JUSTICE IN THE POSITION OF #8 STRENGTH. WHAT DO YOU THINK?

**The position on the tree of #8 and # 11 many times is switched. It is said that Justice belongs in the position of #8.**

In some ways this is true. Decide after reading the following and make your own decision.

Attaining and maintaining equilibrium is what this card is all about. If this card is positioned on the Tree at path #19 (9) where Strength was, it shows that Man can act from one's free will (planet Mars on the left pillar in Geburah). The planet Jupiter, Chesed on the right pillar, stands for the law. Law reacts to his action. Law is interposed between the freedom of man and the Law of God.

Note on the card for Justice that she sits between two pillars. Justice does not act, she can only react. This is why it is said that she is a woman. She has the sword in her Masculine hand and speaks with authority, and the scales in her Feminine hand, which allows her to weigh everything with feeling, again the balancing of the two pillars.

These pillars can represent the pillars on the Tree. The one on the right is Fire and masculine and considered the positive one. The one on the left is Water and feminine and considered the negative one. Or one may say the balance of positive and negative or right and wrong. The card of Justice is in the middle of these two pillars when placed on path #19 and connects them together. These two pillars are the same ones in the card of The High Priestess and the Hierophant. One is Boaz (no) and one Jachin (yes).

The left pillar on Sephirah #5 (Geburah) has the planet Mars which stands for the actions that we take for ourselves. It also brings with it Sephirah #8 (Hod) which is below it, and the planet Mercury, which is our thought process. Now there is action and thoughts. On the right pillar on Sephirah #4 (Chesed) is the planet Jupiter and under it is Sephirah #7 (Netzach) and Venus. Jupiter is the spiritual law and freedom and Venus is the planet of love.

Now think of the card Justice as the scale of balance and picture the two pillars on the right and left as if they were hanging as a scale does. Place the card of Justice in the middle of the path or rod which connects the two together. On path #19 she is in-between the individual will of beings and the universal will of the Supreme Being. She has the power to establish balance each time the individual will overpowers the universal laws. An action (which is the planet Mars) finds justice (which is the planet Jupiter).

Note that the rod or path that Justice would be on is straight across and supported by the path coming up. These two paths form the cross called the Tau. The cross which is like the T is Greek and one of the earliest forms of the cross used by the first Christians. It is the point of balance supported by the cross, balance in the World of Formation.

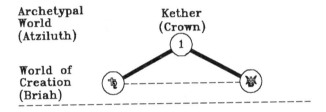

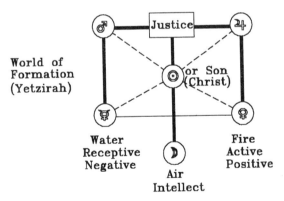

TAU − CROSS

Since we always have as above, so below, we look above to Kether. Kether is the scale of balance which balances Binah and Chokmah. It is the balance of the World of creation (Atziluth), the balance of Understanding and Wisdom. Isn't this what the lower scale is balancing also? The only difference is that the upper scale is of the higher, spiritual, and universal world and the lower scale is of the mundane world of form. The balance of Heaven or the balance of Earth.

Our thoughts and mind (which is the planet Mercury), can keep us in bondage, imprisoned in hell, so to say, or give us knowledge that can free us. The Soul imprisoned or the Soul freed to climb higher. Don't forget that we are trying to get back to the Garden of Eden of eternal Bliss. That is the scale or Supernal Triangle above.

To think is to judge. To judge is to decide if something is right or wrong. Therefore, one has to know the extent of their knowledge and ignorance when one makes a judgement. We may think something is right because we know at the time that it is that way. We may think something is wrong because at the time this is how we perceive it. We are all looking at life and spirituality from our own ability to comprehend. One is always ignorant of the Soul of another; therefore, do not judge one another. Thoughts (Mercury) which contain love (Venus) never accuses. It always perceives the image of God in everything. Words (Mercury) coming from only one side of the Tree and including the force of Mars, can hurt. When we balance our thoughts (Mercury) and action (Mars) with love (Venus), we are expressing ourselves on a higher spiritual wave. We make our judgement on the basis of the data supplied by our senses. We have, here, the balancing of the mind and actions with spiritual Jupiter and love which is Venus. Justice can be called the balancer of the equilibrium.

Remember that, in this World of Formation, we are learning to deal with the earthly attributes that we all have. We are dealing with the earthly lessons. We are controlling of the beasts within us. We are turning those beasts into super beings. This is the same as was done on the Wheel of Fortune when the beasts were elevated to the spiritual Supernal Triangle.

The World of Formation contains the Sun ☉ as the center and the inner personal planets around it. The Sun has the gravity to keep all in order. The power of the Sun was worshipped until it was changed to the Son Christ. The first religion was the worship of the power of the planets. The Sun is the center and the 12 signs of the Zodiac are around it. During the reign of Justinian, 6th century AD, it was decreed that from that day on, a new form of religion would be taught. The Sun was changed into the Son and the 12 signs into the 12 disciples. These planets Mercury ☿ the mind, Mars ♂ our actions, Jupiter ♃ our spiritual philosophies, Venus ♀ our love, the Moon ☽ which is also our memories and mind and emotions, are what we use in the earthly realm. They are the planets that are the closest to the Sun and deal with the subjective part of us.

The square that is formed, which is the World of Formation, is our earthly battle that we go through without the help of the higher spiritual planets.

These are the squares in our chart that are stumbling blocks until they become building blocks. The planet Jupiter is the first one which takes us up to a higher mind. Jupiter is the last before we rise higher. Jupiter is the planet of growth which shows us there is more. Jupiter is the bridge to heaven. The Sun sign, in astrology, is also ourselves which is the self, ego and God-given talents. It is surrounded by the planets that represent our mind, actions, love and emotions.

Y - Yod

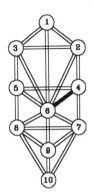

**THE HERMIT**

The Hermit represents all men/women of wisdom that are thought of as spiritual fathers. A few that come to mind are Socrates, Aristotle, Plato, and Hermes Trismegistus. These men were looked up to for their wisdom and many have studied their works. A person who has this knowledge, as previously talked about in the cards of The High Priestess and The Chariot, magnetically draws those to them that want to learn. They come under the heading of The Hermit. This card represents a person who is a teacher of the true meaning of life on this planet and also on the spiritual path. Christ himself was one of these learned people as well as Buddha and Mohammed. There are so many more that it would take pages to list them all. We are what we are today because of all of these people.

The Hermit indicates union with the supreme self, which is the true "I Am" of the cosmos. The Hermit stands alone and is isolated. He stands on a snowy mountain peak (Spiritual attainment). As the snow melts, it fertilizes that which is below. He is the most Holy Ancient one, like The Hermit in the Himalayan mountains, who has all knowledge and is sought out for this knowledge. His lantern is a beacon. It is light shining in the darkness. The path is pretty dark but the light in the distance guides us along the way. In the lantern is a 6 pointed star which is the Star of David, the lamp of the mysteries.

All beings know of their common origin and that they are created in the likeness and image of God. We come in with this knowing. Once we are here, sometimes the light is shut off and one has to grope along the path of darkness, until the beacon of the light shines again. This beacon then gets them back on the path. The Hermit is the source of all, yet he is also the goal of all endeavors. We learn from him and then become him to teach others. The true light is God or spirituality, whose word is the true light that enlightens every man on his path. This card aims at personal consciousness with the cosmic will. The Hermit represents the teacher, one who lights the way for others. "I AM THOU AND THOU ART I AM."

**KEYWORDS** - Guided by wisdom offered
**SIGN** - The Hebrew simple letter Y (Yod) rules path #20 (10), represents the astrological sign of Virgo ♍ and rules this card. The Hermit searched and now deciphers with discrimination and digestion. Virgo rules the intestines. Virgo is the assimilation of spiritual knowledge. Virgo is the sign of perfection.

**CARD NUMBER** - 9 represents completion. It is the last of the single digit numbers. 0-9 denotes perfection and realization. Perfection is prior to and behind all manifestation. It is also beyond and above all things. (Number 3 is square root of 9 (3x3). (Reread #9 in numbers) Three degrees of life make three triangles. The third is the one dealing with The Hermit and indicates completion on three levels of consciousness.

**HEBREW LETTER #10** - Y (Yod). This is a Hebrew simple letter and stands for the astrological sign Virgo as well as hand. This is on path #20 (10). An open hand shows freedom of the supreme spirit. In astrology the Yod aspect is considered to be the finger of God, pointing to you, telling you to use this energy in an important way, as though you have been chosen to do the work that is best for your soul's evolution. The Yod is in all of the letters in the Hebrew alphabet. If you look at the Hermit, his cap looks like a Yod.

**PATH #20 (10)** - Path #20 (10) is called *Intelligence of Will*. Sephirah #10 is called *Resplendent Intelligence*. Path #20 connects Sephirah #4 (Chesed Mercy, Fire pillar and Jupiter) to Sephirah #6 (Tiphareth, Beauty, Air pillar and the Sun). The 20th path is the path of Intelligence of Will and is so called because it is the means of preparation of each created being. By this intelligence the existence of the Primordial Wisdom becomes known. Since Tiphareth is the Sun (Son of God) and connects to all of the planets, it is now joined with Chesed (where the philosophical planet Jupiter resides) and all knowledge is available. Chesed connects to Chokmah-Wisdom Sephirah #2, which is part of the Supernal Triangle. Look at the diagram on page 149 and notice that path #20 (10) leads to Sephirah #6. Picture the Hermit standing on this path with his lantern. He is illuminating the path that leads above. Are you going up the path or down the path?

**PATH COLOR** - yellow green, slate gray, green gray, and plum

**HAT**- His hat looks like the Yod. This shows that he is crowned by the knowledge of the Christ energy and the #1.

**STAFF** - is yellow representing intelligence. He knows he can lean on his intelligence. In a different deck of cards, The Hermit's staff has the 12 signs of the Zodiac on it, representing all knowledge. Remember the story that I told about in the riddle of the sphinx. ("Who in the morning goes on four legs, at midday on two and in the evening on three?" The answer was Man.) We crawl when we are beginning our spiritual path, then evolving humanity walks on two (2) legs, and the illuminated man adds the staff of wisdom as the third (3).

**GRAY ROBE** - gray is wisdom, the blending of white and black, positive and negative. He is dressed in simple clothing.

**BEARD** - also shows wisdom. When we are old with a beard we have experienced a lot.

## SUMMARY

+ This card denotes knowledge in the form of a book, teacher, or class. The client may be a teacher, one who has been initiated with all knowledge. One can be taking a course that is giving him greater knowledge or he may know a person of this sort.

- Reversed, one is ignoring or not searching or growing in knowledge, or has wrong knowledge. They are still on the path of darkness. They need to learn to tune into self in order to have the wisdom needed.

K - Kaph

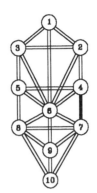

WHEEL of FORTUNE.

## CARD #10 WHEEL OF FORTUNE
## ON PATH #21 (11)
### Wheel of Life-Fate-Destiny

**WHEEL OF FORTUNE**
The Wheel of Universal wisdom. This card combines the ideas of rotation and cycles. What goes around, comes around; as you sow, so shall you reap. If you're down, next is up; when up, next is down; around and around; the law of harmony and order. Seek and ye shall find. One thing that we can be sure of, is change. However, in order to change we must get out of the cycle.

**KEYWORD** - Ups and downs of life, good luck, or a change

**PLANET** - The Hebrew double letter K (Kaph) represents the planet Jupiter ♃. This falls on path #21 (11). This is like law and justice. What goes around, comes around. As we go through life and experiences, we need to have faith and optimism (Jupiter) that our new beginnings will have great rewards. Jupiter is the planet of expansion and growth. We need to expand our consciousness to a high spiritual and philosophical level.

**CARD NUMBER** - The 10 of Cups or Pentacles are lucky as are the 10 of Hearts or Diamonds in a regular deck of cards. The 10 of Spades and Clubs are unlucky as are the 10 of Swords and Wands. Number 10 is 1, Aleph. 0 is mystery of beginning.

**HEBREW LETTER #11** - K KH (Kaph) This is a double Hebrew letter standing for the astrological planet Jupiter, also closed hand. It is the act of grasping to hold, to comprehend or to master. It is like when you grasp something mentally. It is also known as the spoon. A spoon is used to feed one.

**PATH #21 (11)** - Path #21 (11) is called *Intelligence of Conciliation and Reward.* Path #21(11) connects Sephirah #4 (Chesed, Mercy, Fire pillar and Jupiter) to Sephirah #7 (Netzach, Victory, Fire pillar and Venus). It is so called because it receives the divine influence which flows into it from its benediction upon all and each existence.

**PATH COLOR** - violet, blue, rich purple, bright blue, rayed yellow

**MUSICAL TONE** - Sol-Jupiter (Sagittarius)

**WHEEL** - We are going to refer back to the Snake with his tail in the mouth. If you reread the page on the number 0 and the closed serpent, it will now mean more to you than it did when you first read it. This is on page 103.

The Wheel is the symbol of the fall of man after Eve succumbed to the serpent's temptation. It is said that, after the earth was created, the circle of movement of the world was not closed but remained open. The 7th day was sanctified and blessed as the open part of the circle of movement of the world, in such a way that the beings of the world had access to the Father and the Father had access to them.

In this card you see the wheel. As they say, what goes around, comes around. The snake headed down is the descent into life. The jackal headed up, is our ability to move higher. In order to get out of the circle, we must engage in the studies represented by the letters and figures in the circle.

There are 4 wheels in all, representing the four worlds. The center of the wheel is a dot and called the Archetypal world.

The 2nd wheel is the Creative world.

The 3rd wheel is the Formative world. In the third circle one spoke has the sign of the architect, the symbol of Mercury. Right one, symbol for Sulfur. Bottom one, sign for Aquarius. Left one, symbol for Salt. The alchemical philosophers used the symbols of mercury, sulfur and salt to represent not only chemicals but the spiritual and invisible principles of God, man and the universe. This is the philosophers' mercury, sulfur and salt, not the crude substances taken from the earth. Each of these three substances contains the other two substances. They are each three fold. Each being three fold equals the number 9. Added to this is Azoth (universal life force) which makes number 10. The element Air is mercury and represents the Father, the element Fire is sulfur and represents the Son (Christ) and the element Water is salt and represents the Holy Ghost.

The 4th wheel is the Material world. The letters T A R O T are around the 4th wheel. Or T A R O. How many words can you make out of it? As the wheel revolves, the letters seem to form the words: Rota (wheel), Taro, Tora.

The Torah is the Jewish religious book of law. Orat, Ator (Latin for Hathor) is the Egyptian goddess. The wheel of Tarot speaks the law of the Tora and the law or Hathor, which is the law of nature or the law of cause and effect. Interspersed are the letters of the Holy Name JHVH in Hebrew, the signature of God. No other is ruler of your destiny.

**SPOKES** - 8 like the 8 pointed star on key 17. This represents universal radiant energy.

**SPHINX** - Sits on the top of the wheel with the sword of knowledge and his tail between his legs. Will is controlled when knowledge is applied. He signifies the perfect equilibrium of Universal Wisdom. Blue symbolizes that emotions start us thinking. This is like the cherubim with the flaming sword that was placed at the Garden of Eden to bring us back to the land of bliss.

**SNAKE** - The snake is yellow which is intelligence and represents vibrations and wavy motion. The snake was responsible for inspiring in us the desire to change and to set the wheel into motion. The snake is headed down, the same as we were in our involution.

**JACKAL** - is sometimes known as Anubis (Egyptian god of the underworld). It represents the evolution of consciousness from the lower forms to the higher. Red is desire put into motion.

**BLUE BACKGROUND** - emotions and feelings

**CLOUDS** - gray-wisdom

**FOUR FIGURES**- represent the four fixed astrological signs: Aquarius, Scorpio, Taurus, and Leo. Also the four Apostles Matthew, Mark, Luke and John. It is also said that these four figures represent the four Archangels Michael, Gabriel, Raphael, and Anael. They are all reading a book: the Bible, Thoth or Tora. So what gets us out of the circle or wheel????

Notice that the tails are again in submission, except one which is the Lion/Leo.

The four figures in the corner of the cards can be referred back to page 113 on the Symbols of the Four Evangelists. The Bull, Lion, Man and Eagle also form the sphinx. The sphinx is the unity of the human and the animal kingdom. Notice that they have wings which symbolize that they have been elevated to the Supernal Triangle. Remember, too, that these were the signs of the seasons when the cards were designed. These are the four fixed signs of the Zodiac. They form the fixed cross. You also see the statues for the four evangelists on the altar in Episcopal churches.

Quietness is the state that leads to elevation of the spirit and of the heart and is the eagle. This can be done through meditation. The eagle is a bird capable of rising to tremendous heights and is considered to be the only creature able to look directly at the Sun. It is a symbolic source of spiritual life and light. The Lion symbolizes the instinct that can be designated as moral courage. The Bull is the symbol of the instinct of productive concentration. It underlies deep meditation. The Angel or man is the inspiring companion and instinct of man to rise higher in evolution.

<u>SUMMARY</u>

+ This is a lucky card showing a change for the better. One wants more than to just go around and around in a situation or life. One wants to progress.

- In reverse it is an unlucky change for the worse or a delay. The client is in a period of time when everything is going around and around and not progressing. A recurring problem exists.

L - Lamed

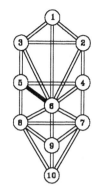

## CARD #11 JUSTICE ON PATH 22 (12)

**JUSTICE**
Justice is to balance. We have to learn to eliminate useless, worn-out forms. This includes people, situations and things. Education is completed by action or work. Just hearing the word or reading it is not true education. You have to act or apply it. A balanced personality is faithful, constant and confident because the right use of reason has been established and ensures certainty as to the just outcome of all activities. You really learn when you have to act (Mars), judge (Jupiter) and balance a decision.

**KEYWORD** - balance, decision, judgement, legal matters
**SIGN** - Lamed, the Hebrew letter, represents the astrological sign Libra ♎. Libra rules the courts. The scales are seen there. The weighing of justice. The final decision.
**CARD NUMBER 11**- 11 is a spiritual master number and is not usually reduced.
**HEBREW LETTER #30 (12)** - L (Lamed) Word for Lamed is oxgoad. This is a simple Hebrew letter standing for the astrological sign Libra. Lamed is the power of 30 (3+0=3), which again associates with the Triune Powers of Spirit; it is the triple power of 10. This shows that man must be purified by continued communication with the higher dimensional worlds. Truly, humanity hangs upon the cross of matter and suffers the wounds inflicted by the goad of Karma until, by its own efforts, through sacrifice, love and service, it releases itself.
**PATH** - Path #22 (12) is called *Faithful Intelligence* and is so called because, by it, spiritual virtues are increased. All dwellers on earth are nearly under its shadow. Faith comes from the Sephirah #3 Binah above Geburah. This is a path of Karmic Adjustment. This path connects Sephirah #5 (Geburah and Mars on the Water pillar) to Sephirah #6 (Tiphareth and the Sun on the Air pillar). It is said that here one is judged by higher law. Geburah represents the condition of the Spirit in action in the higher levels of form and the subsequent descent to Tiphareth via this path.
**PATH COLOR** - emerald, medium dark blue, deep blue green, pale green
**MUSICAL TONE** - La-Libra
**PILLARS** - He sits between the two gray pillars of wisdom; this is the same as the pillars of Fire and Water on the Tree. Purple cloth draped between them is spiritual. Purple is the blending of red and blue. Desires and emotions are balanced. He is not blindfolded.
**RED ROBE** - is active desires and the green cape is growth.
**SQUARE** - is white with a red center. Shows activity (red) of spirit manifested in form (square).

**YELLOW** - The hair is yellow showing that he thinks with intelligence. The crown, background and scales are also yellow.

**SWORD** - in an upright position shows that he is not finished or hasn't made a decision.

**WHITE SHOE** - a peek of purity

**SCALES** - are the symbol of justice. It was the belief of early Christians that there would be a day when all the activity of their life would be judged as if it were laid on the scales. St. John Chrysostom, one of the early writers, recorded, "In that day our actions, our words, our thoughts will be placed on the scales, and the dip of the balance on either side will carry with it, the irrevocable sentence." The balance scale was a symbol associated with the archangel Michael, who was considered to be the judgement angel.

SUMMARY
+ This can be a court decision pending. A positive decision. The client is using his intelligence, weighing and balancing, in order to come to the right decision about a matter.

- The decision delayed. One must contemplate longer before a decision can be made since he/she does not have all the facts. There could be a misjudgement or postponement.

**JUSTICE IN THE POSITION OF #8 . WHAT DO YOU THINK?**

**The position on the tree of #8 and # 11 many times is switched. It is said that Justice belongs in the position of #8. (See path #19 (9).)**

**Should #8 STRENGTH become #11 and be on PATH #22 (12)?**

**STRENGTH**
The law states that the subconscious is at all times in control of every sub-human manifestation of cosmic energy.

**KEYWORDS** - decision, judgement, handling a difficult situation with intuition and love

**SIGN – If you change Strength to Path #22 (12) bring with it the Hebrew letter Teth, astrological sign of Leo and musical note Re.**

**THE CARD NUMBER 11, PATH #22 (12) and PATH COLOR,** can be read on page 158.

**GIRL** - Closing the jaws of the lion. This shows she is in control of her energy and of the lion (notice his tail is in a submissive position). Look at the card. It is as though she was psychically tuning in to the mind of the lion, to control him.

**WHITE ROBE** - is purity and spiritual consciousness showing she has accomplished her spiritual growth.

**MOUNTAIN** - is spiritual attainment.

**CHAIN OF ROSES** - around the waist twines around like the snake. It is twisted like the figure 8. The same is above her head. When we learn to weave our desires together into a chain, reflecting all desires which are compatible with our main purpose, we shall be able to make wonderful applications of creative imagination to the control and direction of the serpent power.

SUMMARY

+ This card shows the client is using his strength, intuition, and psychic ability to perceive and be in control of any situation that may seem too powerful to handle.

- Card in reverse shows that the situation is out of control.

M - Mem

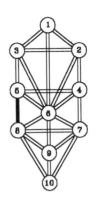

## CARD #12 THE HANGED MAN ON PATH #23 (13)

**THE HANGED MAN**
This card is the law of reversal. It represents the suspended mind. The title refers to the utter dependence of human personality upon the cosmic life. The Hanged Man is a T and is hanging on living wood. There is green growth on the tree. His leg is crossed like a #4 which is the symbol for sulfur. Sulfur feeds the vital Fire. His arms are 2 triangles. He looks like a suspended pendulum at rest, a state of cosmic consciousness. It implies the complete conquest of the personality when subjugated by the forces of Spirit.

**KEYWORDS** - reversal, self surrender. Enlightenment brings a complete change of ways.

**SIGN** - There is no sign for this card because the Hebrew mother letter Mem is the Water element and does not represent a sign.

**CARD NUMBER** - 12 divine manifestation. A 12 fold expression. Number 12 is also 1+2=3.

**HEBREW LETTER #40 (13)** - M (Mem). A Hebrew mother letter means seas and represents the element Water. Mother is the seed and root of all. Water was the first mirror, which reflects images upside down. Water reflects the heavens. Mem represents reflected life. The Spirit of God moved across the waters and the great deep, the ocean of life. Water is feminine. Nearly every name given to the mother of the Sun Initiates begins with an M. The month of May is sacred to motherhood (Mother's Day). Moses was taken from the water. Water washes away the soil or contamination-not the garment itself.

**PATH #23 (13)** - Path #23 (13) is called *Stable Intelligence*. On the Tree, path #23 (13) connects Sephirah #5 (Geburah, Severity on the Water pillar with the planet Mars) to Sephirah #8 (Hod, Splendor also on the Water pillar and the planet Mercury). Since he is upside down, he is really looking up to Geburah and Binah above which includes the Supernal Triangle. He has the knowledge of Mercury (Hod) and realizes there is more above. The energy of Mars above energizes him.

When you look at The Hanged Man, his eyes are open with a glow of enlightenment around his head. Since he is on path #23 (13), he is in the position of being between the intellectual planet Mercury on Sephirah #8 and the aggressive planet Mars on Sephirah #5. He is between thought and action. Mercury is where his head is and Mars is where his feet are. He has awareness that he is traveling up and knows that he is better off if his feet are rooted in the spiritual, instead of the earth. He is going up the path to the higher spiritual life. So, he has an awareness and is awakened; that is why there is a yellow halo around his head. He is enlightened by the spiritual knowledge. If he includes that which is above with his thinking, and changes his viewpoint while on earth, he is headed toward his initiation. He tells us that we must think everything through and realize that we are part of the earth, having come here to learn earthly lessons. If we keep ourselves anchored to our decisions and thoughts, we remain attached to the earth.

**PATH COLOR** - deep blue, sea green, deep olive green, white flecked purple

**JACKET** - is blue. Blue is emotional sensitivity. On some cards there are two pockets which are crescent shaped Moons on the blue of emotions. Also on some cards there is a cross on the jacket and 10 buttons representing the 10 Sephiroth on the Tree of Life.

**PANTS** - are red. Red shows active desires. The left leg is crossed under the right, which is like the combination of the triangle and cross.

**EYES** - are open, showing awareness.

**GLOW** - shows his intellectual enlightenment. When we walk with our feet in heaven, we are enlightened. This inverted position is contrary to that in which we find most people. St. Peter was crucified upside down. He was the rock or foundation. The foundation of everyday practice of a person who lives the life of obedience to the esoteric law is the reversal of the most usual way of speaking, thinking, and acting.

The great secret is to walk, in all things, contrary to the world. Silent reversal of one's own way of life, combined with perfect tolerance of the ways of other people, is the method to practice. This reversal consists of primarily the reversal of thought in a point of view, which is just the opposite to that accepted by most people.

At first there may seem to be no practical advantage to this. Most people are sick, troubled or not getting along with the self or world. This indicates that most people have put the cart before the horse in their practice of life. Everything is an expression of the working law of cause and effect. The misery afflicting most people is the result of their negative use of the law. In every moment of a human life, a special application of the law and the outcome depends wholly on whether we think positively or negatively. Speech and action come from thoughts and the interpretation of the patterns for experience. That which happens to us is what we have selected, whether the selection is unconscious or conscious.

The emphasis is upon the importance of a change of viewpoint, and this change is none other than total reversal. Every human personality depends on the God force, symbolized by the Tree of Life. As soon as truth is realized, self surrender begins in the mind. It is the submission of the personal consciousness to the direction of the universal mind. Say "let it be your will and not mine," meaning complete surrender to the will of God. Practice of mind control and body direction are often laughed at by the world and considered upside down. Yet the world's ridicule would be the best evidence that the occultists are right. The world is sick, writhing in pain, experiencing wars, pestilence and famine. The wise have found the way to health, happiness and peace.

Out of these sacrificial experiences, elevation of consciousness and spiritual perception result if they are accepted in the right spirit and assimilated. Such elevation and expansion is in man's fulfilling of his destiny and being crowned with eternal light. One's outlook is different from others.

<u>SUMMARY</u>
+ The card is straight up when his feet are at the top. He is walking with his feet in heaven. This opens up drastic change. Give up thinking of earthly desires as your support and walk on the floors of heaven. Stable intelligence comes from removing our feet from terrestrial ground and placing them solidly on spiritual reality, letting God take care of the rest. "Seek ye first the Kingdom of Heaven and all things shall be added unto you." He has voluntarily bound himself to his goal. Look at what is happening with a different point of view.

- When the card is upside down it shows that the client is walking with his feet on the ground. One insists on keeping the ways of the earth and being caught up with earthly frustrations, not incorporating a spiritual understanding. Things are not as they appear on the surface. Look beneath for true understanding. Sacrifice the self to what is happening in life.

If you develop life in accordance with the ideas developed through the Tarot series, and willingly bind yourself to spiritual development as The Hanged Man has, it will lead to a complete transformation. The following card, Death, shows this.

N - Nun

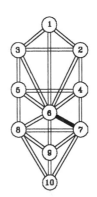

DEATH.

# CARD #13 DEATH ON PATH #24 (14)

## DEATH

The forces of change which result in physical death are unfriendly because we misunderstand and fear them. Death, like every other event in human life, is a manifestation of law. When we understand the law, we can direct the forces of change to overcome death. Understanding never will be ours until fear, not only of dying but of death itself, has been overcome by the right knowledge, and by the right interpretation of the phenomena of physical dissolution.

The serpent wanted you to believe that he was life, but he was death. Christ tells you that death, when you die, is when life begins. His death showed us that this is possible. When we forget, it is like being asleep and not remembering the spiritual. When one remembers, one awakens and is born.

When we are here on the earth and look at the mundane part of life (including people and relationships as well as everything that we are tied to), we get very upset when people we love die. This is because we are looking at it again through our earthly way of seeing it. We need to look at death as a transformation that takes us into a higher dimension and see that each life we go through brings us to a different Soul level. We can then realize that we are going up our spiral and that there is no such thing as death. We go on forever.

Death comes in many forms. It means an ending of a matter as it was. It cannot continue in its usual way but must be given new life by transformation and regeneration of the situation. If this is not possible, then complete release may call for help through therapy and psychology, which is ruled by the sign of Scorpio and the planet Pluto. This sign and planet in astrology rules the 8th house in the chart which is the house of death.

The card Death is describing what we are involved with here on the earth. A cycle ends and, if it was difficult, it helps you to become more aware. It feels like total death when one is going through it. As we suffered, it helped us with our transformation and to grow and evolve higher. Every day becomes a resurrection to the awakened soul. All the old motives, all the petty ambitions, all the foolish opinions and prejudices gradually die out. Little by little, there comes a complete readjustment of one's personal conceptions of life and its values. It happens because of the patterns created through the imagination. Do not think of death as death alone, but as a rebirth of your consciousness to a higher plane.

The river from the High Priestess' gown brings with it all of her knowledge. The boat is going up the river headed towards the towers and the rising Sun (Son Christ). The boat is so tiny you almost don't see it. Everything on one side of the river is mundane and everything on the other side is totally different (spiritual).

**KEYWORDS** - transformation, death, inability to continue as is. Death and rebirth.

**SIGN & PLANET** - Scorpio ♏, a fixed Water sign, is ruled by the planet Pluto ♇. It rules the 8th house of the horoscope which relates to death and transformation. The Hebrew simple letter N-Nun represents the sign of Scorpio.

**CARD NUMBER 13** - is considered an unlucky number. Friday the 13th comes from the Crucifixion which was on Friday and 13 was the number for Christ. (12 disciples plus himself). The crucifixion was the death that allowed new life to come when he was resurrected or raised from the dead. 13 is also 1+3=4. One is the Divine plus the trinity (3) or Supernal Triangle. Four is the number of starting a new cycle.

**HEBREW LETTER #50 (14)** - N (Nun). This is a Hebrew simple letter standing for the astrological sign of Scorpio. It means fish. As a verb it means to sprout, to grow. The essential idea is fertility, productiveness and generative power. These ideas are bound up in thought and language with such words as cause and origin.

**PATH #24 (14)** - Path #24 (14) is called *Imaginative Intelligence*. Path #24 (14) on the Tree connects Sephirah #6 (Tiphareth, Beauty and the Air pillar and the planet Sun) with Sephirah #7 (Netzach, Victory on the Fire pillar and the planet Venus). It is the ground of similarity in the likeness of beings. All changes are primarily changes in mental imagery. Change the image, and ultimately the external form will change.

**PATH COLOR** - green blue, dull brown, very dark brown, livid indigo brown

**MUSICAL TONE** - Do-Scorpio

**SKULL** - skeleton inside armor as well as on the harness of the horse. Even in death we are prepared to do battle. The horse is white with black trim, showing the positive and negative.

**PEOPLE** - All ages are here, showing that no matter what our age, we all go through the stages of death or transforming situations in our life by getting rid of debris and starting over. The man on the ground has blue on and is putting his emotions to rest. The Pope has a cross on his hand and is showing dispensation. The people and earthly matters are on one side of the river. Everything spiritual is on the other side.

**RIVER** - is coming from the High Priestess. It moves from West to East and the reaper moves in the same direction, showing that which has been is being transformed.

**BOAT/SHIP**- The boat is going up stream to the East. It takes you from one side to the other and represents a new beginning. The sail is purple, a spiritual color. Purple is the combination of red (action/desires) and blue (sensitivity). Again, this is Fire and Water or the blending of the conscious and the subconscious to make the super-conscious. The ship has long been a favorite symbol of the church. The picture of the ship, plowing through the stormy water with the waves lashing up on the sides, is a reminder of the church as it sails through the troubled waters of adversity in the world. The ship of the church has a good captain at the helm, Jesus Christ, and he will bring the ship and all her faithful to the safety of the shores of heaven. You will also see a ship on the King of Cups card.

**TOWERS** - is like a gate which we pass through to get to the other side. The Sun is there. Remember that the Sun is the Son of God. We are trying to cross through those barriers. It is like crossing from the World of Formation to the Supernal Triangle. The towers or pillars look like the ones on card #18, The Moon, and the 10 of Pentacles in the Minor Arcana. This shows that once we pass through the gates there is a new sunrise, or beginning. Eternal Life.

**SUN** - rising in the East shows new beginnings.

**BANNER** - Mystic Rose of the Rosicrucian order. Five petal mystic white rose signifies not death, but life.

SUMMARY

+ & - The client is going through a life and death experience. A divorce can be a death to many people. At times this card can show a physical death. Note the card next to it to see what is ending. If the card is upright, it will be an easier transition. Upright shows it is time to make the transformation and recognize that there has to be a change in order to progress. Reversed makes it difficult because one finds it hard to move on. The client is stuck, cannot let go, is at an impasse.

S - Samech

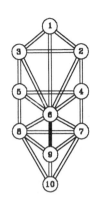

## CARD #14 TEMPERANCE ON PATH #25 (15)

**TEMPERANCE**

Temperance suggests adaptation, blending, and measurement. To adapt is to equalize, to adjust, to coordinate; it is what the Supreme Alchemist does. Equilibrium is the basis of the Great Work. Adaptation is the basis of all practical work in Hermetic science.

**KEYWORD** - balancing emotions and practicality. Modification in all things.

**SIGN & PLANET** - The Hebrew simple letter S (Samech) represents the astrological sign of Sagittarius ♐, which rules this card.

**CARD NUMBER** - Numbers are like sounds. The idea here is that *vibration* is the basis of manifestation, and that all vibration is essentially like sound. Sound is the kind of vibration which is particularly associated with The Hierophant. The Hebrew letter for The Hierophant is Vau and represents hearing. Vibration is fluctuating motion; it makes wave-forms. Temperance here shows that everything blends into everything else. As she pours the water from one Cup to the other, one foot in the water and the other one on land, everything blends together. If you look at card #17, The Star, the same thought is shown as the water on the land flows back and joins the water in the pool.

Number 14, when reduced, is the #5 which stands for man and adaptation. Card #5 is The Hierophant which relates to that stated above.

What this shows is that one number vibrates into the next. This is the same as when you put energy out to start something. It will begin to vibrate and continues to do so until it is completed. One thing blends into the next.

**HEBREW LETTER #60 - (15=6) - S (Samech).** This Hebrew simple letter looks like a serpent swallowing its tail. It means peg or prop. It is what makes something secure, such as the foundation of our house. It is, therefore, the letter-symbol of that which is the basis or support of our house of life. It is that which sustains, preserves and maintains our personal existence. Renewing intelligence is the kind of consciousness attributed to Samech. When we find a fact that does not fit in with our beliefs, we are obliged to revise our theories, unless we prefer a comfortable lie to an uncomfortable truth. This is a simple Hebrew letter standing for the astrological sign Sagittarius. This sign is on path #25 (15).

**PATH #25 (15)** - Path #25 (15) is called the path of *Intelligence of Probation or Temptation* and is so called because it is the primary temptation, by which the Creator tries all righteous persons. Path #25 (15) connects Sephirah #6 (Tiphareth, Beauty on the Air pillar and the Sun) to Sephirah #9 (Yesod, The Foundation also on the Air pillar and the Moon). Look at the Tree and see how Temperance connects the Sun and Moon together. Astrologically the Sun is your outer self and the Moon your inner self. These two are joined together. As you look at the Tree, notice how the other paths connect to these two Sephiroth and how these two go directly up the Air pillar to Kether, which is Divine Light. The Moon, having no light of its own, reflects all of that above.

**PATH COLOR** - blue, yellow, green, dark vivid blue

**RAINBOW** - In Greek history Iris, the Greek goddess, is referred to as the goddess of the rainbow. She and Mercury were messengers. She wore a cloak of many colors. Notice the iris flowers which symbolize her. In the Albano-Waite tarot deck, there is a rainbow over the head of the angel. A rainbow is caused by the sun shining through mist made up of water droplets in the atmosphere. It causes the refraction of the Sun's pure white or colorless light into its 7 component parts, the colors of the solar spectrum.

**POOL** - At the bottom of the picture is a pool. This corresponds to the 9th Sephirah (Yesod and the Moon on the Tree of Life) which has to do with the depth of our unconscious. Remember the pool started from the High Priestess' gown. The path rising from the pool appears again in card #18 and will be more fully explained in connection with that card. It rises over rolling ground, and thus imitates the wave-motion which is characteristic of all forms of vibration. This path is like the one on the card, The Moon. Our path of Life is full of ups and downs. Notice that her foot in the water is like having an attachment to Yesod and the Moon. The crown is like being attached to Tiphareth, the Sun, which connects to Kether.

**CROWN** - At the upper end of the path is a crown. It signifies attainment and mastery. The path of attainment is the realization of the crown of perfect union with the Primal Will. The Crown is also the symbol of Kether. This is like the pot of gold at the end of the rainbow. Twin Peaks are Wisdom and Understanding (the two pillars on the Tree).

**ANGEL** - Michael is the archangel of Fire, angel of the Sun and ruler of the South. The solar symbol ☉ on his head establishes his identity as does his yellow hair and the rays streaming from it and the fiery wings. Michael means "One with God" and is called the Holy Guardian Angel. His white robe represents purity and wisdom. On his clothing at the neck are written the letters HVHY. This is the same as on the Fool. Below the letters is a cube and triangle. The cube represents spirituality. It has the triangle representing #3 (the Supernal Triangle and the Trinity) and the #4 (the cross or square of matter). One foot rests in the water, symbol of the psychic or subconscious world. The other is on land, symbol of concrete, physical manifestation.

**CUPS** - The Angel pours water from the Cup in his right hand, which should be gold and represent the Sun (masculine and Tiphareth) to that in his left, which should be silver and represent the Moon (feminine and Yesod). The stream of water vibrates between them. This is the blending of Fire and Water, the + and -, the conscious and subconscious. Action and reaction are intimated because, when the lower Cup is filled, he will reverse the position of the Cups, and that which is now above will become that which is below. Finally, all your experiments will be in equalization of vibratory activities. There is nothing in the cosmos but vibrations, and all forms of vibration may be modified and changed by mental control.

SUMMARY
+ The client is showing that he is keeping the balance between his emotions and stability. Some days he may be emotional and some days stable, or he can work both together by synchronizing and blending all he knows to bring about satisfactory results.

- A reversed card shows that the above control is not being put into force. One is unable to handle what is happening because of lack of complete understanding.

O - Ayin

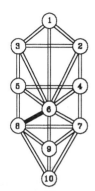

THE DEVIL .

**THE DEVIL**

Devil in Greek means slanderer. This card represents the first stage of spiritual unfoldment. It is the stage of conscious bondage. The Devil personifies the false conception that man is bound by material conditions and the negative understanding of the problems we deal with. He is limitation created by ignorance, taboo and blindness in the sense of passing judgement on outward appearances only. We should understand our essential freedom in order to take into account the hidden side of existence. We need to realize that our bondage comes from our negative thinking and our imagination playing tricks on us, allowing us to reverse the real meaning or view of a situation.

**KEYWORDS** - Deception, escapism, mistaken ideas and negative thinking keeps one in bondage.

**SIGN & PLANET** - The sign Capricorn ♑ goes with this card because the Hebrew simple letter Ayin represents that astrological sign. Therefore Saturn ♄, its ruling planet, can be involved. Saturn is a planet that shows bondage. Saturn is the Karma (life work) that our Soul took on. Notice the symbol on the palm of the Devil. That is the hieroglyphic for Saturn. I also believe that Neptune ♆ comes into play here. Neptune is like the negative you receive when you take a picture with your camera. It is a total reversal of the real picture. What is white on the picture is black on the negative and vice-versa. This is how the devil works, allowing us to see in reverse what really is. Neptune is deception, confusion and illusion. Neptune, in the positive, stands for religion and our psychic ability. When used improperly, it brings in pictures from the Devil. Again the balance of the positive and negative is seen here. Drugs and alcohol are ruled by Neptune which, when used, allows us to see things that are not there. It allows us to escape from facing the truth. The positive versus the negative. Remember that the word for Jehovah written in Hebrew and spelled backward says Devil. Every positive has a negative. We cannot get around this because we need the molecules made up of both positive and negative to make the world of matter. Neptune rules magicians that hide the truth of what is happening. Only the spiritual understanding of life can set us free from our bondage.

**CARD NUMBER** - 15 reduces to #6. It is said that the Devil is #6. Number 6 is also the Sephirah #6 Tiphareth (where the Sun is placed). Remember that the Sun is also the Son of God, Christ. See how this number represents both. As said above Jehovah spelt backward says Devil. The Devil represents evil. Evil spelled backward says live.

**HEBREW LETTER #70 (16)** - O (Ayin Ah-Yeen) means eye and signifies also the external, superficial appearance of things. As an organ of sight, the eye is the most important sense-tool. Vision is limited by the circle of the horizon. Through the eye we see appearances only. The eye represents the limitations of the visible, and the bondage of ignorance resulting from the acceptance of those limitations as the true reality as being all there is. We are limited by our knowledge. This Hebrew simple letter stands for the astrological sign Capricorn. This letter and sign is on path #26 (16).

**PATH #26** - Path #26 (16) is called *Renewing Intelligence.* Path #26 (16) connects Sephirah #6 (Tiphareth, Beauty on the Air pillar and the planet Sun) with Sephirah #8 (Hod, Splendor on the Water pillar and the planet Mercury). Hod the lower mind is joined to the Conscious Moral Soul in Tiphareth. The mind has to realize its idea about God.

**PATH COLOR** - indigo, black, blue-black, cold very dark gray

**MUSICAL TONE** - Fa-Capricorn; Sol-Pisces (Neptune)

**TORCH** -The Devil is afraid that we will see what he is, so he is holding his torch down, to hide the light and to keep us in darkness. The Devil is sensation divorced from understanding by ignorance. He also brings renewal, because we can make no real effort to be free until we feel our limitations.

**BLACK** - symbolizes ignorance. The bat's wings also shows this. Bats live in darkness and caves and only come out at night. They can't handle the LIGHT. They have to return before the Sun (SON) comes out. Evil cannot exist when Christ is there.

**CHAINS** - By keeping everything dark, the Devil does not allow one to see that they are not really bound up. Notice that the chains are loose and can be easily removed. When they irk us we make the effort to throw off our chains change our thinking about our limitations, and exercise our freedom.

**MAN & WOMAN** - Man (+ positive) represents conscious and woman (- negative) represents subconscious mentality. This is the same as the right and left pillars of the Tree of Life. Their horns, hoofs and tails show that, when beliefs are formed based on surface appearances, human consciousness becomes set aside. The tails represent the two trees on the card of The Lovers.

**HAND** - His hand is held open. It is not like the Hierophant's hand which showed two fingers down (not everything is revealed). The Devil's hand wants you to believe that what you know, and see, is all there is. On the palm of his hand is the symbol for the planet Saturn ♄.

**GOAT'S HORNS** - the goat is the animal for the sign of Capricorn. The Devil's face is that of a goat, his ears of a donkey, which suggest the obstinacy and stubbornness of materialism. His body is thick-set and gross, of an earthy color to represent the earthy quality of the sign of Capricorn. His claws are like a vulture's.

**PENTAGRAM** - It is on the top of his head. It is inverted. Heading down in involution instead of up in evolution. The pentagram is the symbol of man walking in the white light. When it is inverted it shows that the white light turns into the darkness. The God energy changed into the Devil energy, positive vs. negative.

**CUBE** - The Devil sits on a half cube showing he is only allowing one side to be seen. There is no dimension. A false pedestal and a false god. When only the surface of the cube is shown, it depicts that only surface knowledge of the physical plane is available.

**THE POINT OF CHOICE** - What have we learned? This is the true test of our worthiness to enter a higher level. Do you see things all negative, black, with only earthly pleasures of this world? If one is evolved, one can turn away and say - GET THEE BEHIND ME, SATAN. The battle is then won and you flow in spirituality.

SUMMARY

+ This card shows confusion. They feel that they cannot get away from a certain predicament. They are not looking at reality and are allowing the imagination to build pictures that are not there. It can symbolize drugs, alcohol, deception or a need to escape. If it appears next to a person card then it is saying to be alert, that this person is not what they appear to be. There is a deception or they could be on drugs or alcohol. This could also be a wrong dosage or just wrongly prescribed medicine. Get more facts before making a decision.

- When upside down this card is not as bad. The issue hasn't become a full blown problem yet but could be if approach is continued.

176

ℷ

P/ Ph - Pe'

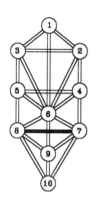

THE TOWER.

## CARD #16  THE TOWER ON PATH #27 (17)

### THE TOWER

The tower is the "Lightning-struck Tower," "The Fire of Heaven," and "The House of God." Destruction will happen to anything built on the foundation of blocking any aspect of the Life Force. When lightning hits, it brings a tremendous force of electricity and breaks up what was constructed. It was thought that this tower built out of concrete could be added to, brick by brick, to get higher and higher. It was believed that, when material substance was used it could build this tower as high as one wanted. The higher it was built the closer to heaven one gets--right? Wrong! That's what they thought when they built the Tower of Babel. Divine Fire destroys only that which is evil and purifies good. The Tower of Babel, which was built high enough to reach God, came tumbling down, showing that we do not need a tower to reach God. God is within!

Many times we build strong structures in our lives in relationship to our beliefs. When we become too set or are following the wrong path, a sudden unexpected change happens. It destroys our foundation if it was built on wrong precepts. Many times we can only see life in the way that our knowledge at the time allows. When we study more and are spiritually awakened, we then tear down and rebuild.

One feels that the mundane is going to get us where we want to go. When we build our foundation with spiritual substance and change the tower into a spiral, we can go as high as we want to. We can only build the tower in this card so high. We do the work. However, if we do not do the work we have to do, through our studies or our own personal growth, we are not really building anything. When the lightning comes on the day of reckoning, all which has been built, that wasn't done in the spiritual way, is going to fall apart. Earthly things fall apart. As the old saying goes, do not store up things that corrode and carry dust. Store up those things that you can take with you. So here is the tower that man had built. This he thought was going in the right direction to get him up to heaven. He topped it off with the crown and all of a sudden the lightning comes (Uranus brings changes unexpectedly) and it shocks that base or foundation of what we thought was right and it is destroyed. You fall out of your tower or your beliefs.

When you came here in a whirlwind and tumbled down as in involution, it was a shock to the system. We almost have to start over again to build a new foundation which is of spiritual substance and understanding so that, in our evolution, we can go back up.

**KEYWORD** - awakening, turmoil, unexpected change

**PLANET & SIGN** -The Hebrew double letter is P (Pe') and stands for the planet Mars. Mars is energy turned into action that can destroy if put to that use. The old books say, Mars rules this card and so it does according to the Hebrew letter. The planet Uranus had not been discovered or understood at that time or included as one of the planets. The lightning bolt can be Uranus since it is known to bring sudden changes and destroy old concepts. Uranus wants to push us ahead into the future and awaken our consciousness. Capricorn ♑ a hard working sign, allowing one to lay a strong foundation by working hard and steady at one's goals. Uranus ♅ is the only planet that can destroy what Capricorn or Saturn ♄ puts together.

**CARD NUMBER 16 (7)** #7 is made of 3+4. Number 3 is completion and the trinity and #4 the new beginning through hard work.

**HEBREW LETTER #80 (17)-** P, ph, f, (Pe'). This is a Hebrew double letter standing for the astrological planet Mars. Pe' means mouth. It symbolizes the power of utterance. The mouth receives food, the food of experience. Speech brings vibration which triggers our psyche.

**PATH #27 (17)-** Path #27 (17) is the *Active or Exciting Intelligence* and it is so called because through it every being receives its spirit and motion. It stirs up activity, sets things going, produces changes, affects transformations. It connects Sephirah #7 (Netzach, Victory on the Fire pillar with the planet Venus) with Sephirah #8 (Hod, Splendor on the Water pillar and the planet Mercury). This is the last of the three paths that connect the two sides of the Tree together, the pillar of Fire and the pillar of Water. The Tower, placed on this path, is in-between the planets Venus and Mercury.

**PATH COLOR** - scarlet, red, venetian red, bright red rayed azure, and emerald

**MUSICAL TONE** -Fa-Capricorn, Fa-Uranus, Do-Mars

**LIGHTNING** - Lightning is a masculine symbol. When it flashes artificially, it is shown to be spirals rather than zig-zags. The Chaldean Oracles of Zoroaster speak of the supreme spirit as "the God who energies a spiral force." The lightning flash breaks down existing forms in order to make room for new ones: a flash of inspiration which breaks down structures of ignorance and false reasoning or worn out ideas. It is like the inventive mind that takes us into new realms and the future. Anything man made can be destroyed, but what God made cannot. Therefore, that which is built of the "*Rock*" (God) will stand. That which is built of *Cement* (Man) will tumble.

**TOWER** - One deck of cards shows the tower built of 22 bricks, referring to the 22 Hebrew letters. There are 22 Yods hanging in the air on either side of the Tower, 10 on one side represent the Sephiroth on the Tree of Life. The 12 on the other side represent the 12 zodiacal signs. They hang in the air to indicate that the forces they symbolize rest on no physical foundation. The tower is built on a lonely peak, and suggests the fallacy of personal isolation which is the basis of all false philosophy. The 3 windows represent the Sephiroth Binah, Kether and Chokmah. This is manifestation of force since these three form the Supernal Triangle. The advanced seeker of wisdom suffers the destruction of his whole former philosophy, because this tower is built upon a foundation of misapprehension. If we build our tower out of spirituality, it will be in a form of a spiral; then one can go as high as one wants and will eventually reach Kether and receive the true Crown of the Divine.

**BLACK BACKGROUND** - shows wrong beliefs

**FIGURES** - The falling figures correspond to the chained prisoners in the preceding card, The Devil. They fall head first, because the sudden influx of spiritual consciousness represented by the lightning-flash completely upsets all their old notions about the relationship between subconscious and self-consciousness. The figures are clothed. The man wears both red and blue, to show a mixture of conscious and subconscious activities. The woman has red shoes but wears a blue robe. She is crowned in false knowledge; subconscious motives are permitted to dominate the personality.

**CROWN** - The crown, which was on the top of the Tower, is knocked off by the lightning flash and is the materialistic notion that matter and form are the ruling principles of existence. "Crown" is a term relating to the #1 (you won) and to "will." It should be the Crown of Kether if the Tower is a spiritual one. This crown refers to the false doctrine of the materialist and the false interpretation of will which makes it something personal, something which may be set against the cosmic purpose.


SUMMARY

+ This card shows that there has been a sudden unexpected happening which has brought a change into the person's life. The cards surrounding it will tell you what changed. If The Lovers card is there it can be a relationship. If it is a Wand card a change of job. What one thought would never change all of a sudden has. The way that you used to look at everything is now changed because of your growth through what you have learned. An awakening which brings an exposure of the untruth.


- Upside down this card is not as bad. The upsetting quality of the change may have been minor. The people look like they are going up instead of down. They wanted the change so it was not a shock to them.

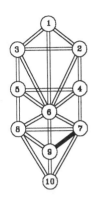

Ts/X - Tzaddi

XVII

THE STAR.

**THE STAR**

This picture shows the third stage of spiritual unfolding. It is the calm which follows the storm depicted by card #16. It is a period of quest and search. The light is dim, like starlight, but these stars are distant Suns. "When you have found the beginning of the way, the star of your Soul will show its light."

The Tarot cards help us, through concentration, to arouse our psychic centers. Behind their symbols are practical secrets of occultism which cannot be put into words. Lesser secrets, too, are hidden there, which might be written out, but the first rule in occult teaching is that the pupil should be told almost nothing that he can find out for himself. The teacher puts you on the track of discovery, but your own work with the tarot keys is the only thing that will bring you to the point where you will possess actual first-hand knowledge of the secrets of practical occultism.

**KEYWORDS** - Revelation, past experience allows emotional control.

**SIGN & PLANET** - The Hebrew simple letter Ts, Tzaddi represents Aquarius. The sign Aquarius ♒ is represented by the water-bearer. However, Aquarius is not a Water sign, it is an Air sign. What is being poured out is not water, but cosmic knowledge. The earth is thirsty and absorbs. Its astrological symbol ♒ is shown on the Wheel of Fortune. This is also an alchemy symbol. It is one of many Hermetic representations of the axiom "as above, so below." The planet Uranus ♅ also leads us into the future by our intuition and inventive ideas. Aquarians are highly intellectual people. #17 reduces to 8, so this picture has occult correspondence to the card Strength or Justice. (See the section on card #8 Strength and/or card #11 Justice). It shows the method by which that knowledge of the Great Secret is attained. This method solves the mysteries of nature and, as the picture shows, unveils her to the enlightened seer. Astrology is ruled by this sign and planet and gives to us a knowledge far superior to our everyday knowledge.

**CARD NUMBER 17** - reduces to #8, the life force, unending, unbreakable force.

**HEBREW LETTER #90 (18)** - This is a Hebrew simple letter representing the astrological sign Aquarius. Ts, Tz or Cz as in "czar" (Tzaddi). Means fish hook and signifies that which draws the fish out of the water. The indication is for the activity which lifts the fish up and out of the material relations of personal existence, and utilizes the reproductive and revitalizing forces as a regenerative agency: quest and research, groping, feeling one's way-fishing. What is clearly intimated here is that whatever the fish-hook symbolizes must be some agency or instrument whereby one investigates the unseen and unknown, whereby one makes attempts to solve enigmas, or to discover secrets, or to follow a more or less faint trail leading to the solution of a mystery. Meditation is the function attributed to Tzaddi. It has been defined as "an unbroken flow of knowledge about a particular object." It is fishing for the truth in the depths of the subconscious. The Hebrew word means literally "conception." It refers to the budding or germination of ideas. Moon, water and the sea, flux and reflux, always moving, birth and death. Out of the sea we came. Aphrodite was born of sea foam and carried to land in a mussel shell. The pool is the same as shown in cards #14 and #17 and is the "great deep" of cosmic mind stuff, out of which emerges the "dry land of physical manifestation." From it all, organic life proceeds.

**PATH #28 (18)** - Path #28 (18) on the Tree is called the *Natural Intelligence*; by it, the nature of all that exists beneath the Sun is completed and perfected. Awareness of the hidden qualities of nature is arrived at by meditation. It joins Sephirah #7 (Netzach, Victory on the Fire pillar and Venus) with Sephirah #9 (Yesod, Foundation on the Air pillar and the Moon). It is a path of great power and force. By it, the pure forces of the creative imagination pour into the subconscious mind. On this path is the Hebrew letter Tzaddi and the astrological sign Aquarius.

**PATH COLOR** - violet, sky-blue, bluish-mauve, white tinged purple

**MUSICAL TONE** - Fa-Aquarius

**STAR** - The great yellow star signifies the cosmic radiant energy, which is sent forth from the various Suns and fixed stars of the universe. It has 8 points. Its geometrical construction is like that of the Wheel of Fortune, or the symbols of Spirit embroidered on the dress of the Fool. The inventors of the Tarot used innumerable devices to remind us that, in our mental and magical work, we are using an actual force, which has definite psychic forms of expression. Meditation modifies and transmutes the personal expression of this cosmic energy, and that personal expression is what we term nerve-force.

**7 STARS** - represent the 7 planets, 7 chakras, the 7 metals and the 7 rays. (Refer to the section on numbers #7.)

**MOUNTAINS** - symbols of our spiritual attainment

**BIRD & BUSH** - is a scarlet Ibis. This is the Egyptian bird sacred to the god Hermes. Some say it is Thoth, counselor to Osiris and scribe to the Egyptian Gods. Both names can be the same person. He was also the measurer of time and inventor of numbers. The bird's long bill is a natural container. Perched on a tree which represents the human brain and nervous system, it symbolizes the act of bringing intellectual activity, or the thought process, to rest by concentration. We have to stop thinking in order to meditate properly, and when we stop thinking truth unveils herself to us.

**WOMAN** - Hathor, Isis Mother Nature, The Empress and The High Priestess. She is also the woman who tames the lion and controls his mouth in the Tarot card Strength.

183

**POOL** - The Pool is like Sephirah #9 (Yesod and the Moon). The Moon is queen of the subconscious and was the main symbol of worship in matriarchal times when life was lived on a subconscious, intuitive level. Universal consciousness, or reservoir of cosmic-mind power which is stirred into vibration by the act of meditation. This is indicated by the stream of water flowing into the pool from the right-hand pitcher (gold and Sun +). It indicates direct modification of the cosmic mind power apart from sensory experience. This is similar to Temperance, but in this card she has her foot on the water instead of in it, showing that she is in control. The stream flowing from the other pitcher in her left hand (silver and Moon -) divides into five rivulets, which flow back to the pool along the ground. They indicate the 5 senses. One rivulet flows to the pool and unites matter and Soul. Meditation stabilizes the psychic waters and makes them solid.

The two people falling from the Tower are shown by twin vessels (conscious/subconscious) held in the hands of the Great Mother of Heaven. She is replenishing them with waters of Eternal Life. God made the firmament and separated the waters under the firmament from the waters above the firmament and it was so. As above, so below. ♒

SUMMARY
+ Many times this card shows the client has the knowledge of astrology or the higher sciences. The client is using a higher source and meditation to direct the life. Experiences of the past allow one to be on top of the situation.

- The client has not been using the above or has not been initiated into it as yet if the card is reversed.

Q - Qoph

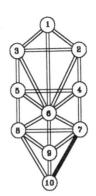

# CARD #18 THE MOON ON PATH #29 (19)

## THE MOON

This is the fourth stage of spiritual unfolding, where the knowledge gained by meditation is incorporated into the bodily organism. It is the building of the subconscious mental patterns, like the prodigal son and the final journey home, when man realizes the better life (spiritual source).

**KEYWORD** - a crisis

**PLANET & SIGN** - The Moon ☽. (Water is our perception and feelings). The drops of light falling from the Moon corresponds to the 15 Hebrew Yods and #15. 1+5=6, which is Sephirah #6 Tiphareth where the Sun (Son) resides and signifies "life." The falling Yods refer to the descent of the life force from above, into the conditions of corporeal existence. The Moon has risen from her seat as High Priestess to reign supreme in the heavens. She produces the ethereal substance from which all is made, but now works from a higher level to transmute this substance so that the vehicle of man may become sufficiently spiritualized to receive the light of Christ.

Since the Sun/Tiphareth is mediator between God/Kether and Nature/Malkuth, Yesod, the Moon, is the mediator between the Sun/Tiphareth and Nature/Malkuth. Note on the card that the Moon is joined with the Sun and shows an **Eclipse**. This is like the joining of Tiphareth/Sun and Yesod/Moon. Eclipses are formed from New and Full Moons with the Sun. Full Moon eclipses pull the gravity of the water, pulling us to a higher consciousness. When an eclipse happens, there is usually an important event or break through. Pisces ♓ is also a Water sign and a very spiritual sign.

The Hebrew simple letter Qoph represents the astrological sign Pisces, ruler of this card. Pisces rules the 12th house in astrology which is the department of our life that has to do with our subconscious and our dream state, the level where messages come through or where we wrestle with problems. Pisces rules the feet and the feet are the path makers. The foot is a symbol for understanding the Soul and its direct relationship with earth. The feet of the Great One shows a path for others to walk which leads to higher consciousness. Note in the Bible that they were always washing the feet. The symbol for Pisces is two fish joined, going in different directions, representing the pull between the personality and the Soul.

Neptune is the planet that rules Pisces. It is the planet that symbolizes our picture-making ability, our beliefs, our psychic ability. When the cards were designed Neptune was not known.

**CARD NUMBER** - #18 = 9. The Hermit is also #9. The goal of this path is to work through knowledge.

**HEBREW LETTER #100 (19)** - This is a Hebrew simple letter standing for the astrological sign Pisces. Q (Qoph) means the back of the head. This is the part of the skull which contains the cerebellum and the medulla oblongata. When there is an approach to the back of the head, one feels a funny vibration. These parts of the brain are related to the functions of human personality which man shares with the rest of the animal kingdom. The medulla, in particular, governs some of the most important bodily functions. The cells of the organ remain awake when the rest of the brain is asleep. Sleep is the period of time of psychological repair during which the cells of the body undergo change. Dreams come to make one ready for experiences. Being behind or in back of shows what has already been accomplished.

**PATH #29 (19)** - Path #29 (19) is called the *Corporeal Intelligence,* so called because it creates everything that is formed in all the worlds and the reproduction of them. It connects Sephirah #10 (Malkuth, Kingdom Earth on the Air pillar) to Sephirah #7 (Netzach, Victory on the Fire pillar and Venus). On this path is the Hebrew letter Q (Qoph) and the astrological sign Pisces and the card, The Moon.

**PATH COLOR** - crimson, buff flecked silver-white, light translucent pinkish-brown, stone

**PATH** - At its very beginning, where it rises from the margin of the pool, the path is bordered by stones and plants. The path rises and falls, worn by many feet traveling over it and suggests waving and vibratory action. Yet it continually ascends, so that as one progresses, the time comes when his most depressed states of consciousness are at a higher level than some of his earlier exaltations. The path passes between two dogs.

**STONES AND PLANTS** - are symbols of the mineral and vegetable kingdom.

**MUSICAL TONE** - Ti-Moon (Cancer) Sol-Neptune (Pisces)

**SHELL FISH** -The shell fish climbs from the pool and is the symbol of the early stages of conscious unfoldment. In these first developments of consciousness, the individual seems to be isolated from the rest of nature. Note he is purple--he made it!!!!! In Egypt the shell fish symbolized the God Khenbra. Sometimes a scarab is shown here. The scarab is a holy bug in Egypt. It is said that it writes the word for God with its hind legs.

**TWO DOGS** - Dogs are a symbol of the animal kingdom, one a wolf and the other a dog: the extremes of nature or the evolution. Dog evolved from the wolf.

**CULTIVATED FIELD** - The path moves through a cultivated field which symbolizes matters of more or less general knowledge, until it comes to the towers.

**TWO TOWERS** -The towers mark the boundaries of the known. It then continues into the beyond, rising and falling through planes of consciousness which are open to us during sleep and trance. Towers also are man made and imply terminal ends or openings which separate the mundane from the spiritual.

SUMMARY

+ Usually a major crisis of an emotional nature has happened, and this card says to be aware. This is also the card of a psychic.

- Reversed, the client is allowing the upsetting emotional state to make everything so confusing that there is no perspective or detachment.

R - Resh

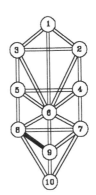

**THE SUN**

This key represents the fifth stage of unfolding. It is a degree of adapting, that of liberation from the limitations of physical matter and circumstances. It is also a grade of conscious self-identification with the One Life. Yet it is not final. It is a stage where all physical forces are under the control of the adept who, having himself become childlike, realizes in his own person the fulfillment of the promise, "A little child shall lead them." Yet a person who has reached this level still feels himself to be a separate or at least a distinct entity. This is not full liberation, though it is a higher stage than any of those preceding it. It is a particular stage in which all physical forces are dominated by the will of the adept, because he is an unobstructed vehicle for the One Will which always has ruled those forces, since the beginning.

**KEYWORD** - attainment

**PLANET & SIGN** - The Sun ☉ is the planet corresponding to this card, because the Hebrew double letter Resh represents the Sun. The Sun (Fire +) is a very positive power but creative only when harmoniously blended with Water. It has been known to scorch land dry on its own. To receive its ever enriching potential we must facilitate this blending within us. This blending takes place by blending the conscious and subconscious, the Fire and Water together. It is said that what makes flowers (Sunflower) grow is moisture (Water) and warmth (Fire-Sun). This was shown by the joining of the Moon and Sun together in card #18. The Sun sign in the astrology chart shows the God-given talents that come to one through that sign and expresses the ego of man. Leo ♌ is the sign for this card.

**CARD NUMBER** - 19=10=1 This shows the beginning. A successful time to start new ventures.

**HEBREW LETTER #200 (20)** - R (Resh) is a Hebrew double letter standing for the astrological planet the Sun. Resh means head or face. In the head all the distinctive human powers are gathered together or collected. The head of any project is its organizer, director, guiding power, manager, or controller.

**PATH #30 (20)** - Path #30 is called the *Collective Intelligence.* Astrologers deduce from it the judgement of the stars and celestial signs, and perfect their science according to the rules of the motions of the stars. To collect is to assemble, to bring together, to combine, to synthesize. The collective intelligence concentrates all the consciousness which has gone before and combines them together in a new form. Path #30 connects Sephirah #8 (Hod, Splendor on the Water pillar and Mercury) with Sephirah #9 (Yesod, Foundation on the Air Pillar and the Moon). Visualize this and see that the combination is definitely Collective Intelligence. Any time that Mercury and the Moon are combined, thought and perception are joined together. This is a tremendous amount of knowledge. This is, therefore, called the teacher's card.

**PATH COLOR** - orange, gold yellow, rich amber, amber rayed red.

**MUSICAL TONE** - Re-Sun (Leo)

**CHILD** - The child is fair, like the Fool, and like the Fool wears a wreath and a red feather. The feather has the same meaning as for The Fool. The wreath is of flowers, instead of leaves, intimating the near approach to the harvest of final realization and liberation. The child is naked, in accordance with an old Kabalistic saying that Spirit clothes itself to come down, and divests itself of the garments of matter to go up. The nipples and navel of the child form a triangle representing the water triangle, hinting at the Hebrew letter Mem. Child is the fifth stage of spiritual unfolding, the ultimate stage of transformation, where the Christ Light is absorbed by the prepared being. "Man becomes reborn as a little child, who knows himself to be in truth, a Son of God." "Suffer the little children to come unto me for they shall inherit the earth." The child holds no reigns and is using mind control and intuition to direct the horse. He rides without saddle or bridle because he represents perfect balance. The balance is maintained by his outstretched right hand, which represents self-consciousness. The gray horse also shows the blending of black and white.

**BANNER** - is red showing action. Carried in the left hand (feminine), it shows that the subconscious is automatic and triumphs.

**WALL** - The wall is man made and represents human adaptation of natural conditions. Wherever stone appears in Tarot symbolism, we are to understand it as a reference to the Hebrew word ABN, and thus to the perfect union between the Divine Wisdom which Kabalists call ALB, the Father, and the One Self of the entire human race, which they call Bn, the Son.

**SUNFLOWERS** - They represent the four Kabalistic Worlds, and the four kingdoms of nature: mineral, vegetable, animal and human. Although sunflowers always turn to the sun, in this card they are turned to the child as if to hint that all creation turns to man for its final development. Remember that the child is a product of the man and woman, the conscious and subconscious. It represents the blending of the two consciousnesses to raise them up to a Super-consciousness. The Sun (Son) admires what the child stands for.

SUMMARY

+ This is a card of success. It is like saying "Look what I did, and I did it all myself!" No one can do anything for us, We must do the work ourselves if we are to be successful. We also cannot do the work for others.

- Card in reverse says success is delayed.

Sh - Shin

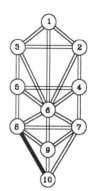

JUDGEMENT.

**JUDGEMENT**
Judgement, sometimes THE LAST JUDGEMENT, implies completion, decision, termination. It is the final state of personal consciousness, because that which is represented by the next card is a state wherein personal consciousness is wholly obliterated in a higher realization. This indicates God and man united.

**KEYWORDS** - spiritual awakening, completion, time for a decision about reincarnation. By throwing off limitations imposed upon us by our attitudes and environment, our judgement is improved. An outstanding person will have access to his subconscious, which is the foundation of success.

**CARD NUMBER** - #20=2 the polarity of the positive and negative, + and - or The High Priestess. 20 stands for free will, where man with his developed will and the power to use it decides which path he shall tread, which is shown in #21 and #22. It is called the breaker of the elements, one who has separated the elements and has gained control over them. 20 is the highest expression of duality. Man realizes his responsibility and has completed his cycle and is now God's ambassador. He is responsible for Self and answerable to God.

**HEBREW LETTER SHIN # 300 (21)** - Sh (Shin) is a Hebrew mother letter and stands for the Fire element. It is the Holy Spirit.

**SIGN** - There is none since the Hebrew letter stands for the element Fire.

**PATH #31 (21)** - Path #31 (21) is called *Perpetual Intelligence*, so called because it directs and associates the motions of the 7 planets, directing all of them in their proper courses. This path connects Sephirah #8 (Hod, Splendor on the Water pillar and Mercury) with Sephirah #10 (Malkuth, Kingdom and Earth on the Air pillar).

**PATH COLOR** - glowing orange scarlet, vermilion flecked crimson and emerald

**PEOPLE** - Man, woman and child. Man is the conscious, woman the subconscious, and the child is the blending of the two together into the Super-conscious. Bodies tinted gray show wisdom. Arms refer to the symbolic gestures used in certain occult societies to represent the letter L (woman's extended arms), V (upraised arms of child) and X (crossed arms of man) which spell the Latin noun LVX meaning "Light". The child's back is toward us, because he represents the return to the Source of all. This card shows the 6th stage of spiritual unfolding, in which personal consciousness is on the verge of blending with the Universal.

**COFFINS** - Coffins show restriction. Child is in a square coffin, which can form a cross. "As a child." Others are rectangular, to represent the three dimensions of the physical plane. They float on the Water, which is the final reservoir for the Major Arcana of those waters which began in the robe of the High Priestess. At this stage, the adept realizes that his personal existence is nothing but the manifestation of the relationship between conscious and subconscious. He sees, too, that self-consciousness and subconsciousness are not themselves personal but are really kinds of Universal consciousness. He knows that his personality has no separate existence. At this stage his intellectual conviction is confirmed by fourth dimensional experiences which finally blot out the delusion of separateness forever.

Man moves from the limitations of his old third dimensional existence with its mortal encasement, comparable to the sleep of death, to be transformed into a new, awakened consciousness where one is functioning on all levels simultaneously, and coming into the reception of his true being. The *Spiritual Summons--Man Joyfully reaches out.* Man must become attuned to the harmony of the Universe. John baptized with water. Jesus was baptized with the Holy Spirit. Power belongs to he who knows and, therefore, he is responsible in proportion to his knowledge, for the use he makes of his power. Therefore, the initiate, by toil, self sacrifice and suffering, has sought out the hidden mysteries of life and has, like Job, stood face to face with the Lord (for Judgement).

**ANGEL** - is Gabrielle, not only because he carries a trumpet, but also because Gabrielle is the element of Water, he creates Air, the substance of breath. Breath is specialized in sound, and is the basis of sound and is sevenfold. These seven basic tones are indicated by seven lines radiating from the bell of the trumpet utilizing sound vibration. These 7 tones are those which affect the 7 interior planets. Do Re Me Fa Sol La Ti-Do. Do is a repeat and starts the next octave.

**SNOWY MOUNTAINS** - represent the heights of abstract thought.

**BANNER** - measures exactly 5x5 units. The arms of the cross, equal in length, show measurement and form, the blending of the Fire and Water, male and female, positive and negative. The first cross was made for measurement and drawing of right angles. The angles represent North, South, East and West.

**CROSS** - Greek cross. It is of equal length and is used in art, science, and math. It is also the identification symbol in the Red Cross. It is like the carpenter's square, used to draw and measure. It is the same cross that is on The High Priestess' gown. When I was in Greece, I saw this cross. It was first used to measure the depth of the river Nile. Here it is also measuring up what has been. We are measured by our works.

## SUMMARY
+ This card shows that which has gone before must now come to a decision and be judged. Gabriel blows his horn and it is the time of reckoning. It cannot be delayed....it is now!!!!

- Card in reverse is delayed judgement.

### THE FOOL #0 is also on path #31 (21)

## THE FOOL
The Fool coming from universal energy began as 0 upon entering life. He went through lessons and paths #1-20. In #21 the Fool can become one who finds it necessary to continue, to review, to reincarnate only because lessons were not thoroughly learned. The Judgment #20 was severe and not passed. The Fool begins his lessons again.

On the other hand, at this point the Soul could choose to climb to the height of the completed individual. Passing each of the lessons of the paths and Sephiroth, the Soul can now take the next step and enter The World, card #21 (11). At that point, feeling complete, the Soul can spiral up the Air pillar and go directly to Kether the Divine Light and receive the Crown of Life. Not until fully reaching this stage had there been this strength or wisdom. He not only holds the Rod of Power but has become the Rod himself. The higher self now has greater and harder work to do. The more evolved you are, the more that is required of you.

Reread pages #97-108 about The Fool.

**LETTER** - The letter Shin (pronounced "sheen") is on the Fool's clothing (lower right hand corner). It means teeth, probably a serpent's fangs, and suggests sharpness, acidity, active manifestation. We may understand this letter as being a symbol of the power which tears down the limitations of form, as teeth break up food to help our digestion. As the serpent's fang, it represents the power which "kills" the false personality and its sense of separateness. The #300 or 21 is the value of the Hebrew words RVCHALHIM, Ruach Elohim which means "Life Breath of the Divine One" or "Holy Spirit." Therefore, the Kabalists call Shin the "Holy letters." It has three flames representing Binah, Kether and Chokmah (the Supernal Triad of the Tree of Life). The Fool has a triple flame over his heart and symbol of Shin on the lower right corner of his cloak. Shin completes man. No creation can be completed until the force of Shin or heat (Fire element) has done its perfect work. Shin, being on path #31 (21) and also on The Fool's garment, shows that he is connected to this path.

**FIRE** - is the element attributed to SHIN. It is the particular quality of the solar force and the Mars vibration.

**NUMBER** - Number 21 is connected with 12, the number of fruition as well as The Hanged Man. This is because both are reduced to 3. (2+1=3) 7+7+7=21. 21 is 2+1=3. Three sevens mean perfected man in the Three Worlds, totality of the mystery of life in the Three Worlds.

Th/T - Tau

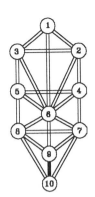

## THE WORLD

The World is the common title but it sometimes is called 'The Universe' to indicate that the consciousness it represents is not merely terrestrial, but truly cosmic. This key signifies cosmic consciousness or Nirvana. One knows that through God the governing and directing power of the universe flows out into manifestation. This is the seventh stage of spiritual unfoldment. We must leave it to our intuition to combine the suggestions of the picture with the meanings of the letter Tau. Here is a representation of what you really are and of what the cosmos really is. The universe is the Dance of Life, the immortal, central self of you-that is THE ETERNAL DANCER. The Fool looked up but here we look within, indicating completion.

KEYWORDS - feeling balanced, centered, completed evolution

PLANET - The Hebrew double letter Tau represents the planet Saturn. Saturn ate his own children. He represents that which absorbs its own expressions back into itself. Sephirah #3 and path #22 both represent Saturn. Esoterically, Saturn is the planet of inertia, concrete and weight. Saturn is exalted in Libra. We have here a power which is the source of those apparent limitations, which make us seek a way of escape from bondage, and which is expressed in the equilibrated action symbolized by Justice. As you sow, so shall you reap. Karma. If we do not use the discipline of Saturn to work on our evolution, we have to repeat our Karma. In astrology, Scorpio and Pluto are the sign and planet that rule the house of death as well as what one changes or regenerates. Once Pluto has made a change, you can never go back to using the old way. Transformation and Regeneration. The Karma has been completed here.

CARD NUMBER 21 - 21 when reduced becomes #3 the Trinity.

HEBREW LETTER 400 (22) - Hebrew double letter Tau Th T value 400 or 22 means cross. (Signature or mark). As a mark, it represents a signature, the sign of the cross. The letter Tau therefore indicated the final seal and witness of the completion of the Great Work of Liberation. The Tau cross is the earliest cross used. It is the cross used by Moses to lift up the brazen serpent in the wilderness See Numbers 21:8. "Even so must the Son of man be lifted up: that whosoever believeth in him should not perish, but have everlasting life. For God sent not his Son into the world to condemn the world; but that the world through him might be saved."

The brazen serpent in the lifted hands of Moses in the Old Testament was an instrument of deliverance to those who looked upon it. This symbol reflected the spiritual deliverance that was realized through faith in the crucified and risen Christ. It was called the prophetic cross because it foretold the redemptive powers of Christ. At this point #22 puts one in this position also.

**PATH #32**- Path #32 is called *Administrative Intelligence*. Wisdom, for he who possesses it, is brought into a condition of responsibility: namely cooperation with the creator of all, to do his part in helping direct the administration of the universe. This path is said to "direct all the operations of the 7 planets" and concur therein. He has opened self up to divine consciousness.

**PATH COLOR** - indigo, black, blue-black, black rayed blue

**MUSICAL TONE** - I feel we should sing the song of the whole scale here.

**ANIMALS** - There are four at the corners of the card and have been explained in connection with the 10th card. In this card the Bull faces the Lion, but in card #22 the Bull faces away from the Lion. This is because the Bull corresponds to the last letter of the Tetragrammation, IHVH, which symbolizes the physical plane. These four animals are the four fixed signs of the Zodiac (Taurus, Leo, Aquarius and Scorpio). This also refers to the four Apostles.

**ELLIPSE** - The ellipse surrounding the dancing figure is 5 units wide and 6 units high. This gives a very close approximation to the quadrature of the circle and is related also to the dimensions of the sides of the vault described in the Rosicrucian Fama Fraternitatis. The proportion is derived from the geometrical construction of the hexagram, or figure of 2 interlaced triangles.

**GREEN WREATH** - living state-crown of the Initiate, given only to those who master the four guardians and enter into the presence of the whole truth. In other packs the ellipse is formed of 22 groups of 3 leaves, 11 groups on either side. These represent the 22 forces corresponding to the letters of the Hebrew alphabet and the Tarot paths. There are 3 leaves in each group, because every one of the 22 forces has three levels of consciousness. Any one of these forces may manifest itself in integration, according to the way in which it is applied. Note that the ellipse is a 0 sign and 0 is the numerical symbol of super-consciousness. It takes us back to the beginning and the FOOL as the circle has been completed. The bindings look like #8 and the sign for infinity.

**DANCER** - represents the merging of consciousness with subconsciousness, and blending of these 2 with super-consciousness. She is the All-Father, All-Mother and the Bride as well as the Bridegroom. She is the Kingdom and the King, even as Malkuth, the Kingdom is by Kabalists called the "Bride," but has also the Divine name ADNI KLK, Adonai Melek, Lord King. The red wreath on the head is fruition.

**WANDS** - show the balance of the polarities + & -. The right hand turns clockwise and the left counter-clockwise. The wands represent the spiral forces of the life power. One hand is masculine and one is feminine, giving equally balanced power. Posture of the leg is the symbol for sulfur or that

Divine Fire which is the heart of the Great Mystery. This is the same as the leg in The Hanged Man.

**SCARF** - Shaped like letter Kaph "grasp" and denotes that here the grasp of truth itself has become complete. THE TRUTH SHALL MAKE YOU FREE. It looks like she is coming over the finish line. She has won the race!

<u>SUMMARY</u>

+ This card shows a successful completion of what one is working on. A triumph.

- Card in reverse shows that completion is delayed. Further work has to be done.

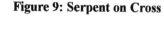

**Figure 9: Serpent on Cross**

We started with the serpent in the Garden of Eden and we end with the Serpent.

# PART TWO

# THE MINOR ARCANA

# TREE AND SEPHIROTH

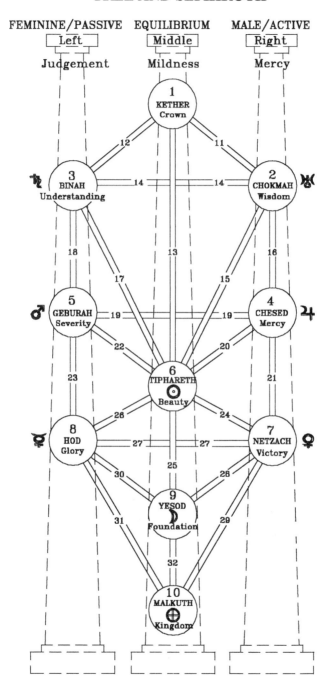

FEMININE/PASSIVE     EQUILIBRIUM     MALE/ACTIVE

Left         Middle         Right

Judgement      Mildness       Mercy

1
KETHER
Crown

12         11

3
BINAH
Understanding

14 ——— 14

2
CHOKMAH
Wisdom

18       13       16

17      15

5
GEBURAH
Severity

19      19

4
CHESED
Mercy

22      20

23      21

6
TIPHARETH
Beauty

26      24

8
HOD
Glory

27 ——— 27

7
NETZACH
Victory

25

30      28

9
YESOD
Foundation

31      29

32

10
MALKUTH
Kingdom

# PART TWO: MINOR ARCANA

## EXPLANATION

The Tarot is an interpretative system involving a set of 78 cards. 22 are called the Major Arcana, which we already discussed. The remaining 56 cards are called the Minor Arcana. All of these cards unlock the wisdom of the ancient philosophers.

The Minor Arcana consists of 56 cards having four suits: the Wands, Cups, Swords, and Pentacles. Each of these suits has a King, Queen, Knight, Page and cards 1 through 10.

When working with the 56 cards of the Minor Arcana, we will be incorporating the three pillars on the Tree. We are also going to use the 10 Sephiroth. It would be a good idea for you to read the following pages to refresh your memory about information relating to The Tree and the Minor Arcana discussed previously.

When I refer to the Kabalah and the Tree of Life, I am **facing** the Tree. Reference to the right pillar means the pillar on the right hand side of the paper. The left pillar is on the left hand side of the paper as I face it.

When talking about the King, Queen, and Knights in reference to their hands, it would be as if you placed yourself in that position. Just take the card and place it on your chest with the King facing away from you. You can see that your right and left arms line up with those of the card. Now, walk straight ahead into the Tree. Your right arm is on the right pillar and your left arm is on the left pillar. The right pillar and right arm is masculine/positive in energy and the element of Fire. The left pillar and left arm is feminine/negative in energy and the element of Water. The middle pillar of the Tree represents the element of Air and aligns with the spinal column, kundalini or chakras. The base of the Tree is Sephirah #10 Malkuth, the element Earth.

# PILLARS

The Kings, Queens, Knights and Pages represent the elements. The Kings are Fire, the Queens are Water, the Knights are Air and the Pages are Earth. There are three pillars on the Tree of Life.

The **right pillar is positive, masculine or assertive.** It, therefore, is the element of **Fire. The Kings** are placed here and represent men of over 30 years of age.

The **left pillar is negative, feminine or receptive.** It is the element of **Water. The Queens** go here and represent women of over 30 years of age.

The **middle pillar** symbolizes the consciousness of Man and his efforts to balance the positive and negative of life. It is the element of **Air. The Knights** are on the 6th Sephirah on the Air Pillar. The Knights can be either male or female. They are age 20-30.

The **base** of the Tree is **Earth. The Pages** are placed here on the 10th Sephirah. They also can be either male or female. They are young, up to age 20.

The elements also relate to the four suits: **Fire is Wands, Water is Cups, Air is Swords, and Earth is Pentacles.**

The above cards will depict people in the life of the client. When describing the astrological sign for the individual card, you can refer back to pages 15-17 and get a brief description of each sign. Remember that the person may not be the sign shown by the card. However, if you describe the qualities of the sign, the client will know whom you are talking about.

These same principles hold true for homosexuals. If your client is a gay man, he will be interested in relationships the same way everyone else is. When a masculine or feminine card shows up, this can be his person of interest. The masculine person would be the one that takes the masculine role in the relationship. If a female card appears, that would be the one that takes the feminine role in the relationship. The same is true when reading for a lesbian.

When studying the Minor Arcana, the number on the top of the card will be important as it relates to the Sephirah corresponding to that number, as well as the astrological planet that goes with each Sephirah of the Tree of Life. It will also relate to the same number previously discussed in the section on numbers.

The objects Wands, Cups, Swords and Pentacles on each card will add up to the number of the card. The placement and arrangement of them also gives clues to the meaning of the card.

## TIMING OF AN EVENT
The timing of an event can be seen according to seasons. This is shown in all of the Minor Arcana.

Wands are the **Spring**.
Cups are the **Summer**.
Swords are the **Fall**.
Pentacles are the **Winter**.

## LINE UP OF CARDS
The Tree of Life and the 10 Sephiroth (10 commandments).

Each Sephiroth will be placed on a pillar. The pillar will be one of the four elements: Fire for the right pillar, Water for the left pillar, Air for the middle pillar and Earth for Sephirah #10. There will be four cards on each Sephiroth. There will be one card that will have primary rulership over the pillar and element. This card is the pure, unblended elemental energy. For example, when the four cards are placed on Sephirah #2, they will be on the Fire pillar. These cards are the #2's. The most important card here will be the one that relates to the Fire element. Since the Wands are the Fire element, the 2 of Wands will be of the pure energy of the element.

All three of the other cards are combinations of two different elements. Example: the 2 of Cups is a combination of Fire and Water. Cups are Water and, being placed on Sephirah #2 on the Fire pillar, blends the Water and Fire together. The 2 of Swords is a combination of Fire and Air. Swords are Air and, being placed on Sephirah #2 on the Fire pillar, blends the Fire and Air together. The 2 of Pentacles is a combination of Fire and Earth. The Pentacles are Earth and, being placed on Sephirah #2 on the Fire pillar, blends the Earth and Fire together. The combination of two different elements gives these cards unique qualities and strengths.

The card that has the primary rulership will always be listed first in the interpretations. The rest will follow in the order of Fire, Water, Air, Earth or Wands, Cups, Swords, and Pentacles. When the cards are numbered in the suits, they go by this order also. Reread pages 39-41.

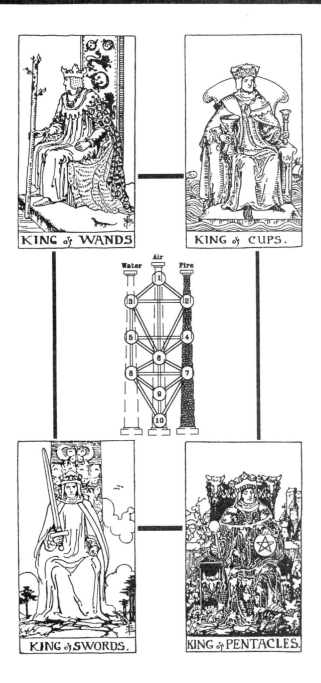

# THE KINGS - YOD

The four Kings in the four suits of cards represent the Hebrew letter Y (Yod) and the element Fire. It is the start of material forces and follows through with completion in the other cards. The Kings are always masculine and the age of about 30 and over. The Kings are of the Fire element which is + (positive). They are placed on the right Fire pillar of the Tree of Life. Since the pillar is Fire and the Kings are placed there, the first one we will start with is the King of Wands. Wands are Fire also.

## KING OF WANDS    23-5
*Fire & Fire     Astrological signs: **Aries, Leo, Sagittarius***

**ELEMENT/PILLAR** - This King is pure Fire and brings with it the Fire element and the whole Fire pillar, representing Primal Fire. This is tremendous energy and force.

**CROWN** - His crown is yellow representing the intellectual. It is made up of flames because he is of the Fire family.

**LIONS** - Lions are on the back of the throne and are a symbol for the astrological Fire sign Leo. Yellow and gold are Leo's colors. His necklace has the head of a lion on it.

**CAPE** - is yellow and green. Green stands for growth.

**WAND** - Notice that there are leaves on the Wands which shows that the enterprise has life.

**THRONE** - He sits on a solid piece of concrete (cubic). He has firm convictions.

**SALAMANDERS** - Notice that the salamanders on his cape, throne and concrete slab. The spirits that are seen for the element Fire are the salamanders. They symbolize a radiant state of matter. Sometimes they are seen as small balls of light and are also called spirits of Fire. Without them it is said that material fire cannot exist or a match be struck. A salamander can be evoked by friction. You will see these also on the cards for the Page and Knight of Wands.

## SUMMARY

+ The King of Wands is a proud man who likes to own or rule in a majestic way. He has great charm and likes everything first class. He is frank, honest, and a gentleman, a man with warm leadership abilities. (Reread the astrological signs Aries, Leo and Sagittarius.)

- This card in reverse can be a man who is domineering and rules by fear, a self-seeker, and egotistical. One who is not living up to the positive attributes of the signs.

## KING OF CUPS     37-10-1
*Fire & Water     Astrological signs:* **Cancer, Scorpio, Pisces**

**ELEMENT/PILLAR** - This King is the Water element and on the Fire pillar, a combination of Water and Fire. He has enthusiasm and sensitivity. He draws from the Fire and Water pillars. This is Fire in the World of Primal Water. The King of Cups (Water) visits the Fire pillar. The fire stirs up the emotions (Water).

**THRONE/WATER** - He is a man of emotional sensitivity who is strong, shown by his throne made of concrete. He is able to balance his throne on a sea of Water, which stands for emotions. Notice that the water is rough, but he still can balance on it.

**SHIP** - Notice the ship in the background. It stands for commerce as well as a symbol of the church. The picture of the ship plowing through the stormy water is a reminder of the church as it sails through troubled waters of adversity in the world. The ship of the church has a good captain at the helm, Jesus Christ, and he will bring the ship and all her faithful to safety, onto the shores of heaven. This same ship is seen in the card Death in the Major Arcana.

**FISH** - There is a fish on his neck and on his right in the water. Fish is the symbol for the astrological Water sign of Pisces.

**COLOR** - Blue stands for emotional sensitivity. Green is for growth and red is for desire. His subconscious sustains him.

**RING** – Ring on right masculine hand and on the Saturn finger representing structure and stability.

SUMMARY
+ He is compassionate and sympathetic, a man of the sea, a counselor, doctor, policeman, homebody or carpenter. A strong, sensitive man in control of his emotions and is artistic and musically inclined. (Reread the astrological signs for Cancer, Scorpio and Pisces.)

- In reverse he can be too sensitive and easily hurt, lacks backbone, strength or courage. He can drift or be involved with alcohol and drugs. One who has emotional problems and is fearful.

# KING OF SWORDS   51-6
*Fire & Air     Astrological signs:* ***Gemini, Libra, Aquarius.***

**ELEMENT/PILLAR** - This King is of the element Air and on the Fire pillar, therefore, a combination of Air and Fire.  The enthusiasm is being released in an intellectual way.  The elements Fire and Air are both positives, which results in a harmony of energy: Fire in the World of Primal Air.  Both the Fire and Air pillars are drawn from.  It is as if the King of Swords visits the Fire pillar, which fires him up, to become more productive intellectually.
**THRONE** - Notice his throne is in the Air.  He rules the Air signs.  His sword is up, initiating aggressiveness and uncompleted matters.
**SWORD** - The sword is a symbol for communication.
**BUTTERFLIES** - Butterflies are on the back of his throne.  Butterflies flit around the same way as the Air signs do.   It is also a symbol for the resurrection, because of the three stages in the butterfly's life: 1) the caterpillar, 2) the entombment in the cocoon, and 3) the emergence in new life as the beautiful butterfly.  These are clear, natural symbols of finite life, death, and the resurrection to new life.
**HAT** - The yellow hat shows he thinks with intelligence.  Red under the hat shows that the intellect controls his desires or aggressive nature.  Notice the face on the hat within the wings.  Read sylphs below.
**BLUE GARMENT** - The blue garment shows that he also has intuition or an emotional nature.  He is a King who sees the crux of the matter and, with swift justice, sets matters aright.  He speaks the truth.
**SYLPH** - The spirits that are seen for the Air element are called Sylphs.  They are very quick, darting to and fro, like lightning.  They work through the gases and ethers of the earth.  They are winged or tiny cherubs and delicate fairies.  The two people over his shoulders could possibly be Sylphs.  This also represents the duality of Gemini, being the sign of twins.

## SUMMARY
+ The King of Swords can be a domineering and aggressive man, possessing shrewd insight into human nature.  He is a man of strength who enjoys a position of rulership, management or control, a man who uses his intellectual ability in his career.  He could be a lawyer, teacher, broadcaster, salesman, writer, magician, auctioneer, etc.  He can give advice and is a jack of all trades and highly intellectual.  (Reread the astrological signs for Gemini, Libra and Aquarius.)
- Card in reverse shows that he scatters his energy.  He can be a scatterbrain and all over the place accomplishing nothing.  This is a man of duality who is changeable.  One who gossips, and finds it hard to stay in one place.  He can be unstable, a swindler, or fast talker.

# KING OF PENTACLES   65-11-2
*Fire & Earth     Astrological signs: **Taurus, Virgo, Capricorn***

**ELEMENT/PILLAR** - This King is of the Earth element and on the Fire pillar, a combination of Earth and Fire. He is Fire in the Primal World of Earth. He has enthusiasm, practicality and caution. He draws from the Fire and Earth pillars. This is an earthy, practical man. He has a business sense and has accomplished a lot. The fire energizes the ambition.

**GRAPES** - Note the grapes, which show fulfillment for hard work. It takes a long time and patience for grapes to grow.

**COLORS** - red and green are desires and growth.

**BULL** - The bull's head represents the astrological sign of Taurus, a hard working sign. Castles are material accomplishments.

**GNOMES** – The spirits of the Earth are called Gnomes. There is one beside the bull's head on the lower right as you look at the card.

**STONE WALL** - The stone wall is behind him. He has put the hard work behind.

**ARMOR** - He has a suit of armor under his garment which shows he is prepared to battle if necessary.

**CROWN** – Notice the lilies and roses on the crown.

**WILD BOAR** – His foot on the boar shows that he is in control.

SUMMARY
+  He is a dependable, hard working, man.   A man who has stick-to-itiveness, control and accomplishment. A Capricorn can be an engineer, Virgo is very precise, and Taurus likes banking, investing, real estate or building.  These signs can make money grow.  They are workaholics and have achieved through perseverance and hard work. (Reread the astrological signs Taurus, Virgo and Capricorn.)

- Card in reverse shows that he can have an uncontrolled desire for money, not living up to his nature and can be corrupt. One who is stubborn and over-spends caring only for material possessions.

QUEEN of CUPS.

QUEEN of SWORDS.

Water    Air    Fire

QUEEN of PENTACLES

QUEEN of WANDS.

# QUEENS - HE'

The Queens are of the element Water, and the Hebrew letter H (He') also stands for this. Water is - and receptive/negative. The Queens are always female and the age of about 30 and over. They are placed on the left pillar (Water) of the Tree of Life. They work through the Eternal mother. Since they are of the Water element, we start with the Queen of Cups. Cups is Water.

## QUEEN OF CUPS 38-11
*Water & Water      Astrological signs: **Cancer, Scorpio, Pisces***

**ELEMENT/PILLAR** - This is pure Water energy. She is the Water element and on the Water pillar. Sensitivity, psychic ability and subconscious knowledge abounds.

**SEA SHELL/CHERUBIM** - Sea shell on back of throne and cherubim represent the ocean, which is the Water element.

**CHALICE** - Notice her chalice. There is a cross on the top and the wings of angels in the shape of the Moon. The wings are the phases of the Moon when it is waxing and waning. It also represents gothic architecture and the church. The church represented the Holy Mother in the 14th century. The Virgin Mary was referred to as a church. The church was a building that held all wisdom. This chalice is thought of in this way.

**CROWN** – Circles are the 8 phases of the Moon around the Earth.

**COLOR** - Her blue garment gives her an emotional and nurturing quality. She sits on red, symbolizing that she sits on her desires.

**TOE** - Her toe touches the water but is not all the way in. This means she knows emotions, but she is in control of them.

**UNDINES** - The spirits that relate to the element Water are called Undines and they appear in the form of mermaids, sea-maidens, water spirits and water nymphs. Note that they are on her throne at the top and side.

SUMMARY
+ A very sensitive, motherly woman with psychic ability. She is a real homemaker, nurse, cosmic mother and guide. She is a woman who truly exhibits divine love in her motivation to aid others. (Reread the astrological signs of Cancer, Scorpio, and Pisces.)

- Card in reverse shows an overly sensitive, frustrated, pouting, emotional person who needs help in directing and handling her emotions. She worries, has an overly active imagination and is possessive.

## QUEEN OF SWORDS   52-7
*Water & Air    Astrological signs: **Gemini, Libra, Aquarius**.*

**ELEMENT/PILLAR** - She is of the Air element and on the Water pillar. This is a combination of Air and Water. She draws from the Water and Air pillars. Whatever is placed on the Water pillar has the backing of the emotions behind it. In this case the Queen of Swords (intelligence) is combined to give good perception.

**SWORD** - The Sword represents communication.

**BUTTERFLIES** - Butterflies are on the yellow headpiece. Butterflies show evolution and flit around like the astrological sign Gemini.

**COLOR** - The yellow shows an intellectual ability.

**HAND** - The sword is in the right, masculine hand and is up to initiate action. She faces the East, waiting for new beginnings.

**CLOUDS** - Clouds on her cape and clouds in the background as well as the bird symbolize the Air signs. Her throne is floating in the Air.

**TOE** - Her red toe represents that she has enthusiasm.

**SYLPH** - The winged cherub could be a Sylph. The spirits for the Air are called Sylphs. They are tiny winged cherubs and delicate fairies. They work through the gases and ether of the earth.

SUMMARY

+ An intellectual woman who knows a lot about a variety of things. One who is shrewd and uses her intellectual ability in a career teaching, selling or writing. The receptive left hand extends to the unknown to receive. A communitive person. (Reread the astrological signs Gemini, Libra, and Aquarius.)

- Card in reverse shows that she can be sarcastic, scattered, a gossip, of a dual nature and fickle. One who is very nervous and never sits still, jumps in and out of everything.


## QUEEN OF PENTACLES   66-12-3
*Water & Earth    Astrological signs: **Taurus, Virgo, Capricorn**.*

**ELEMENT/PILLAR** - She is of the Earth element and on the Water pillar. This is a combination of Earth and Water. She draws from the Water pillar and the base of the Tree which is Earth. The Queen of Pentacles (Earth) being on the Water pillar, allows the emotions to become productive. This is like surrounding water with earth so that it is contained or controlled.

**PENTACLE** - The pentagram in the enclosed circle also shows that man can work in a confined space. This is the same as mentioned above.

**ROSE ARBOR** - She has found fulfillment, which is symbolized by the roses overhead that have been growing a long time.

**MOUNTAINS** - Mountains are spiritual attainment.

**GOAT** - The goat on the throne is symbolic of the astrological sign Capricorn.

**FRUIT** - There are pears and apples on the back of the throne to show fruitfulness.

**RABBIT** - A rabbit in the right corner of the card symbolizes that she is fruitful.

**COLOR** - The outer garment is red and represents desires, an under garment is white, for purity. The red shows that the desires and activity are there to use. Green is growth.

**THRONE** - The throne is on the earth and is very big, showing stability and accomplishments.

**GNOMES** - The spirits of the Earth are called Gnomes. They look like a brownie or elf. If you look at the side of her throne, there appears to be one there and one also on the top of her throne.

SUMMARY

+ A woman who has attained growth on the path through developing the will. A strong, practical, business person holding the Pentacle. One who likes good quality. Works well in banking, real-estate and interior design. A woman in control of her finances. (Reread the astrological signs Taurus, Virgo, and Capricorn.)

- Card in reverse shows a person with a poor sense of values. One who is confused in ambitions and is egocentric, fault finding and critical. She is not handling her life in an organized way.


## QUEEN OF WANDS    24-6

*Water & Fire    Astrological signs: **Leo, Aries, Sagittarius***

**ELEMENT/PILLAR** - She is the Fire element and on the Water pillar. This is a combination of Fire and Water. She draws from the Water and Fire pillars. The Queen of Wands (Fire), being on the Water pillar, can energize the emotions, or the Water can put a damper on the ambitions.

**WANDS** - The Wand symbolizes that the energy is there for one to use in working for what one wants.

**LIONS/SUNFLOWERS** - Note the lions on the back of the throne. They are symbolic of the astrological sign Leo as well as the sunflowers and her lion pin. Sunflowers always face the Sun.

**PLANET** - The Sun is the planet that rules the sign of Leo.

**CROWN** – Has a wreath and also ☉ which is the symbol for the Sun.

**FEET** - Her feet are on solid concrete.

**BLACK CAT** - The black cat shows clairvoyance.

**MOUNTAINS** - Mountains in the background show attainment.

**COLOR** - The yellow robe represents being clothed in intelligence.

**HAND** - She rules with power since her wand is in her masculine, positive right hand. A sunflower is in her feminine, negative left hand.

SUMMARY

+ A woman of her word. One in whom you can confide. She is dignified and glamorous. She stands like royalty and walks with pride. She has leadership ability, being aggressive and outgoing, to pursue and accomplish. (Reread the astrological signs of Aries, Leo, and Sagittarius.)

- Card in reverse shows a person with scattered energies, needing a lot of attention. Can be egocentric and rule by fear. Can be selfish with a disregard for others' feelings. Only interested in the self.

# KNIGHTS - VAU

The Knight is about 20-30 years old and can be either male or female. He takes the energy or idea from the Page and puts it into action according to the suit of the card. The Knight is always considered Air, of positive polarity, masculine and aggressive. The Hebrew letter V (Vau) also means Air. They are placed on Sephirah #6 Tiphareth on the Air pillar. Being on the Air pillar places them between the two pillars Fire and Water. They are also thought of as being between the Father (King) and Mother (Queen). When the element Air is added to the other elements, it makes movement. We start with the Knight of Swords. Swords are the Air element. Notice the armor on the Knights. They are prepared for battle or to be aggressive.

Each suit of cards has a horse that is appropriate for it. The Knights and Pages show the seasons when an event can happen. The Wands are the Spring, the Cups are the Summer, the Swords are the Fall and can represent the day and the Pentacles are the Winter. Each of the Knights has the object representing their suit (Sword, Wand, Cup or Pentacle) in the right, masculine, aggressive hand. This shows that there is aggressive power behind what they pursue. Knights can mean the coming or going of a matter as well as what the matter is. This is shown by the object they are holding which represents the suit of cards.

## KNIGHT OF SWORDS 53-8

*Air & Air*  **Fall**  *Astrological signs: **Libra, Aquarius, Gemini.***  Intellectual people.

**ELEMENT/PILLAR/SEPHIRAH** - He is the Air element and on Sephirah #6 and the Air pillar. This is pure Air and relates to the Air pillar.
**DIRECTION** - He comes from the East, so he is someone or something new. The Air signs can do more than one thing. He faces the West, ready to charge at what is there.
**SWORD** - Raised sword means action and that these ideas are being given quick energy.
**HORSE** - He is dressed in armor and on a swift horse, ready for battle. Swords represent the Air signs, which are positive and aggressive. The horse is moving fast to show this also.
**BUTTERFLIES & BIRDS** - Butterflies on the horse represents reincarnation and fast movement. The birds on the horse and the Knights garment also represent fast movement and being able to fly quickly from one place to another.

**COLOR** - Red shows he acts fast. Red wings also on helmet. Wings on armor behind his knee.

**CLOUDS** - Clouds show he is an astrological Air sign. Note that he is suspended in the Air.

SUMMARY

+ No effort is too great, no obstacle too severe. He has the ability to face adversity and overcome strife. This is the coming or going of a matter and can be a man charging into your life. He acts fast with reason. Challenging situations arise and he forges ahead on a new endeavor. He is delivering news or bringing ideas. (Reread the astrological signs Gemini, Libra and Aquarius.)

- When the card is upside down he appears to be leaving the situation, giving in to negative thinking, unwilling to defend issues. A person always ready to start a fight. Bad news. A narrow minded individual with no stability.

## KNIGHT OF PENTACLES  67-4

*Air & Earth*  ***Winter***  *Astrological signs:* ***Capricorn, Taurus, Virgo.***

**ELEMENT/PILLAR** - He is the Earth element on Sephirah #6, which is on the Air pillar. This is a combination of Earth and Air. Down to earth dependable people.

**PENTACLE** - Time to invest in new endeavors.

**HORSE** - Notice that he is on a work horse. This shows that he is prepared to work hard for his money. Notice that the 5 pointed stars on the bridle. It has the same meaning as the pentacle. There can also be one behind his knee. The Earth signs are receptive and the horse being calm shows this.

**LEAVES/FIELDS** - Leaves on the helmet and horse are grape leaves. This is the same as on the King of Pentacles. This shows that there are fields to cultivate.

**DIRECTION** - he is coming from the West, contemplating new endeavors as he faces the east and waits for its arrival.

SUMMARY

+ New endeavors are coming which, when completed, will be profitable. (Reread the astrological signs Taurus, Virgo and Capricorn.)

- Card in reverse shows a loss of money, poor investment or a warning to guard money.

## KNIGHT OF WANDS   25-7

*Air & Fire*   **Spring**   *Astrological signs: **Aries, Leo, Sagittarius**.* Outgoing energetic, friendly people.

**ELEMENT/PILLAR** - He is the Fire element and on Sephirah #6 on the Air pillar. This is a combination of Air and Fire, the Air pillar and the Fire pillar. Fired up ambition. He has an intellectual yellow garment on.

**WAND** - shows being fired up with new endeavors.

**SALAMANDERS** - Salamanders represent reincarnation and the ability to change. They are also the spirits of Fire.

**HORSE** - Notice his theatrical parade horse. He is coming from the East so this is something new. Fire signs are aggressive and the horse in motion shows this.

**FIRE** – He has fire for his plume of his hat, on his elbow and behind his knee.

### SUMMARY

+ Represents a man in early manhood, a generous friend or lover who can be cruel and brutal also. He is an active person who brings messages representing a change in business or residence for the better. Thoughts about a new enterprise (coming from the east) and desire to win. Putting action behind your new venture. This can be a job offer. (Reread the astrological signs Aries, Leo, and Sagittarius.)

- Card reversed can indicate a setback in business or career. Loss of esteem, pessimism in job. Not disciplined in the mental processes. A jealous lover. Discord and frustration. Does not put energy into succeeding or to develop the mind to the inner wisdom or study subjects of higher value for ones inner advancement.

## KNIGHT OF CUPS   39-12-3

*Air & Water* **Summer**   *Astrological signs: **Cancer, Scorpio, Pisces**.* Cups represent sensitive, caring, nurturing people.

**ELEMENT/PILLAR** - He is of the Water element and on Sephirah #6 on the Air pillar. This is a combination of Air and Water. He uses the two pillars of Air and Water. This is shown by the combination of the wings representing the Air and the cup and fish representing the Water.

**WINGS** - The wings on the cap remind us of the god Mercury the bearer of messages, and are involved with the Air sign Gemini. This also shows that he is swift in motion and draws from the Air pillar on the Tree of Life.

**FISH** - on his suit reminds us of the sign Pisces. He is gentle and unhurried, holding a Cup of affection.

**HORSE** - He sits on a passive horse. Water signs are receptive.

**ROBE** - His robe has fish on it, representing the Water sign Pisces.

**STREAM** - Stream is serene and calm showing the emotional, sensitive nature, like Pisces, and tells us that the knowledge of the High Priestess is here.

**DIRECTION** - He faces the East waiting for inspiration.

SUMMARY

+ It represents an invitation coming to you. This brings a gift of love. This card represents happiness in love and romance, merriment and emotional satisfaction. (Reread the astrological signs Cancer, Scorpio and Pisces.)

- Card in reverse shows a disappointment in love. An unhappy event, lack of joy, and unrealistic. Tends to reject the higher love for earthly pleasure. Needs to work toward the Divine Love of life's expression.

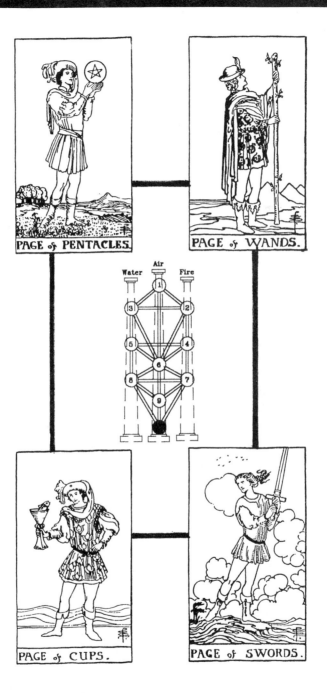

# PAGE - HE'

The Page is a young adolescent, either male or female. Note that they gaze at their object, contemplating and aware of it but not acting upon it. Awareness of what can be. Aware of abilities we have within and contemplating how to use them. The Page can deliver messages relating to the suit of the card. They represent the element Earth as does the second He' and are on Sephirah #10. The Earth Sephirah is also connected to the Air pillar. Notice that they are all standing still, concentrating, planning, and taking their time. The Earth signs have this ability. Since they are of the Earth we start with the Page of Pentacles. Pentacles are Earth. The Pages and the Knights tell us of the seasons and when events happen.

**The Page gets the idea or inspiration and then gives it to the Knight to put into action.**

## PAGE OF PENTACLES   68-5

*Earth & Earth*    ***Winter***    *Astrological signs:* ***Capricorn, Virgo, Taurus.***
Down to earth, dependable, people.

**ELEMENT/PILLAR** - He/she is the Earth element on Sephirah #10 which is Earth. This is pure Earth.
**PENTACLE** - He holds a pentacle lightly. He is calm and concerned about making right choices to deal with material opportunities. He is thinking, "How can I take this pentacle and let it grow into an abundance?" He is using both hands representing the positive and receptive energy combined.
**MOUNTAINS** - Mountains of attainment are in the background.
**FLOWERS** - Flowers in the foreground show what has been developed. He is aware of goals at hand and in the future.
**COLOR** - Garment of earth colors shows a practical person.
**DIRECTION** - He is looking to the East for inspiration to deal with material substances.

### SUMMARY
+ This is one of the lucky cards involving money. This is a small sum of money. The Ace of Pentacles is a large sum of money. Waiting for a message to do with a small amount of money or raise. (Reread the astrological signs Taurus, Virgo and Capricorn.)

- Card in reverse can show that he is obsessed with desires for material possessions. Waste and loss can result. Exaggerated materialism.

## PAGE OF WANDS 26-8

*Earth & Fire   Spring   Astrological signs: **Aries, Leo, Sagittarius***. He is outgoing, energetic, and friendly.

**ELEMENT/PILLAR** - He/she is the Fire element on Sephirah #10 which is Earth. This is a combination of Fire and Earth. This is the Earth and Fire pillar. He takes measure of his power. He uses both hands representing the blending of the positive and receptive.

**MOUNTAINS** - Mountains in the background means that there is attainment. He has ambition internally but has not yet used it.

**SALAMANDER** - Salamanders on the robe show changes of self as well as reincarnation and the spirits for Fire.

**WAND** - He looks and inspects his wand. Thoughts of a new enterprise come to him but no action yet.

**FLAMES** – Flames on his hat and boots shows he is the Fire element.

**COLOR** - Yellow garment means he uses his intellect.

SUMMARY
+ Check out all details of thoughts or messages. News comes about a proposition, which could materialize, into a big enterprise. (Reread the astrological signs Aries, Leo and Sagittarius.)

- Card in reverse shows bad news, still check for deception. Ideas do not materialize.

## PAGE OF CUPS 40-4

*Earth & Water   **Summer**   Astrological signs: **Cancer, Scorpio, Pisces***. Sensitive, caring, nurturing people.

**ELEMENT/PILLAR** - He/she is the Water element on Sephirah #10 which is Earth. This is a combination of Water and Earth. It uses the pillars Earth and Water.

**LOTUS** - Lotus or water lilies decorate a garment of red and blue. Lotus is a self-renewing plant, which contains both male and female elements.

**COLOR** - Red is desires and blue emotions, which is Fire and Water. The conscious and the subconscious mind have made him or her aware of eternal life. He has yellow boots showing he walks with intelligence.

**FISH** - A fish in the cup is a symbol of divine messages of all kinds to do with emotions.

**WATER** - The water is not calm and peaceful but wavy, showing an upset. Water in the background is sensitivity to emotional situations.

**BRAID** – Braid around his left shoulder should be gold and shows achievement.

**DIRECTION** - He stands on solid ground. He is not looking to the East. He/she is looking at what is already in the Cup, thinking, "What am I going to do with this?" Notice he is only using his right masculine hand. Being a Water element he needs strong structure.

SUMMARY

+ Fully aware and appreciative of what God has given him. Has love and compassion. A Cancer with some Pisces influence makes him psychic and gives intuition. (Reread the astrological signs Cancer, Scorpio, and Pisces.)

- Card in reverse shows that he only sees the difficulty and obstacles in the life and wallows in it. Confusion and disorder. Unhappy messages to do with emotional aspects of life.


## PAGE OF SWORDS 54-9

*Earth & Air    Fall    Astrological signs: **Libra, Aquarius, Gemini.*** Swords represent intellectual people.

**ELEMENT/PILLAR** - He/she is the Air element on Sephirah #10 which is Earth. This is a combination of Air and Earth. The Earth and Air pillars are used. He/she has a practical mind. He holds the sword with both hands + & -
**COLOR** - Has yellow pants and shirt showing intelligence. Red shoes show that he walks with quickness. Ideas and messages are acted upon. He has no hat showing that he wants his intellectual head open.
**BIRDS** – There are 10 birds representing the 10 Sephiroth.
**CLOUDS** - Clouds represent the Air element. Notice that he is in the air.
**SWORD** - His sword is up, showing he is working on a decision.

SUMMARY

+ His practical mind attains goals. Witty, intelligent and eloquent. News demands your attention. Always talking, communicating and spreading the word. (Reread the astrological signs Libra, Aquarius and Gemini.)

- Card in reverse shows too much restlessness of the mind gives scattered thoughts. Information is all mixed up, unsettled.

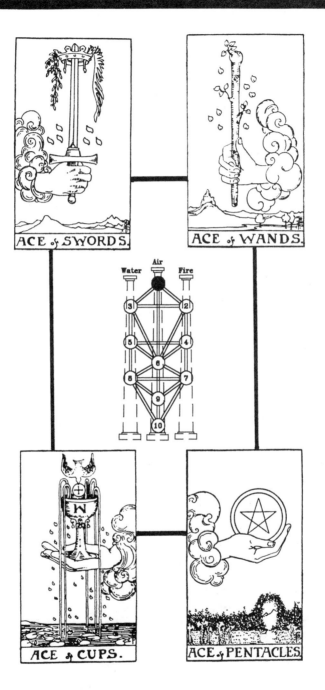

There are 10 Sephiroth on the Tree of Life. Each of the cards 1-10 will be placed on the Sephirah that corresponds to the same number. To refresh your mind about the meaning of each number, reread the section on numbers.

## ACES (#1) are placed in Sephirah #1 KETHER on the Air Pillar
### FROM SPIRIT
### Kether is Divine Light & The Crown
#### Admirable or Hidden Intelligence

Reread #1 and Sephirah #1.

Remember that when the Fool came into this incarnation, all he had in his bag was a Wand, Cup, Sword and Pentacle. He had just come from Sephirah #1 (Kether). In Kether, all sources of energy exist. Kether has three of the four elements in its makeup. They are Wands which is Fire, Cups which is Water and Sword which is Air. The Earth which is matter is created when these three elements are blended together. The Air is the God force of intelligence. Kether is on the intellectual Air pillar. This shows that intelligence or studies are very important, because they allow the consciousness to open up and tune in to Kether.

The Fool looks up to this higher power and knows he has the ability to tap into those resources. He knows that, through thinking or meditating, he can have contact with the God force above. This gives him sensitivity, perception and ambition to be able to acquire what he needs. So, looking up to Kether reminds him of this and, in Sephirah #2 (Chokmah), he finds out how he can use it.

The four suits of the cards each have an Ace. **The Aces are the seeds that grow the pillars.** Each suit of cards brings with it an element. When the element is placed on Kether and the Air pillar is blended with it, it gives us an understanding as to how each element can react when intermingled with the four worlds. It is also important, for interpretation, to use the planet that goes with the Sephiroth when blending energy. I will walk you through the Aces to show how this happens.

Kether, therefore, consists of the three elements Air, Fire and Water. The hand of God in each of the Aces reminds us of our connection to Kether or the supreme being. The hand of God says it's a sure thing. The Aces tell the seasons.

Kether also starts the first triangle on the Tree called the Supernal Triangle. There are three triangles on the Tree but this one is the highest in spiritual attainment. Sephirah #1 (Kether is on the Air pillar), Sephirah #2 (Chokmah and Uranus is on the Fire pillar), and Sephirah #3 (Binah and Saturn is on the Water pillar) giving us the Yod, He', Vau to complete the triangle.

### The Air Pillar

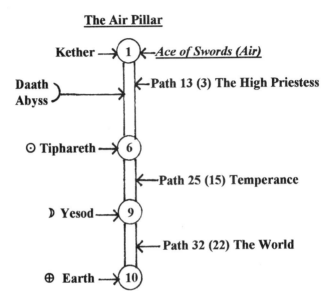

### Ace of Swords

**Wirling energy up and down the Air pillar**

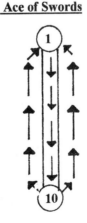

# ACE OF SWORDS 55-10-1
*Air & Air - Fall*

**ELEMENT/WORLD/SEPHIRAH** - The Ace of Swords is of the Air element and is on the Air pillar, meaning pure Air with nothing added. It is the whirlwind that propelled us and the Fool here. It is the intelligence that we connect to. There is nothing to blend here except what is on the Air pillar. Air represents also the World of Yetzirah. It is pure energy. The Ace of swords is on Sephirah #1 (Kether.)

**PILLAR** - The Ace of Swords is the seed for the Air pillar. This pillar, which these four cards are on, expresses that everything connected to this pillar is available to each of the Aces. Air creates movement.

The High Priestess is on the Air pillar and path #13 (3) with the planet the Moon and her knowledge. This tells us to develop our perception and understand the mysteries of life, to be able to see that life is full of positive and negative circumstances and learn how to balance them.

Sephirah #6 Tiphareth on the Air pillar brings with it the planet the Sun. Work with the concept of astrology and understand one's Sun sign. Why did the soul want to be incarnated into this life?

Temperance, and the astrological sign Sagittarius, are on path #25 (15) on the Air pillar, which shows us that everything in moderation is good. that everything is a part of the whole.

Sephirah # 9 on the Air pillar has Yesod, which holds the planet the Moon. We need to put our emotions and perception behind everything that we want. Creating the energy for this will help it to become. After all, this pillar is very powerful since it relates to the Kundalini and the chakras.

The final path on this Air pillar is #32 (22) which holds The World and Saturn. Saturn puts everything into a state of matter and brings stability. It is the root of the tree. This complete Air pillar connects with Sephirah #10 (Malkuth), which is the Earth and matter. Number 10 reduces to 1 which tells us that what is in Kether, is also in Malkuth. As above, so below. Kether is the Macroprosophus and Malkuth is the Microprosophus. This pillar allows one to zip straight up and down. This path also goes over a spot in the tree called Daath, a place where all knowledge is gathered, and the Abyss, a place to let go of what is not needed. Daath and the Abyss are explained on page 34.

For a deeper understanding of the above, you can reread the cards The High Priestess, Temperance and The World in the Major Arcana.

**HAND/SWORD** - The hand of God holds an upraised sword. The sword is the symbol for the Air sign and intelligence. This shows the power of Air.

**CLOUD** - The cloud means it is from spirit.

**DIRECTION** - It is coming from the west. When something is coming from the West, you already have it. It is already in motion. This is like the whirling sword at the Garden of Eden which symbolizes that knowledge brings us back.

**CROWN/BRANCHES** - The Golden Crown studded with rubies is to honor those who use their intellectual powers. The crown is shown in the following cards and reminds us that we are reaching for that achievement, The Crown of Life. When we have completed this life and hopefully the 9 lessons that lead to spirit, we will receive the Crown. The Crown will always remind us of Kether.

The palm and olive branches show us of the suffering and celebration that can be achieved and remind us that Christ's resurrection was a victory over death and provides all of his followers with the Crown of Life. "Fear none of those things which thou shalt suffer: behold, the devil shall cast *some* of you into prison, that ye may be tried; and ye shall have tribulation 10 days (the lessons of the 10 Sephiroth). Be thou faithful unto death, and I will give thee a Crown of Life." Revelation 2:10. The palm branches were strewn on the ground for Christ on Palm Sunday. It is also another Messianic symbol of prophecy. Jeremiah said, "Behold, the days come, saith the Lord, that I will raise unto David, a righteous Branch, and a King shall reign and prosper, and shall execute judgement and justice in the earth." Jeremiah 23:5. "Ye shall receive a crown of glory that fadeth not away." 1 Peter 5:4. The image of the crown and the branches symbolize this prophecy.

**YODS** - The 6 yods tell us of the Sephirah #6 Tiphareth which is on the Air pillar and reminds us of our connection with the Christ center.

**MOUNTAINS** - The mountains show that we can attain our spiritual goals.

SUMMARY
+ When this card shows up, it tells us that the mind is the greatest tool. Coming from the West, it is something that has been already worked on. It shows success in completing a course or graduation or just the awakening to the connection above. It can also show that people look to you for ideas. You are equipped to explore any project or concept.

- When the card is upside down, it is described in a negative way. Each card has a positive and negative ability. In the negative, it can be that one does not use the intellectual connection that comes from above. Also one may have dropped out of school. They are not using the abilities of the intellect and need to take more courses.

## The Fire Pillar

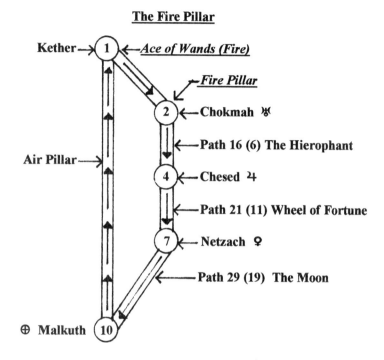

**ACE OF WANDS 27-9**

*Air & Fire- Spring*

**ELEMENT/WORLD/SEPHIRAH** - Air and Fire combined reminds one of the World of Atziluth. Here we are combining the energy of Air-Kether with Fire. The Ace of Wands is on Sephirah #1 (Kether.)

**PILLAR** - The Ace of Wands is able to use everything on the Air pillar since Kether is on that pillar. The Ace of Wands is the seed for the Fire pillar. The energy comes from Kether and creates the Fire pillar. Fire is what is needed to start propulsion. Here we are combining the Ace of Wands, Fire with the Air pillar. Everything mentioned above about this pillar is now energized with the Fire. When Fire and Air are combined, this is powerful. They are both masculine, outgoing elements.

The entire Fire pillar comes through this card. There is Sephirah #2 (Chokmah and the planet of cosmic knowledge, Uranus), Sephirah #4 (Chesed and the philosophical planet Jupiter) and Sephirah #7 (Netzach and the love planet Venus). On path #16 is The Hierophant. On path #21 (11) is the Wheel of Fortune and on path #29 (19) is The Moon. At the end of the Fire pillar and path #29 (19), it connects to Sephirah #10 (Malkuth). This connection allows the energy to run up the Air pillar and to rejoin Kether.

**HAND/WAND/CLOUD** - This is represented by the hand of God holding a living Wand. The cloud shows that it comes from Spirit. Being a Wand tells us that there is a new endeavor coming. Of course, it is if one applies the Fire energy. The Wands being Fire shows it has to be applied. The hand shows that one is given this ability.

**YODS** - Some leaves are falling, forming Yods, which is the spark of inspiration and creation (Kether). There are 8 loose leaves representing Sephiroth #8 Hod, which is the planet Mercury. This tells you that the mind and our breathing has to be applied here. If you count all of the leaves, there are 18. 18 reduces to #9 which tells us the 9 lessons are involved.

**DIRECTION** - It comes from the East, therefore it is new.

**RIVER** - There is a river in this card which says that the wisdom of the High Priestess is flowing through. There is also a castle showing the accomplishments when this energy is applied.

SUMMARY
+ A new enterprise or job is presented to you. Start a new venture.

- Card in reverse shows that what you are waiting for is delayed. Perhaps one has to work harder.

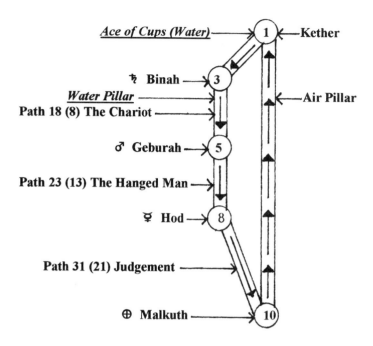

## ACE OF CUPS 41-5
*Air & Water-**Summer***

**ELEMENT/WORLD/SEPHIRAH** - The Ace of Cups is of the Water element and reminds one of the World of Briah. This is the unfolding of the divine consciousness in the Water element. It is the maternal force. The Ace of Cups is on Sephirah #1 (Kether).

**PILLAR** - The Ace of Cups is Water and on Sephirah #1 (Kether). It can use everything on the Air pillar, since Kether is on that pillar. The Ace of Cups is the seed for the Water pillar. The energy propels from Kether and creates the Water pillar. Now we have the Sephirah #3 (Binah with Saturn), Sephirah #5 (Geburah with Mars) and Sephirah #8 (Hod with Mercury). The paths and Tarot cards that are involved are path #18 (8) The Chariot, path #23 (13) The Hanged Man, path #31 (21) Judgement. This last path connects to Malkuth (Earth) and allows one to go up the Air pillar again and return to Kether. It is the whirlwind of energy.

**HAND/CUP** - The hand of God holds forth a Cup. It comes from the East. Therefore, there is a new emotional experience.

**DOVE** - The white dove is a symbol of peace, love, truth and the Holy Spirit. It drops the seal of Jehovah (communion wafer) into the Cup.

**WATER/LILY** - 5 streams of water represent the 5 senses overflowing into the lotus or lily pond. A water lily is the only plant that uses all of the elements. It has its roots in the Earth, its stem in Water, its blossom in the Air and draws in the Sun for the Fire. We create an unending supply of water. The 5 streams also represent the #5 which includes the name for God, Yod He' Vau He' and Shin, the Holy Spirit. The drops of water are in the form of yods and there are 26 drops. 26 reduces to 8 the number for infinity. The word GOD in numbers is 7,6,4 =17=8

**W** - The letter W can refer to the Hebrew mother letter for Shin representing the element Fire and the Holy Spirit. Turn it upside down and you have an M, which is the Hebrew mother letter Mem and is the Water element.

SUMMARY

+ Your cup runneth over. Something you want with all of your emotions is being given to you. Everyone wants something different. It can be a child, job, love, home, etc. It is said that this card can say that the love of your life is coming. You are offered all pleasures of the world, in abundance.

- A reversed card can show an over indulgence, too much pleasure seeking. A love relationship falters.

### The Earth Pillar (Sephirah #10)

Kether / 1 \ *Ace of Pentacles (Earth)*

Air Pillar

Water Pillar                    Fire Pillar

Hod ☿ (8)          (7) Netzach ♀

Malkuth ⊕ \ 10 / *Earth*

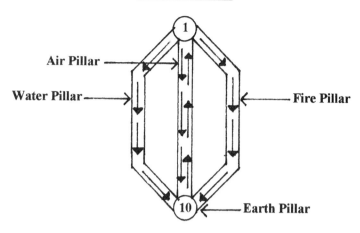

**Whirling Energy**

Air Pillar

Water Pillar

Fire Pillar

Earth Pillar

## ACE OF PENTACLES  69-6
*Air & Earth - **Winter***

**ELEMENT/WORLD/SEPHIRAH** - The Ace of Pentacles is of the Earth element and reminds one of the World of Assiah.  The Earth is Sephirah #10 (Malkuth).  The pentacle is a magical symbol representing the Earth element.  It is made up of a double circle and a pentagram.  The double circle shows the confined space that the element Earth works in.   The upright pentagram stands for the #5 and the Hebrew letters for God, Yod He' Vau He' plus Shin (the Holy Spirit).  The pentagram is all the elements: Air, Fire, Water, Earth and Shin (Holy Spirit).  It also represents Man.  The Ace of Pentacles is on Sephirah #1 (Kether).

Being the last element, it shows that when you have the elements. Air, Fire, and Water, you automatically have matter, which is Earth.  Notice that the three pillars all connected to Malkuth which is Sephirah #10 and represents the Earth element.  There is no pillar for Earth, but it does connect to the Air pillar as well as the Fire and Water pillars.

**HAND/PENTACLE** - The hand of God holds a pentacle.   The hand is coming  from the West saying that you already have this.
**LILIES/ROSES** - The lilies represent purified desires.  The roses represent an energetic drive.  It takes a lot of work and patience to form and grow an arbor.  It shows accomplishment.

**MOUNTAINS** - There are 2 mountains on the other side of the arbor which show that once you have done the work there is spiritual attainment.

<u>SUMMARY</u>
+ Fortune, honor and fame. You have all the talents necessary to create a life of material success. There is a raise of pay or large amount of money coming to you.

- The card in reverse shows that there is too much pursuit of worldly goods. One is hoarding or did not get the money they thought they were entitled to. More is going out than is coming in.

## Attention:
"The Pattern of the Trestleboard" on page 94 explains very well the Ace of Pentacles. Number 4 says; From the exhaustless riches of its limitless **SUBSTANCE**, I draw all things needful both spiritual and material.

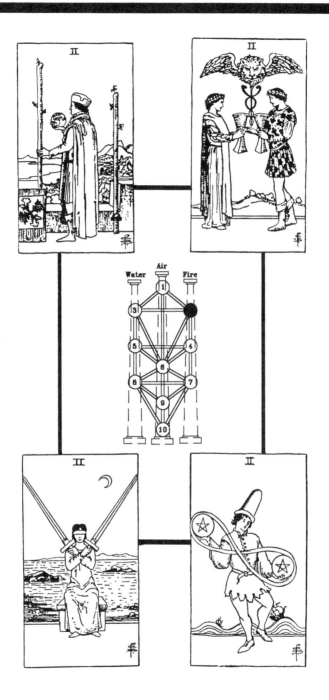

# TWOS are placed in Sephirah #2 CHOKMAH on the Fire Pillar
## WISDOM
### Illuminating Intelligence

Reread #2 and Sephirah #2.

In #2 balance is required or the polarity of aggressive/positive and receptive/negative. The Tree is always balanced with this polarity. Sephirah #2, which is on the positive Fire pillar, has to balance with Sephirah #3 on the receptive/negative Water pillar. This is like waxing and waning, the building up and the tearing down, pushing out and pulling in. There is always an opposite force involved in all things. We need this in order to continue. Positive can be good or bad when used in excess. Negative/receptive can be bad, but it is good when the energy is used to create a needed change.

These two energies can be used in both ways. I will use Sephiroth #2 and #3 for an example. In Sephirah #2 Chokmah, the planet Uranus exists. Uranus is the planet that takes us into the future. It brings about change through new concepts and ideas. It is the planet that deals with cosmic understanding. It is intuition that tells us that we are still connected to the higher power. It is a planet of rebellion when one wants change. This is like when the Fool wanted to leave heaven and come to earth as well as the lightening bolt on The Tower card. To like to do something different or make a change is typical of Uranus.

In Sephirah #3 Binah the planet Saturn exists. The only planet that Saturn will bow down to is Uranus. Saturn realizes that without Uranus we would still be in the dark ages. Saturn is father time and the disciplinarian. Everything has to be stabilized and proven with Saturn. It goes by the facts and what has happened in the past. Uranus brings new concepts and hands them to Saturn. Saturn then tests them and proves them out to see if they are worth keeping and developing. As these two planets work together, we progress into the future. Everything that Uranus stands for would be for naught, if Saturn did not work in cooperation with it. Saturn gives us our karma/responsibility for this lifetime. Through analyzing the planet Saturn in one's horoscope, it can be seen why the Soul chose to be incarnated into this life.

See how the cards #2 and #3 respond to each other.

The Fire Pillar was created by the seed of the Ace of Wands in Kether. The twos are placed on Sephirah #2 (Chokmah) and the Fire pillar. Since the twos are on the Fire pillar, we will start with the Wands which is Fire also. The twos also tell the seasons.

## TWO OF WANDS 28-1
*Fire & Fire* **Spring**

**ELEMENT/PILLAR/SEPHIRAH** - The Wands are the Fire element and the pillar is Fire, so this is pure Fire energy. The Two of Wands is placed in Sephirah #2 (Chokmah) with the planet Uranus.

**WAND** - The Wands have to do with endeavors. One Wand is "secured" meaning it is finished. It is behind him. This was the #1 as shown in the Ace. One Wand he holds onto by his left, feminine, emotional hand. This shows he is still emotionally attached to it. It is still active.
**HAND** - A man holds the world in his right, masculine hand, showing that he can achieve by hard work.
**ROBE** - The purple robe and red hat means that he activates desires in order to be productive.
**WATER** - He looks over Water, which shows he is using his subconscious powers. Water also reminds us of the power of the High Priestess.
**GARDEN** - The garden shows that which has been started and accomplished.
**LILIES/ROSES** - The crossed lilies and roses show physical desire and that the spiritual nature is blended.

SUMMARY
+ There are many opportunities. Take time to consider all of them. One can be looking into the future contemplating a new enterprise or work. They have finished and secured what they were doing and can now move on.

- The card in reverse shows that it is difficult to make a decision. The time is not quite right. That which is behind may not be completed.

## TWO OF CUPS 42-6
*Fire & Water* **Summer**

**ELEMENT/PILLAR/SEPHIRAH** - Since all the twos are on the Sephirah #2 (Chokmah, Uranus and the Fire pillar), we blend the energy of the card with the pillar. This is the blending of the Fire and the Water (Cup) elements. There is a need for a balance here. The Two of Wands did not show this need because it was pure Fire. Because of the polarity here, it is calling for cooperation, an exchange or sharing. A blending of the two elements or two ideas that come from each other. This is a positive and negative energy; there will be friction that will produce action.

**PEOPLE/COLOR** - Fire is initiating and Water is emotions. Man and woman exchange Cups. The male and female, positive and negative, is being exchanged. The law of give and take. The Cups show this is an emotional experience. The woman is dressed in white with blue over it. This is symbolic of purity and emotions or the subconscious. She has red shoes which shows that she walks with desire and energy. The man's costume is yellow, showing he has an intellectual nature. They each have something different to offer each other. The shamrocks on the man's clothing are the sign of the trinity. St. Patrick was asked about the mystery of the Trinity. He leaned down and picked up a little three-leafed shamrock and said, "The Trinity is like this flower. This flower has three petals, and the three petals form the shamrock. So God consists of three persons, and yet is one God."

**HOUSE** - There is a house and land in the background showing what they can have together. There is an exchange going on here.

**LION** - There is a winged lion above the caduceus symbolizing will power and higher knowledge.

SUMMARY

+ What one has can be shared with another. The person can be one of these people and have a friendly, cooperative nature and like to help others. An exchange of contracts, vows and agreements. A nicely blended relationship or an engagement. Two people coming to an agreement. If one goes to the doctor, help is now available.

- In the negative this can be a pulling apart through not cooperating and misunderstanding. It is not quite time to make the agreement.


## TWO OF SWORDS  56-11
*Fire & Air* **Fall**

**ELEMENT/PILLAR/SEPHIRAH** - The Two of Swords is the Air element and it is on Sephirah #2 (Chokmah, Uranus and the Fire pillar). This is a blending of the Fire with the Air. Both energies are positive in nature and benefit each. The Air works like bellows to the Fire.

**PERSON** - Dressed in white (gray) for purity or wisdom. The hair is black and bound by a white band of wisdom which is perfect balance. Her eyes are covered so she has to depend on her intuition to make the decision.

**MOON/WATER** - The Moon stands for the subconscious and the water is behind her. She has placed her emotions behind her. The water also is a remembrance of the wisdom of The High Priestess, and her ability to balance the positive and negative in life. The water is choppy, standing for stimulated emotions.

**ROCKS** - The rocks show stability.

**SEAT** - She is sitting on a cubic seat of concrete. This seat has dimension involved with it showing the #4 or the square. This is stability for her. This symbolizes a firm foundation for her convictions.

**SWORDS** - The Swords are up and her arms are crossed. This shows that the masculine and feminine are interchanged. She is balancing the energy as she makes her decision. The Swords still up shows that it is not finished.

SUMMARY

+ You have your feet on solid ground and have placed your emotions behind you, but under control. You are using your intellect (Swords) and perception to make the decision. The Swords still in an upright position show it is still ongoing. Self control is necessary. Do not base decisions on appearances but use your logical (Saturn) and psychic (Uranus) powers.

- The card in reverse shows the person is unable to choose wisely because they are more emotionally involved with the problem.

## TW0 OF PENTACLES 70-7
*Fire & Earth **Winter***

**ELEMENT/PILLAR/SEPHIRAH** - The Two of Pentacles is the Earth element. It is on Sephirah #2 (Chokmah, Uranus and the Fire pillar). This is a blending of Fire and Earth.

**INFINITY** - A clever juggler of money. It is the shape of an 8 which, when placed on its side, is infinity. This is alteration in all matters. The activity needs to be grounded. Reread about the #8. When one side is full it is time to put it to use. He does not have both feet on the ground. However, the ground is solid.

**COLOR** - A desire for balance and continuous activity is shown by the red. There is an ongoing process.

**SHIP** - Ships stand for commerce of the ocean. It also shows that your ship is on choppy water. It goes up and down. There are two ships.

**GARMENT** - The outer garment is leather, showing a lasting, earthly nature. It is placed over red clothing, which shows desires and energy underneath.

**SHOES** - The green shoes show growth.

<u>SUMMARY</u>

+ & - One needs to balance their desires before spending money. Trying to be practical. Indecision on how to approach the matter. Robbing Peter to pay Paul. Cannot handle money or balance the checkbook.

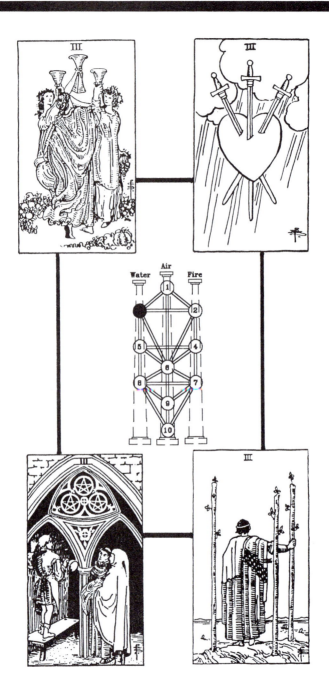

## THREES are placed in Sephirah #3 BINAH on the Water Pillar
## UNDERSTANDING
### Sanctifying Intelligence

Reread #3 and Sephirah #3.

Number 1 starts, #2 reflects, #3 takes form. This Sephirah is the energy from which all life emerges. The threes go on the Water pillar in Sephirah #3 (Binah and Saturn). Binah is the great mother. The threes also stand for seasons. Now that we have a number higher than 2, it will be of interest to you to notice how the objects are laid out in the cards. They will have a special meaning because of this. Since the threes form the triangle (trinity), you can draw a line from one of the objects to the other two and see the triangle.

## THREE OF CUPS 43-7
*Water & Water* **Summer**

**ELEMENT/PILLAR/SEPHIRAH** - The Three of Cups is the Water element. It is on Sephirah #3 on the Water pillar. Pure Water energy. The Water pillar and Sephirah #3, which has Binah and the planet Saturn on it, says that, when disciplines and emotions are used, it brings completion.

**MAIDENS** - A celebration for your accomplishments. Three maidens hold up Cups as in giving a toast. These three maidens are said to be the three graces: Euphrosyne, Aglaea, Thalia. They preside over the joys of life, banquets and dance.
**FRUIT** - The bounty and fruitfulness lies on the ground.
**CUPS** - This is 1+1+1=3 These three Cups are like the three Sephiroth that form the triangle. The celebration of the completion of the Supernal Triangle.

SUMMARY
+ What you started in The Two of Wands has now brought success.

- The card in reverse shows over indulgence, too much partying and not accomplishing your goals.

## THREE OF SWORDS  57-12-3
*Water & Air   Fall*

**ELEMENT/PILLAR/SEPHIRAH** - The Three of Swords is the Air element. It is on Sephirah #3 Binah on the Water pillar. This is the blending of Water and Air.

**SWORDS/HEART** - Three Swords pierce the heart. Notice that the Swords are pointing down. This means that it is over.

**CLOUDS** - Storm clouds and rain in the background show unhappiness and sorrow.

**NUMBER** - 1+1+1=3. These are the three Sephiroth that form the Supernal Triangle.

SUMMARY
+ & - Raise your consciousness to the heart chakra. Speak and think from the heart and it will avoid conflict. Notice that if you turn the card upside down, the swords are pointing up, showing that it can still be worked on. Swords (words) come from the heart. This is one card when in reverse is better.

+ & - Your intellect (Air) and emotions (Water) are doing battle. Use your intelligence to conquer the emotions. You are in an unhappy state and are allowing your mind to stay this way, preventing you from moving ahead. What you heard broke your heart. Learn to talk about it. Maintain a logical approach to emotional situations. There can be a separation and disappointment in love relationships. An argument with a loved one.

## THREE OF PENTACLES  71-8
*Water & Earth   **Winter***

**ELEMENT/PILLAR/SEPHIRAH** - The Three of Pentacles is the Earth element. It is on Sephirah #3 Binah and the Water pillar. This is a blending of Water and Earth. When emotions and patience are applied to what one does, it can be accomplished.

**PERSON** -A laborer working with his talents. Two people ask his advice as they admire his abilities. This shows opportunity in employment and business. The three people also represent the three states of consciousness.

**PENTACLES** - The three pentacles at the top of the arch form the Supernal Triangle on the Air pillar. This shows that one can earn not only money from using his talent but there is also spiritual advancement. Notice the cross in the circle below the pentacles and in the rose below.

**NUMBER** - 1+1+1=3. This is the three Sephiroth that form the Supernal Triangle.

SUMMARY
+ Apply yourself diligently and develop your skills and you will obtain employment which will ensure your financial security. Be dependable, steady and reliable. Take your position as man in the pentacle standing upright.

- The card in reverse shows that you are lazy and do not use your talents the way you could. You accomplish little.

## THREE OF WANDS   29-11
*Water & Fire* **Spring**

**ELEMENT/PILLAR/SEPHIRAH** - The Three of Wands is the Fire element. It is on Sephirah #3 Binah on the Water pillar. This is a blending of Water and Fire, the stirring of activity by applying emotions to the work.

**WANDS** - He is high up. Three Wands are secured in the ground. This shows what has already been accomplished. He holds one as he looks into the future across the water (emotions) to mountains (attainment). The other two are behind him.
**WATER** - He looks like he is in a dilemma and needs to use his subconscious (water) to reach new goals or to figure out what his new goals are. Notice that the water is yellow like the Dead Sea. The boat is going backwards.
**COLOR** - He is dressed in red (desire and energy) with a green cloak over his left shoulder (growth). The left side is your intuitive side. The right arm is blue (emotions) and the right side is the aggressive, masculine side. He has integrated and exchanged these two. There is a yellow band on his head showing thoughts are intellectual.
**NUMBER** - A number can be broken down into many different combinations. The cards will show these combinations. This card shows that 3 can be made out of a 1 and a 2. See how the three Wands are separated. Divine will (1) or light with reflection or wisdom (2) brings completeness. Read about #3.

SUMMARY
+ You have accomplished a lot and secured what you have but are still emotionally tied to one of your projects. Notice the blue sleeve on the right arm showing this attachment. Time to look to future achievements.
- The card in reverse shows that you need to work harder, to secure what you have, before you tackle more.

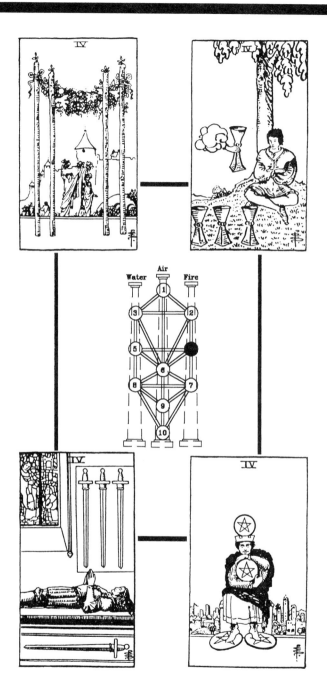

# FOURS are placed in Sephirah #4 CHESED on the Fire Pillar
## MERCY
### Cohesive or Receptive Intelligence

Chesed is interesting as it begins the second triangle and also the square. Sephirah #4 (Chesed and Jupiter on the Fire pillar), Sephirah #5 (Geburah and Mars on the Water pillar) and Sephirah #6 (Tiphareth and Sun on the Air pillar), form the Ethical Triangle. We have the Fire, Water and Air that we need to form the triangle. The Yod, He' Vau.

Chesed, being part of the square which is formed by Sephiroth 4, 5, 7, 8 with Sephirah #6 in the middle, involves the solar system. Number 4 is the expansive, benevolent, philosophical Jupiter; #5 is the aggressive, energetic Mars; #7 is the benevolent, loving Venus; #8 is the intellectual Mercury. Number 6 is the Sun/Son Christ center that keeps the gravitation of all the planets in line. In the horoscope for an individual's day of birth, these planets will tell us what each person is working on to fulfill their karma so that their Soul may evolve. They tell why their Soul decided to be incarnated into this life.

Law, system, order and form. Four is the square and the equal armed cross. The earth was formed on the 4th day. Number 2 is the attraction of ions and #3 led to interaction. Now under #4 the inevitable concentration of energies occurs and is the formation and production of an orderly system. Fours show that you should be able to work spiritually on your life. It is a turning point. It teaches spiritual mercy. The fours are in Sephirah #4 (Chesed) on the Fire pillar. The planet Jupiter is involved here. It is a planet of expansion and increase. We have just finished closing up the Supernal Triangle in #3. In order to continue, we have to add a 1. This starts a new momentum and forms the square which consists of a double triangle. (Reread #4 in numbers.)

You can draw a square from object to object on each of the cards. Reread #4 and Sephirah #4.

## FOUR OF WANDS  30-3
*Fire & Fire*  **Spring**


**ELEMENT/PILLAR/SEPHIRAH** - The Four of Wands is the Fire element. It is on Sephirah #4, Chesed and the Fire pillar. This is pure Fire.

**WANDS** - 4 secured Wands show fulfillment. Two of the Wands have the garland secured to them, two do not. This shows that they are nearly finished but not completely. Note that the growth is on the top of the Wand and not all over the Wands, as previous cards. Now that he has material success he can get on with spiritual growth.

**COLOR** - Red roof on the towers means the desires are being realized. Yellow background shows that the intellect is being applied.

**FIGURES** - Two figures are celebrating.

**NUMBER** - Note the Wands are 2+2=4. The balance of the 2 elements one active and one passive, duplication. It is to remain as it is, a stable form of creation. Two are completed and two are being worked on.

SUMMARY

\+ Rich rewards and material comforts shown by the houses, bounty and people. You have the abundance and success that life has to offer because of the hard work and obstacles that you surmounted. Remember that the squares in astrology are stumbling blocks in the beginning and become building blocks once overcome. Your fondest hopes and dreams are being fulfilled. Completed negotiations. Nothing is accomplished unless we have squares in our chart. They irritate us until we do something about them.

\- The card in the reverse shows a delay in realizing the above. Perhaps success makes you lazy. More effort is needed to complete goals.


## FOUR OF CUPS  44-8
*Fire & Water*  **Summer**


**ELEMENT/PILLAR/SEPHIRAH** - The Four of Cups is the Water element. It is on Sephirah #4 (Chesed on the Fire pillar). This is a combination of Fire and Water.

**FIGURE** - Figure seated quietly--yoga position--meditating. He sees and knows from past experiences what to expect. This is symbolized by the 3 Cups in front of him. Does he want to take another chance?

**HAND** - he seems unaware of the 4th Cup being offered by the hand of God (gray cloud is hidden wisdom.)

**DIRECTION** - It is coming from the West showing that it is already in the making.

**COLOR** - His clothing is red for desire and activity, blue for emotions and intuition and green for growth. How can I accomplish more? He meditates and a new opportunity comes through. He will now have to work hard to accomplish the 4th.

**NUMBER** - Note the cups are 1+3=4 A new cycle of creation. 4 appears when a new impulse (1) is added to the already existing 3.

SUMMARY

+ You have the time to re-evaluate your present circumstances that relate to emotional fulfillment. Your emotional situation makes you think, "Is this all there is?" Your intuitive side (Cups) shows you there is more if you want to accept it. You must find the answer within yourself (intuitive work and completion).

- The card in reverse shows that you may be missing your intuitive link. The opportunity to develop is at hand. You are ignoring it. Work on becoming aware of what you cannot see. Tune into your inner self. Actions first inspired on the inner plane.

## FOUR OF SWORDS  58-13-4
*Fire & Air* **Fall**

**ELEMENT/PILLAR/SEPHIRAH** - The Four of Swords is the element Air. It is on Sephirah #4 Chesed on the Fire pillar. This is a combination of Fire and Air.

**FIGURE** - The figure rests. Rest is earned. Note position of fingers.

**SWORDS** - The Swords are put away. 3 are hung up with points down (completed). One Sword is under him. He is waiting for inspiration.

**WINDOW** - The window shows a man kneeling before a woman. Man (conscious mind) is still a slave to subconscious mind (female).

**NUMBER** - The positions of the Swords say that this is a 3+1=4, the same as the Four of Cups.

SUMMARY

+ By using his intellectual abilities, he has reached a point of fulfillment and is resting. He dreams, and his intellectual mind asks his subconscious what is next. One needs peace and quiet to gather strength. The conclusions your subconscious comes up with will affect your future goals. Conflicts have ended.

- Can be convalescing. You need peace and quiet to gather your strength before starting something new.

## FOUR OF PENTACLES  72-9
*Fire & Earth*   ***Winter***

**ELEMENT/PILLAR/SEPHIRAH** - The Four of Pentacles is the Earth element. It is on Sephirah #4 (Chesed on the Fire pillar). This is a combination of Fire and Earth.

**FIGURE** - A figure sitting on a concrete seat. All parts of his body have pentacles touching them. He appears to be either thrifty or miserly.
**COLOR** - Dressed in brown (earth) tattered shawl. Robe edged in blue (subconscious), red (desire), shoes unlaced. Desire can be removed quickly.
**HOUSES** - Houses in background show material gain.
**NUMBER** - Pentacles are 1+1+2=4. Two are secured to the floor, one in his arms, one on his head. The two single ones are new beginnings which can be the #1 masculine energy. The two on the floor are being reflected by the two above. It also can be that the three that are secured and the one loose on top of his head could make it a 3+1=4 with the same interpretation as the Swords and the Cups.

SUMMARY
+ This shows he has achieved material success and bounty. He is so involved with monetary possessions that it is his whole life. Gets all that he can (value) for his money. Budgets, and has a little left over (pentacle on head) to use for self.

- The card in reverse shows that he has not allowed his spiritual side to develop. Does not enjoy his money by using it (tattered robe). Could also be someone who is poor and has to really watch finances. Your wealth offers little pleasure because you spend every moment guarding it.

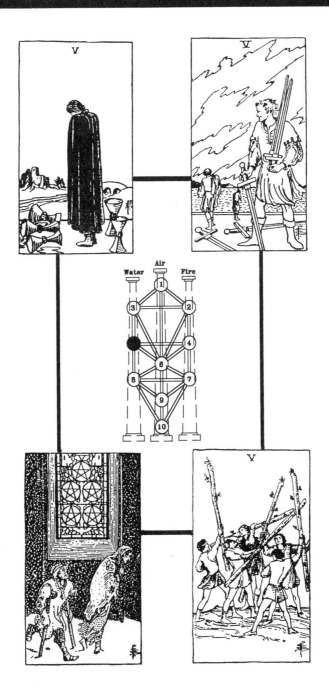

# FIVES are placed in Sephirah #5  GEBURAH
## SEVERITY
### Radical Intelligence

The fives are on the Water pillar of the Tree of Life which is the female side of the Tree and stands for reception and sensitivity. Sephirah #5 is Geburah. Five is strength, discipline, severity plus the warrior as the planet Mars is on this Sephirah. In #4 Chesed and Jupiter started a new beginning by adding 1 to 3 and making it 4. The energy of Mars is for man to use in his battle with life. He can chose how he wants to respond. Notice that all these cards are stressed. Number 5 is the pentagram. Is it pointing up or down?

Note: All four cards are discouraged and lost. Also note the setup for the 5 objects. Reread about #5 and the 5th Sephirah.


## FIVE OF CUPS  45-9
*Water & Water Summer*

**ELEMENT/PILLAR/SEPHIRAH** - The Five of Cups is the Water element. It is on Sephirah #5 (Geburah on the Water pillar.) This is pure Water. A stagnant, deep, emotional problem.

**COLOR** - Black shows negativity and discouragement. A black-cloaked figure looks sorrowfully at three spilled Cups. There are two filled Cups behind him. Yellow shoes say that he walks with intelligence.

**WATER** - The stream of water is emotions. It is also the wisdom of The High Priestess flowing through.

**BRIDGE** - The bridge carries one to the other side. Once you have crossed over the water/emotions, there is a lot to build on.

**NUMBER** - This would be a combination of 3+2=5. This is like the inverted pentagram. It symbolizes the negative energy that keeps us in bondage.

SUMMARY

+ & - Emotional dissatisfaction arises only when you dwell on the past and what you have lost or what did not materialize. With patience and hope, stressful situations can be transformed into lessons, a loss with blessings. Brooding over a partial loss. Do not concentrate on that which did not work out, as it only brings unhappiness. Turn around and see what is still there and concentrate on that. Sometimes we have to evaluate a situation for the positive and negative, good or bad. If there is enough positive, turn your back or accept the negative with understanding. A time of reassessment. Don't cry over spilt milk. This can also be a card that represents an alcoholic problem.


## FIVE OF SWORDS  59-14-5
*Water & Air* **Fall**

**ELEMENT/PILLAR/SEPHIRAH** - The Five of Swords is the Air element. It is on Sephirah #5 (Geburah on the Water pillar.) This is a combination of Water and Air. An emotional battle with words.

**FIGURES/SWORDS** - One figure looks triumphant. There is a smile on his face. Two Swords are on the ground. He still holds Swords. One is down and two are up. When a Sword is down, the battle is over. Up means that it is still undecided. One figure walks away. One is crying.
**WATER/CLOUDS** - Choppy water in the background and storm clouds above show the disturbing emotions involved.
**NUMBER** - Note the setup of the Swords: 2+1+1+1=5 or 2+1+2=5. The divine will is in the middle of the two reflections.

SUMMARY
+ You will stand up for your convictions and defend your rights. Impulsive decisions could hurt those around you. You conquer with your mind. It seems as if you have won, but the problem will come back two more times to be discussed. This is shown by the one Sword down and two up.

- The card in reverse shows that your cruelty or sharpness of words brings empty victories. You think you won but your allies are only retreating to reappear and talk again. A situation looks as if you have won but only temporarily. You get the last word in but don't win the battle. Battle of three levels of the mind.


## FIVE OF PENTACLES  73-10-1
*Water & Earth* **Winter**

**ELEMENT/PILLAR/SEPHIRAH** - The Five of Pentacles is the Earth element. It is on the Sephirah #5 (Geburah on the Water pillar.) This is a combination of Water and Earth. An emotional problem over material matters.
**FIGURES/WINDOW** - Two figures representing physical and mental poverty. They are so caught up with their problem that they do not realize

they have just walked past the anchor of hope. Notice the light in the window and anchor of hope. Notice that the anchor looks like the Kabalah Tree of Life. 1+2+2=5. They have to endure the misery and burdens of life if they deny the spiritual light. The spiritual life brings an anchor of hope and abundance. If you don't believe, you will be left out in the cold.

Our wisdom is attained only through physical, material and financial hardships in which we have to choose between material pursuits and spiritual riches. When you look to the light within, a change of consciousness takes place and the material aspect of life flows easily.

**NUMBER** - 1 pentacle on the top symbolizing the divine and the 2 doubled below showing reflection.

SUMMARY

+ & - Try not to dwell on the unhappy. Do something to change the energy. Look at what else you have in your life. If the spiritual understanding is built in, it is easier to endure hardships.

- This card can symbolize unemployment or poverty. Could be rich but sees self as poor. Welfare and food stamps are available.

## FIVE OF WANDS  31-4
*Water & Fire* **Spring**

**ELEMENT/PILLAR/SEPHIRAH** - The Five of Wands is the element Fire. It is on Sephirah #5 (Geburah on the Water pillar.) This is a combination of Water and Fire. Emotional battle with aggressiveness.

**YOUTHS** - 5 youths battling out of control, going in all directions. There is a need to regain organization. Fight for what you want, competition is around you. By arousing competitiveness in others strife is the result. If you get involved, conflict cannot be avoided.

**WANDS/NUMBER** - Notice that the man entering holds 1 Wand and the other 4 are grouped together. This is a combination of 1+4=5. Number 1 the divine essence and #4 basic necessity of a form. Man is master of the elements.

SUMMARY

+ You must learn cooperation and direction but not to be afraid to jump in when necessary. You have a choice as to whether you want to enter the confusion. You may think that you can help. Everyone is disorganized. It will be a lot of work if you become involved.

- The card in reverse shows that you remain disorganized and live a life of struggle. There are disputes and difficulties. One can be nervous and high strung. Must learn to adjust harmoniously with others.

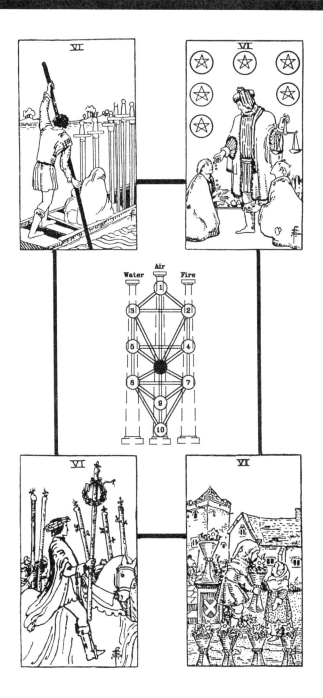

## SIXS are placed in Sephirah #6   TIPHARETH
## BEAUTY
### Mediating Intelligence

The sixs are on the center, positive Air pillar of the Tree in Sephirah #6.  Air is intellectual.  Sephirah #6 (Tiphareth and the planet the Sun) is the heart of the Tree of Life.  It is the Christ center.  This Sephirah has the most paths connected to it.  The powers flow in from them and out to them.  It is the solar plexus in man.  Remember #6 forms the Star of David and the 6-sided cube which, unfolded, forms the cross.

Reread #6 and the 6th Sephirah.

## SIX OF SWORDS  60-6
*Air & Air*  **Fall**

**ELEMENT/PILLAR/SEPHIRAH** - The Six of Swords is the Air element. It is on Sephirah #6 (Tiphareth and the Sun) on the positive Air pillar.  This is pure Air.

**FIGURES** - A man, woman and child (trinity) in a boat.  They also represent the three stages of consciousness.
**WATER** -  Moving water (subconscious) supports them.  On one side of the boat the water is rough.  One side is smooth.  The man is pushing the boat out of the rough waters into smoother waters.
**SWORDS** - The swords in the front of the boat point down.  When swords point down the battle is over.  However, the issues are right in front of them since the swords are in front of the people.
**NUMBERS** - Since #6 is a spiritual number, the 6 Swords can represent that the spiritual is in front leading them.  Notice that the Swords are divided into 2+4=6, 2 reflective and 4 the difficulty overcome.

SUMMARY
+ You are going from rough times to smoother times because  you are allowing your intellect (Swords) to lead the way.  This sometimes denotes travel.  Period of struggle over.  Intellectual movement.  Legal dealings bring a peaceful settlement.

- The card in reverse shows that you are not allowing your intelligence to lead you.  Therefore, you remain in troubled waters and are caught up in your emotions.

# SIX OF PENTACLES  74-11-2
*Air & Earth  **Winter***

**ELEMENT/PILLAR/SEPHIRAH** - The Six of Pentacles is the Earth element.  It is on Sephirah #6 (Tiphareth and the Sun) on the positive Air pillar.  The Sun represents the heart and this card shows generosity from the heart.  This is a combination of Air and Earth.

**FIGURE** - A well-to-do man balances the scales by sharing with those less fortunate.  He holds the scales in his left hand, which is the compassionate hand.  The scale is yellow – intellectually weighing.

**COINS** - The coins that are falling are divided into 2 and 2.  It is as if he is helping out, but the beggar must take them and turn them into 3 or 4 to complete.  He only gives them enough and expects him to work with it.

**COLOR** - He is dressed in red (activity) and blue (sensitivity).

**WAIF**- One waif is blue, showing that he is more emotional impoverished and one yellow showing he is intellectually impoverished.

**BUILDINGS** - Buildings are behind the man, showing previous accomplishments.

**NUMBERS** - Note pentacles 3+1+2=6 The divine #1 is in the middle.  3 is the form that has been productive and 2 are being reflective and still being worked on or will duplicate what is already done.

## SUMMARY
+ You have material prosperity and are using it in a discriminating way.  Not giving to all.  Sometimes an inheritance comes from a well-to-do person.  Can also represent the judge, plaintiff, and defendant.

- You have not used your talents to the most and have not used money wisely, so now you need to get a loan or to ask for help.  You do not have enough to pay both bills, so one must wait.  When the card is upside down it could be that you are receiving the handout instead of giving it.  The coins would be flowing back to you.

# SIX OF WANDS  32-5
*Air & Fire  **Spring***

**ELEMENT/PILLAR/SEPHIRAH** - The Six of Wands is the Fire element.  It is on Sephirah #6 (Tiphareth and the Sun) on the positive Air pillar.  This is a combination of Air and Fire.

**WANDS** - Remember how the previous 5 of Wands showed turmoil.  Here we find that they are all lined up in order, and there is a victory after the strife.

**COLOR** - The green covering over the horse is for growth and the purple cape is a combination of red/activity and blue/emotions.

**LAUREL** - A horseman crowned with laurel and a laurel wreath on his Wand show success and triumph. He rides triumphantly on the horse, a picture of victory.

**NUMBER** - Note the Wands are 1+2+3=6 or 1+2+1+2=6. One is the divine energy, two is the duplicate and 3 is the completion or trinity.

<u>SUMMARY</u>

+ Your goals are high and success comes. Friends will help you. Persistence brings victory. Charm and self control shows confidence. You become a leader and have authority. You reach high goals, success, recognition and honor.

- The card in reverse shows a pompous and haughty nature irritates and turns people off. Develop a spiritual philosophy based on awareness that your present power comes from above. Delayed recognition.

# SIX OF CUPS 46-10-1
*Air & Water* **Summer**

**ELEMENT/PILLAR/SEPHIRAH** - The Six of Cups is the element Water. It is on Sephirah #6 (Tiphareth and the Sun) on the positive Air pillar. This is a combination of Air and Water.

**CUPS** - Six Cups are brimming with flowers showing fruition. There is abundance here. He has plenty to share.

**FLOWERS** - 5 pointed star flower indicates human emotions purified and transmuted into compassionate love. This would be the pentagram pointing up to spirit.

**CAP/COLOR** - His cap is like the Fools cap-0 key representing the highest gift, purified love. He is clothed in blue and red which is sensitivity and action. The yellow background and houses represent the intellect.

**CROSS** - The cross looks like an X and is the St. Andrew's cross. The cross of humility. We "become as little children" or believe as little children.

**NUMBERS** - Note the cups 1+1+4=6 The 4 cups show hard work was successful. The 1+1 shows two new beginnings.

<u>SUMMARY</u>

+ You share your good fortune and are generous, or someone shares with you. You're warm and tender. An old friend that you haven't seen in a long time appears and you go over past memories. There can be a class reunion. You have a lot to share with others and do it in a giving way. You win others through your charm and wit. Joy is giving. A gift from an admirer.

- The card in reverse shows that you live in the past, surrounded by memories, refusing to accept the present. You can be childish and irresponsible thereby attracting, as a natural reaction to your output, a worthless circle of acquaintances. A lack of sharing.

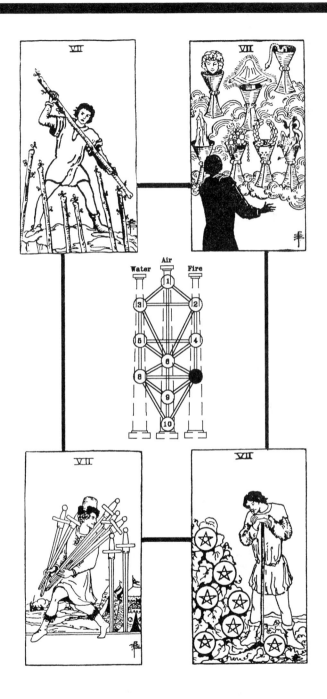

# SEVENS are placed in Sephirah #7 NETZACH
# VICTORY
Occult Intelligence

The four cards in the Minor Arcana numbered seven are on the positive Fire pillar and the Sephirah #7 Netzach, with the planet Venus. Creative Venus represents instincts and emotions out of which evolve the arts. Venus is the planet of love. Is it no wonder that it is one of the biggest lessons of this world. Christ was known to always be saying, "Love one another." It is the expression of this love of one's fellow man and God that will take us to the top--Supernal Triangle. Fire is energy. The sevens can give positive results dependent upon the action taken.

Netzach is the beginning of the last triangle. This reminds us that the elements Fire, Air and Water have to be involved in order to make the triangle. The name Yod He' Vau He' is brought to mind again.

Sephirah #7 (Netzach with the planet Venus) is on the Fire pillar bringing the Fire, Yod energy to this triangle. Sephirah #8 (Hod with the planet Mercury) is on the Water pillar bringing the Water, He'. Sephirah #9 (Yesod and the planet the Moon) is on the Air pillar bringing the Air, Vau energy. These three form the last triangle called the Astral triangle.

The last letter in the name of God is the He'. Sephirah #10 (Malkuth) is the Earth. By adding the Earth we have the complete name. The addition of Malkuth turns the triangle into a square. This is what earthlings respond to first in evolution. If we cannot understand this triangle, then how can we expect to go higher on the Tree? Remember that as one goes lower the tree becomes more dense. This is the lowest part of the Tree. Think of a tree and how it is thicker at the base. After our involution we start to climb up the tree. Starting at the bottom, this Astral triangle plus Malkuth is what we have to hurdle first.

Number 7 can be made up of a 3 (the trinity) and a 4 (form and the cross of matter). The cross of matter is also the square or cube.

## SEVEN OF WANDS 33-6

*Fire & Fire **Spring***

**ELEMENT/PILLAR/SEPHIRAH** - The Seven of Wands is the Fire element. It is on Sephirah #7 (Netzach and Venus) on the positive Fire pillar. This is pure Fire.

**WANDS** - Six wands are coming at him all at once. He is on the hilltop and elevated above the Wands that are coming at him. Each one is a different length, showing that he has worked on each, but some more than others. Which project should he tackle first?

**FIGURE/SHOES** - He is dressed simply and has two different shoes on, showing that he is confused and does not know what to do. This card shows indecision.

**NUMBERS** - Note the Wands (#1) a new beginning or the Divine Will + (#4) the problem to be surmounted + (#2) the polarity of duplication = 7.

### SUMMARY

+ You have courage and tireless energy. Brave and not afraid to stand strong for convictions. Everything coming at you all at once. You are the one always called on. Make a list putting the most important on the top. This will make it less confusing.

- The card in reverse shows a lack of courage, anxious, fearful and indecisive. Responsibility with lack of appreciation.


## SEVEN OF CUPS 47-11-2

*Fire & Water **Summer***

**ELEMENT/PILLAR/SEPHIRAH** - The Seven of Cups is the Water element. It is on Sephirah #7 (Netzach and Venus) on the positive Fire pillar. This is a combination of Fire and Water.

**CUPS** - A figure stands facing 7 Cups filled with gifts and tests. All are floating on a cloud as if he is seeing it in a dream. This card is also called the 7 deadly sins or virtues: 1) The head is ego or vanity; 2) The wreath and skeleton can be success over death; 3) The castle is achieving material success; 4) The one covered is illusion; 5) The snake is overcoming jealousy; 6) The dragon is frivolity; 7) Jewels and glamour represent the love of luxury. Six are recognizable but one is covered. All six are materialistic.

The seventh one looks like there is a robe of white for spiritual growth. It looks like Christ with his arms open.

**NUMBERS** - Note the Cups. 4+3=7. Form and spirit combined.

SUMMARY

+ You faced many tests of character and self development and have accomplished many tasks. A new one appears. It is in your imagination, waiting to be revealed. It is your choice whether you want to unveil it. Since you achieved all of the material goals, now is the time to develop mystical, psychic, and spiritual experiences. It will come in time.

- The card in reverse shows that there are great dreams of success and wealth. Visions of grandeur caught up in worldly matters. Spirituality needs to be developed. It can be that you are in a world of illusions.


## SEVEN OF SWORDS  61-7
*Fire & Air*  **Fall**

**ELEMENT/PILLAR/SEPHIRAH** - The Seven of Swords is the Air element. It is on Sephirah #7 (Netzach and Venus) on the positive Fire pillar. This is a combination of Fire and Air.

**FIGURE/SWORDS** - A figure hurries and sneaks away with an armful of swords. He could be stealing someone elses ideas before they are completed (Swords pointing down).  2 Swords are on the right positive shoulder and 3 on the other negative shoulder. This is 5 in all. He left 2 secured and looks back on them.

**SHOES** - On the old cards his shoes are of different colors showing uncertainty, hesitation, partial success.

**TENTS** - Tents also show instability because they are not permanent.

**NUMBERS** - Note Swords 2+3+2=7 Trinity unfolded in the midst of the pair of opposites.

SUMMARY

+ If the #7 showing positive results depends upon action taken, then this card shows that only two Swords have been completed since they are pointing down and are secured in the ground. This is a partial success. There is a confusion here as he looks back and wonders whether he should stay with those that he is leaving behind. The three swords in one arm and two in the other show they are complete (pointing down) but not secured.

Finish what you start before you reveal it. Don't let anyone know what you are up to, until it is ready to be revealed. Keep your hands hidden like a lawyer does.

- The card in reverse shows confusion. Two different shoes--indecision--2 choices. A break from work. People may find you elusive. You keep a lot of ideas to yourself. Your plans may fail because someone takes what is rightfully yours or someone else attains what you want.


## SEVEN OF PENTACLES  75-12-3
*Fire & Earth*  **Winter**

**ELEMENT/PILLAR/SEPHIRAH** - The Seven of Pentacles is the Earth element. It is on Sephirah #7 (Netzach and Venus) on the positive Fire pillar. This is a combination of Fire and Earth.

**FIGURE** - A young man looks over the fruits of his work. Much material success. He worked hard to cultivate it and made it grow. He rests on his sickle. He remembers the work that went into developing the other vine. He questions whether he wants to do that all over again.
**VINE** - One single vine and Pentacle lies in front of him. If you look at the vine on the left of the card, it looks like half of the Tree of Life. Now perhaps he has to develop this single Pentacle to make it grow to develop the other side.
**SHOES** - He has two different shoes on, showing indecision.
**NUMBER** - Note Pentacles 6+1=7. A strong will and experience brings victory.

SUMMARY
+ You worked hard and accomplished a lot. You pause to evaluate. You're trying to decide if you want to cultivate something new and add it to your pile. Do you want more material success or should you do something different, such as working on your spirituality? Attainment calls for hard steady work.

- Frustrated over financial matters. There are delays and restrictions. Much depends upon your persistence and efforts. It takes time for your efforts to bear fruit. Be calm and patient. Decide which direction to go?

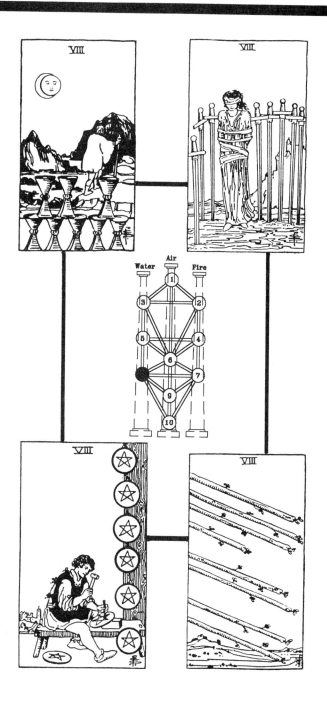

# EIGHTS are placed in Sephirah #8  HOD
## SPLENDOR   Discipline, Accuracy
### Absolute or Perfect Intelligence

Eight is the law of cause and effect--Karma. Moral decision for Good or Evil. The four #8 cards of the Minor Arcana are on the left (Water negative) pillar on the Tree of Life. They are on Sephirah #8 (Hod with the planet Mercury). Hod represents the mind in the same way that Mercury is the intelligence. The #8 is like our lungs as they are used to breathing in and out. As we take in we raise our ideals higher. We can only comprehend new concepts according to the level of our intelligence. Through constant study and learning, not only our level of learning rises but our Soul also awakens. Everyone hears on a different level and everyone is right, according to how they hear it. How we speak and how we think influences our lives. This is the same as the Air pillar on the Tree. Knowledge is what elevates the Soul.

Reread #8 and Sephirah #8.


## EIGHT OF CUPS  48-12-3
*Water & Water*  **Summer**

**ELEMENT/PILLAR/SEPHIRAH** - The Eight of Cups is the element Water. It is on Sephirah #8 (Hod with Mercury) on the negative Water pillar. This is pure Water.

**FIGURE** - A lone figure in red (desire) robe walks toward a mountain (spiritual attainment). He leaves the Cups neatly stacked behind him. He has laid aside old thoughts and ideas and is venturing on to get more. What has fulfilled him emotionally does not any more. It must give place to something higher.
**RIVER** - He just crossed over a river (emotions). He has put the past behind him.
**SUN/MOON** - The Sun and the Moon are together showing an eclipse in the sky. An eclipse means that something very important is happening. There will be a big change.
**NUMBER** - Note the Cups are 5 on the bottom +2 +1 on the top. The will of man #1 reflecting #2 on life connects with the powers of the pentagram #5. Here we see the true meaning of the #8. Man has laid aside old thoughts and ways and ventured on to get more.
**MOUNTAINS** - spiritual attainment

SUMMARY

+ You have just walked away from an emotional situation. You put everything in order (Cups). You leave them behind. You're not emotionally attached to them any more. You have an inner urge to attain something higher (mountains, spirituality).

- The card in reverse shows that your emotional attachments are holding you back from accomplishing what growth you want, or you are neglecting and ignoring the problems at hand.

## EIGHT OF SWORDS 62-8
*Water & Air* **Fall**

**ELEMENT/PILLAR/SEPHIRAH** - The Eight of Swords is the element Air. It is on Sephirah #8 (Hod with Mercury) on the negative Water pillar. This is a combination of Water and Air, emotions and the Intellect.

**FIGURE** - A figure blindfolded and tied can use psychic ability (Water) to lead her away from restrictions. This card also shows how the power of the mind can be used in a negative way to create a prison.
**CASTLES** -Castles in the background show what has been attained.
**SWORDS** - Swords pointed down showing completion.
**NUMBER** - 5+2+1=8 Number 1 (the will) is being reflected upon by 2 and 5, connects man with the power above, as in the pentagram. She sees only what she is deprived of but has the faculties to acquire wisdom. Has a limited conception of understanding and has failed to conquer fears.

SUMMARY

+ & - Her thoughts confine her. Ideas and thoughts have been around a long time (points down). She feels restricted and bound by these. She does not realize that her feet are not tied and she can walk away. By using her intuition and psychic ability, she can find the way out. If you can make your mind look at it differently, you will no longer be imprisoned. Past accomplishments are shown by the castle in the background. If you are not afraid to leave old habits and circumstances behind you, you will be free.

## EIGHT OF PENTACLES 76-13-4
*Water & Earth* **Winter**

**ELEMENT/PILLAR/SEPHIRAH** - The Eight of Pentacles is the element Earth. It is on Sephirah #8 (Hod with Mercury) on the negative Water pillar.

This is a combination of Water and Earth. His mind and emotions are on what he wants and it brings material success.

**FIGURE** - A worker works diligently on making money. He turns his back to everything else in his life. He has accomplished a lot already, shown by the Pentacles stacked up. He is working on one and has two on the ground to go.
**COLOR** - Red stockings show desire and the blue shirt shows he puts his emotions into it.
**NUMBER** - 1+1+1+5=8. The working man is concentrating on his work. Will #1 and the #5 man is connected with the powers above as in the pentagram. He is moving swiftly ahead by using what he has acquired. One reaps what one has sowed.

SUMMARY
+ You are honest and tend to details. You work very hard and have acquired a good bank account. One is a genius, a craft pays off.

- The card in reverse tells you to develop your skills and get some training or be an apprentice.


## EIGHT OF WANDS  34-7
*Water & Fire* **Spring**

**ELEMENT/PILLAR/SEPHIRAH** - The Eight of Wands is the element Fire. It is on Sephirah #8 on the Water pillar. This is a combination of Water and Fire.

**WANDS** - 8 live forces move swiftly through the air over open country unobstructed. They are all going in the same direction. They will soon become complete. One is shorter than the rest. One requires more attention. Perhaps it has been forgotten or overlooked.
**DIRECTION** - They are going toward the East and toward the Light. This means that they are already in the works. They are aimed down towards the Earth and Water.
**NUMBER** - 3+1+2+2=8 Number 3 is the completion and #1 is the will applied. Number 2 is double reflection.
SUMMARY
+ Your efforts travel freely and unobstructed. You have accomplished much. There is something that you have forgotten. Something remains to be finished.
- Need extra effort to finish what started. Can be reckless and impatient.

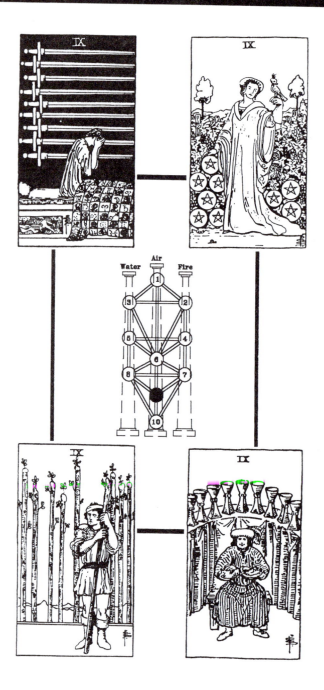

## NINES are placed in Sephirah #9  YESOD
## FOUNDATION  Material we use to build things
### Pure Intelligence

Number 8 was absolute or perfect intelligence. Number 9 is pure intelligence. Sephirah #8 Hod has the intellectual planet Mercury with it.  Sephirah #9 Yesod has the Moon.  In Astrology, both the Moon and Mercury are considered in order to see one's ability to comprehend and communicate. Mercury conducts the information up the nervous system until it reaches the brain where information is stored.  The Moon represents the brain.

The Moon has been shortchanged when it comes to receiving credit for what it does.  The Moon, also being the emotions, shows us that we do not accomplish anything unless we are emotionally driven to it.  It also represents our habits.  Habits are hard to change.  When one sets one's mind and emotions on what one wants to do, anything can be accomplished.  The planet Mercury is on the Water pillar, which is owned and controlled by the Moon. The Moon is on the Air pillar, which is owned and controlled by Mercury. They work together.

Nine is completion of perfection.  $3x3=9$.  It is the completion of the last triangle. It is a time to finish, not to start anything new.  Nine is on the middle, intellectual Air pillar of the Tree of Life.

## NINE OF SWORDS  63-9
*Air & Air*  **Fall**

**ELEMENT/PILLAR/SEPHIRAH** - The Nine of Swords is the Air element. It is on Sephirah #9 (Yesod with the Moon) on the positive Air pillar.  This is pure Air.

**SWORDS/COLOR** - The Swords representing intellectual Air, are the thoughts she has.  They are coming from the West, showing that they have been around for a while.  The black background shows how dark and depressed she is.  Her thoughts and her emotions make her sick.  She mourns the past.  The Swords are not separated.  They are all stacked together as a #9. Unhappy about what is ending.

**FIGURE** - A woman looks with despair, regret.

**COVERLET** - The coverlet has red roses, signs and planets of the Zodiac on it.  This symbolizes the experiences life has brought.  It is one's karma.

**NUMBER** - 9. All swords, together, brings completion.

## SUMMARY
+ Our mind (Swords) brings us sorrow, if we allow it. Understand that difficulties are lessons for growth and development. Courage will replace frustrations. Your mind can make you sick. Bring the memory forward from the unconscious mind to the conscious mind. Understand what the difficulty is, accept it, and let it go. You cannot change the past, only learn from it. Even though the Swords are coming from the West, they point East to new beginnings when the Sun rises. Strength comes from suffering.

- Swamped with sorrows.

## NINE OF PENTACLES   77-14-5
*Air & Earth* **Winter**

**ELEMENT/PILLAR/SEPHIRAH** - The Nine of Pentacles is the element Earth. It is on Sephirah #9 (Yesod with the Moon) on the positive Air pillar. This is a combination of Air and Earth. Ideas and emotions, put to use, have brought material and spiritual gain.

**FIGURE** - A well-dressed woman stands in a garden.
**GRAPE VINE** - She is surrounded with grape vines (abundance). There is a bunch of grapes at the v of her dress.
**SNAIL** – It took a long time- like the snail
**TREES** – Two trees representing the two pillars of the Tree + & -.
**COLOR** - She is dressed in red (desire), yellow (intellect), blue (emotions) and purple (spirituality). Her dress appears to have a design on it that looks like the planet Venus ♀.
**BIRD** - She plays with a falcon. Only the wealthy had time to play with or own a falcon.
**NUMBER** - Notice how the Pentacles are grouped in threes. This is representing the three triangles. They also look like 6+3=9. 6 would be the Sephirah Tiphareth, the Christ center, and 3 would represent completion and the Supernal Triangle. She would then have it all.

## SUMMARY
+ Practicality and thoroughness bring success. Time to enjoy and play. She has achieved a high position and has abundance in material and spiritual achievements. Falcon is a symbol of aristocracy. Only those who have wealth and leisure can indulge in the art of falconry.
- The card in reverse shows that through extravagance you may lose the possessions you love so dearly.

## NINE OF WANDS  35-8
*Air & Fire* **Spring**

**ELEMENT/PILLAR/SEPHIRAH** - The Nine of Wands is the element Fire. It is on Sephirah #9 (Yesod with the Moon) on the positive Air pillar. This is a combination of Air and Fire.

**WANDS** - 8 wands firmly planted between figure and outer world. They are all behind him. The 9th wand is held.

**COLOR** - Yellow (intellect) pants and shoes red (desire.) He stands on a firm foundation.

**NUMBER** - The Wands are divided into 5+3+1=9. Number 5 is man and the pentagram. Number 3 is completion and #1 the will.

<u>SUMMARY</u>

+ You have accomplished a lot. (Wands are behind you.) You have chosen one (your favorite) to finish up. You are contemplating with your intellect (yellow) and your feet are on solid ground. What will be your next endeavor? Should I finish this one and then do something else? You defend your position, always keeping your eyes open for what comes next.

- The card in reverse says that it is doubtful and uneasy. You wonder if you can take on any more pressures of work. Will this one fit in with others? Health can be affected.


## NINE OF CUPS  49-13-4
*Air & Water* **Summer**

**ELEMENT/PILLAR/SEPHIRAH** - The Nine of Cups is the Water element. It is on Sephiroth #9 (Yesod with the Moon) on the positive Air pillar. This is a combination of Air and Water.

**FIGURE/CUPS/COLOR** - He has put all of his intellect and emotions into what he did and succeeded. A well pleased figure sits with 9 Cups organized on a platform of blue (emotions) behind him. He wears red (desire) hat and socks. Yellow (intellectual) background and floor. His arms are crossed, showing he is closed off, not open to anything new. Is pleased with everything that he has completed. However, his legs are open, the same way as The Empress. This shows he is ready to give out.

**NUMBER** - 9 Cups in a row = 9 completion.

## SUMMARY

+ You are pleased. You balanced everything perfectly: intellect, emotions and desires. Well organized and Cups are filled. Success in all matters. This is the WISH CARD. Fulfilled hopes and wishes. The psychic nature is well developed. A very giving person.

- The card in reverse shows a gluttonous approach to life. Overindulgence in food and drink. Delay in wish being fulfilled.

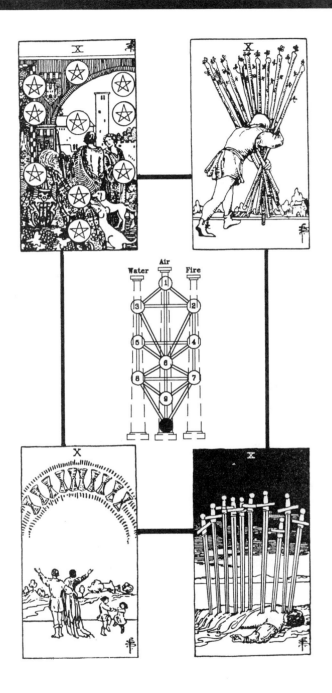

# TENS are placed in Sephirah #10  MALKUTH
## KINGDOM
Resplendent Intelligence

Malkuth, Sephirah #10, is on the opposite end of the Air pillar from Kether Sephirah #1.  If you reduce the number 10 by adding 1+0=1, we return to Kether.  Kether takes one to the heights of understanding spirit and Malkuth grounds us by the Earth, while we are doing it.  Malkuth can come into existence only because of Kether. Earth can be formed only because of when the three elements of Air, Fire, and Water are combined.  They form matter. All things that we know are formed through Malkuth.  "As above, so below" also applies here.

Once the Fool received the Air, Fire and Water, it created form which completed his work to get his body; therefore, we are created in the image of God!  We are God and God is us!  Old time religion told us that we could never be as great as God.  Spirituality tells you that you are him.  Jesus said, "You can do what I can do and even better."  That connection never breaks. It takes the awakening to spirituality to allow one to understand this.  That is why The Hanged Man bound himself to walk with his feet upon heaven.

Malkuth brings the completion to the name of Jehovah Yod He' Vau He'. Malkuth is the last He'. He' is Earth.  The first He' was in the Supernal Triangle, Sephirah #2 (Chokmah and the planet Uranus).  We have a connection here since Uranus is the planet of AWAKENING.  If you reread about the Aces on Sephirah #1, this will remind you of the connection between Kether and Malkuth.  Malkuth rules the Visible Universe and Kether the Invisible world of spirit.

Look on the Tree and see how Sephirah #10 (Malkuth) is connected to the Water pillar and  Sephirah #8 (Hod).  Hod represents the intellectual planet Mercury. Between Mercury and the experiences of the Air pillar we can elevate our consciousness.  On the other side the Fire pillar is connected to Sephirah #7 (Netzach and the planet Venus).  Love is the other element involved.  When this has been accomplished, then meditation and breathing (which is 8) can be used to raise the soul.  The middle pillar is the spine of man and it involves the chakras.  Develop the kundalini through this process and the chakra at the top of your head will burst forth and receive the Crown of Glory.

Once 9 has been completed ten allows us to start a new beginning on a higher spiritual level. Ten, 10, 1+0=1. Ten is Earth and the foundation or roots of the Tree.

## TEN OF PENTACLES 78-15-6
*Earth & Earth* **Winter**

**ELEMENT/PILLAR/SEPHIRAH** - The Ten of Pentacles is the element Earth. It is on Sephirah #10 (Malkuth on Earth). This is pure Earth. This card is #78, the last card in the Tarot.

**PEOPLE** -This card shows the accomplishment of everything. The three states of consciousness are shown here. Man, positive and the conscious mind; woman receptive and the subconscious mind; child, neutral and the Super-conscious mind.

**BEARD** - The old man represents ancient wisdom of the years. He has seen a lot and knows a lot. He not only knows a lot, he has worked hard to accomplish his own spirituality. He holds the rod of The Magician.

**HEBREW LETTER** - At the bottom of his cape is the Hebrew mother letter W (Shin) which means the Holy Ghost and the Fire element.

**GRAPE VINE** - Right under the letter for Shin is the grape vine representing the Vegetable kingdom, as well as plenty.

**SCALES** - To the left of the rod on the arch is the scales. This is where the soul of man is weighed. It can also show a choice of weighing the material side of life with the spiritual.

**HOUSE** - The houses show that one can also own material substance in this life. This is fine as long as it doesn't own us.

**ANIMALS** - The 2 dogs show development of the animal kingdom.

**PATH** - Looking at the card on the left hand side, there is a strip of blue. Take a magnifying glass and look at this. At the top there appears to be a woman, such as The High Priestess or the Madonna, and below is a castle. The castle has an opening that allows one to enter. The path is gone and the water flows into the castle. The High Priestess's knowledge is represented by the Water which leads you inside.

**NUMBER** - Notice the 10 Pentacles. They are in the form of the Tree of Life. They show each of the 10 Sephiroth.

SUMMARY
+ Greatest attainment comes from achieving balance while on the earth plane. Success and fulfillment in every way. Abundance in material and spiritual success.

- The card in reverse says do not allow yourself to degenerate into a state of idleness and dissipation because of the luxury bestowed upon you. Material life is only temporary. Eventually one has to confront the Soul.

## TEN OF WANDS 36-9
*Earth & Fire* **Spring**

**ELEMENT/PILLAR/SEPHIRAH** - The Ten of Wands is the Fire element. It is on Sephirah #10 Malkuth on Earth. This is a combination of Fire and Earth.

In the tens we have two suits that are positive and two that are negative. The positive and negative energy is involved in everything and we definitely have it here. The ten of Wands and Swords are the negative difficult cards. This is the same in a regular deck of cards. The Wands being the Clubs and the Swords being the Spades, are all black. The Cups and Pentacles are the positive. In the regular deck of cards the Cups are the Hearts and the Pentacles are the Diamonds, both shown in red.

**FIGURE** - Man is walking with his head down. He is headed back to the houses and the land. He has chosen to stay with the material side of life. Therefore, he is heavily burdened with the responsibilities that go with this. He has taken on more than he can handle.
**WANDS** - He is heavily burdened with 10 wands.
**NUMBER** - 10 Wands grouped together and holding on. Completion but not letting go of it.

<u>SUMMARY</u>
+ You take on the burdens or responsibility and complete your work by forging ahead. Complete projects.

- The card in reverse shows that you over extended yourself with work and projects. Not sure you can carry the load.

## TEN OF CUPS 50-5
*Earth & Water* **Summer**

**ELEMENT/PILLAR/SEPHIRAH** - The Ten of Cups is the Water element. It is on Sephirah #10 (Malkuth and the Earth). This is a combination of Earth and Water.

**RAINBOW/COLOR** - The 10 of Cups are in a rainbow. The rainbow is red (desires) and yellow (intellect). This shows that there has been success in acquiring the knowledge that one needs and it brings happiness.

**FIGURES** - Man and woman are united in an embrace. They have their arms up in recognition to that above. They have intertwined their natures shown by the colors of their clothing.

**CHILDREN** - Children are dancing. One is a boy (positive +) and one a girl (receptive -).

**HOUSE** - There is a house in the background. They are looking at this. They have accomplished both material and spiritual substance.

**NUMBER** - All ten Cups are in a row, showing completion, and are ready to start again on a new level.

SUMMARY

+ Success and achievement is fulfilled. There is love, family ties, happy changes and public recognition. Promising opportunities. Pleasures in family ties. Life surrounded by family, friends and affection.

- The card in reverse shows wastes and family difficulties.


## TEN OF SWORDS 64-1
*Earth & Air* **Fall**

**ELEMENT/PILLAR/SEPHIRAH** - The Ten of Swords is the Air element. It is on Sephirah #10 (Malkuth on Earth). This is a combination of Earth and Air.

**SWORDS** - Ten Swords pierce the spine (chakras). One Sword is deeper than the rest. It appears to be in the position of the heart. The Swords look like crosses.

**COLOR** - Red robe, of desire or blood, drapes the body. He is dressed in brown, which represents hard work. He has been done in by the hard work. Blood represents ones constitution. Blood is ones ability to survive. When we are in crisis we send the adrenaline through the blood to help it clot in case of injury. Persist through stress and see good in it. He has the ability to fight and handle stress. He's looking at the new horizon, which shows he has the constitution to do it. It also can be the blood that he shed for others like the blood of Christ, which was shed for us.

**FINGERS** - Three fingers on the hand are together. Thumb symbolizes the Father. The love planet Venus and Jupiter is the index finger and is the Son. The second finger is Saturn and the Holy Spirit.

**SKY** - The black sky shows unhappiness. The yellow under the black sky shows that intellectual understanding will lift this blackness. There is a new horizon. The sorrow is over. This card shows that the worst is over. Pick yourself up and shake off the swords and start a new beginning. You have sacrificed yourself long enough.

**NUMBER** - 10 shows it has ended. Can start over, on a higher level.

SUMMARY

+ When things are at their worst and you feel done in, there is nowhere to go but to begin again. #10=1. The yellow shows a new horizon. Intellect and knowledge lifts the darkness and heavy sorrow. Our thoughts can put us down or lift us up. #10 in the Major Arcana is the Wheel of Fortune. When you're on the bottom the wheel turns and up you go. Or are you going round and round.

- The card in reverse says you are allowing yourself to lie in your grief and your grief becomes overwhelming.

# READING THE CARDS

Before you get involved in reading a spread (layout) of the Tarot Cards, there are a few things that you should do. The atmosphere surrounding the place of the reading should be pleasant, quiet or with soft background music. Set your table and chairs so that the chairs are placed in the North-South direction. This will line you up with the energy of the earth's currents. The reader should take the position of the chair that is North. Take the cards from the container that you keep them in. Check your cards to make sure that they are all going in the same direction. Shuffle them to release the energy of the previous reading.

Hold the deck of cards in your hands. Make note that the direction of the top of the card is away from you and the bottom closest to you. Place them in the palm of one of your hands and place the palm of the other hand on top. This will blend the current of the masculine, positive energy with the feminine, receptive/negative energy. Picture the spiritual energy from above, surrounding you, while they are in your hands. Say a blessing, affirmation or the "Pattern of the Trestleboard" (page 94) over them. Remember that these are spiritual cards and should be treated with respect. Decide which spread you will be using.

After the blessing, hand them to your client. Place them in the client's hand so that the top of the cards will be in the same position, with the top away the client and the bottom closest to her/him. Have her/him also hold them in the same way and think about what they want to accomplish with the reading. If they have come with a specific concern then have them think about it while holding and shuffling the cards.

When they hand the cards back to you, take them, remembering that the part of the card that is the farthest away from the client is the top of the deck. Remembering this, place that top on the table in the same position with the top of the card farthest away from you. As you spread your cards out, take them from the deck in the following manner.

The cards will be in front of you. Pick up the first card by just turning it over, right to left. This way you will not be confused as to which end of the pack is up. Do this for each card. If some are upside down, do not be alarmed. This can happen when the client shuffles them. Upside down means that there is a delay. It also means that the client is not fulfilling the positive meaning of the card and that their life is confusing. Look at the summary of each of the Tarot Cards in the previous pages and see how this is so.

Notice if there are a lot of cards that are of the Major Arcana. If there are, this means that the client is on a high spiritual path and another reading of only the Major Arcana cards should be used. When you are finished with the first reading pick up the cards and separate the Major cards from the Minor. Use only the Major Cards in the next layout for the same client. Shuffle the cards well.

You will find the following layouts quite handy.

## TAROT LAYOUTS FOR QUICK QUESTIONS AND ANSWERS

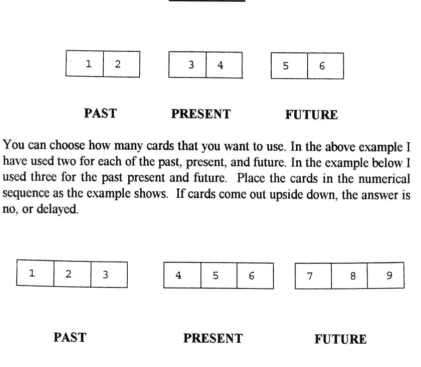

| 1 | 2 |    | 3 | 4 |    | 5 | 6 |

**PAST**        **PRESENT**        **FUTURE**

You can choose how many cards that you want to use. In the above example I have used two for each of the past, present, and future. In the example below I used three for the past present and future. Place the cards in the numerical sequence as the example shows. If cards come out upside down, the answer is no, or delayed.

| 1 | 2 | 3 |    | 4 | 5 | 6 |    | 7 | 8 | 9 |

**PAST**        **PRESENT**        **FUTURE**

# HORSESHOE SPREAD

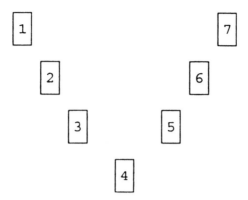

This spread can also answer a specific question.

1. Past influences
2. Querants present circumstances
3. General future conditions
4. Best policy to follow
5. Attitudes of those around you
6. Obstacles that stand in the way
7. Probable, final outcome

# ASTROLOGICAL LAYOUT OR BIRTHDAY LAYOUT

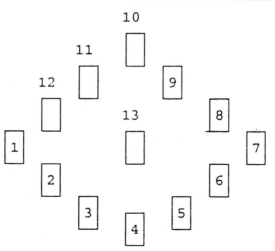

Set up a circle starting at the left and going counter clockwise. After you have placed 12 cards in a circle, place one in the middle.

For a more in-depth reading, you may then go around the circle again starting at card #1 and place an additional card next to each of the 12 cards. Again, place one in the middle.

Do this one more time. Go around the circle and place another card next to each and one in the middle. You will have 3 cards at each number and 3 in the middle. The three cards in the middle give you a synopsis of the year.

When you read all the cards at #1, start by reading the 1st one that was placed there, followed by the 2nd and then the 3rd.

For the birthday reading, this layout can be read as the months of the year for the events. Number 1 would be the start and it would be the birthday month. Number 2 would be the following month.

If you have knowledge of Astrology you may read this layout as representing the houses in the horoscope chart. Number 1 would be the 1st house. A simple listing of the 12 houses of the horoscope chart follows.

1.  Your personal house, what affects you.
2.  House of resources and finances.
3.  Everyday surroundings, short trips, speaking, writing, education, neighbors and siblings.
4.  Your home and one of your parents.
5.  Your self expression, entertainment, risk taking, gambles, talents and children.
6.  Body, health and daily chores.
7.  Partnership, one to one relationships, marriage.
8.  Deaths, wills, legacies, loans, partners money.
9.  Higher education, philosophies, long distance travel.
10. Your reputation before the world, your career and the other parent.
11. Friends, groups, organizations, hopes and wishes.
12. Secrets, dreams, what is going on inside of you.

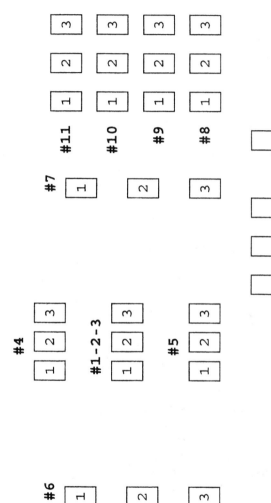

THE TRIPLE CELTIC CROSS

Looking at the example of the Triple Celtic Cross on page 285, I would like to call to your attention that some numbers have a # sign before them. This is the sequence in which you lay the cards down. The numbers without the # is series 1, series 2, and series 3, which makes a Triple Celtic Cross.

The Celtic cross is laid out like the Tree of Life. Start by placing the first three cards in the center. They are listed in the example as #1,2,3. These three cards will tell what is in the client's subconscious. It is the real question that the Soul wants an answer to. They may think that they have come for a different reason, but these cards tell all.

To form the single Celtic cross, place the rest of the cards following the sequence #1-#15. After placing the three cards in the middle, the next card goes above, then one below, one to the left and one to the right. Then place four card to the far right, starting at the bottom and going up. Cards #12, #13, #14, #15 are a synopsis and confirm the reading. (All these cards have a 1 inside of the rectangle (card). Again this can be done by placing a single card on each of the spots. Looking at the example, only use the cards that are numbered 1.

Again, I find, that once around does not give enough to talk about. By repeating the above process, a Triple Celtic Cross is formed. If you decide to go through the layout two more times, then wait to lay down cards #12-15 until the end. For more information, once I have laid down the 11 cards, I then go around again. I do not lay down any more cards in the center. Start by placing a card above and then below, etc. These cards are numbered with a 2 inside of them to make it easier for you to follow. Repeat the process by following the cards with a 3 inside of them. Having completed the three times through, then lay down cards that are #12-15.

When you read the layout, you can then read all three of the cards in each position together. Remember which one you placed there first, second, and third, and read them in that order.

### INTERPRETATION

#1,2,3. Lay three cards down. Some people will tell you to chose a card for the individual. I just take the three top cards and place them here. The individual may think that they have come for a specific question, but these cards tell what is really in the subconscious, needing an answer. They are read as a group and it tells about the situation.

#4. A past situation. It is the nearest past, the real origin of the question.

#5. Probable future events.

#6. What is behind you? This is the farthest away past. Read #4 and #6 at the same time. This will allow you to tell the individual all the past at once.

#7. What is before you, the future? You can consider card #5 with this since both are the future. Also consider #11 (final outcome). These 3 cards are connected in the final interpretation.

#8. Represents your own negative feelings. What is going on in your subconscious mind? What is the deep subconscious emotions surrounding the question?

#9. Represents the feeling of others around you or those who may be involved in the situation or how others regard the situation.

#10. Represents your own outlook. How you really feel about the matter?

#11. Final out come. #11 & #7 are read together influencing each other.

---

287

# TIMETABLE OF LIFE

Louise Fimlaid, p.m.a.f.a

**You don't want to miss this one:**

## Louise is the author of a new Astrological Textbook

- This book is a text which employs an individual's chart to show examples of what is discussed.

- Written in a clear, concise format, it is easy for the student to perfect interpretations.

- There are many books that tackle only one phase of astrology, therefore leaving out the total picture. However, by looking at the individual and incorporating the whole life from conception to death, a total picture is given. This book does just that, by combining the Prenatal Epoch Chart with the Natal and Progressed charts.

- An understanding of fate and destiny, and how the two intertwine with your spiritual development is demonstrated by this process.

- **Unique & Original - it's a must for your library!**

- Astrology teachers are recommending this book to their students. The expert way it is presented makes Astrology understandable and insightful to even a beginner.

ISBN 0-9630409-2-8    8 1/2 x 11    259 pages    $18.00 plus $4.00 P&H

Galaxy Publishing House 7200 Sunshine Skyway Ln. 11-D St. Petersburg, Fl. 33711    (727) 866-2396

723-0120

# COUNSELOR ★ TEACHER ★ WRITER ★ LECTURER

Louise Fimlaid is a well known astrologer who has counseled people throughout the United States. She is certified by the American Federation of Astrologers and is a gifted teacher, writer and lecturer.

**LECTURES:** Louise is available to lecture at your club or to teach a weekend workshop.

**READINGS:** Louise's astrological accuracy and insight will make you want to have a reading with her. Readings are available by phone and are taped for your recall. The following readings are available:

- ★ Life readings
- ★ Yearly updates
- ★ Compatibility charts
- ★ Half hour mini reading
- ★ Choosing the right day for a special event

Please call for prices and to be placed on our mailing list.

723-0120

(727) 866-2396

**ASTROLOGICAL LESSONS:** Available by phone at $20/hour.